James Johnston

Reality Versus Romance in South Central Africa

Being an Account of a Journey Across the Continent From Benguella...

James Johnston

Reality Versus Romance in South Central Africa
Being an Account of a Journey Across the Continent From Benguella...

ISBN/EAN: 9783744799829

Printed in Europe, USA, Canada, Australia, Japan

Cover: Foto ©Andreas Hilbeck / pixelio.de

More available books at **www.hansebooks.com**

Jas Johnston

REALITY versus ROMANCE

IN

SOUTH CENTRAL AFRICA

BEING AN ACCOUNT OF
A JOURNEY ACROSS THE CONTINENT FROM BENGUELLA ON THE WEST
THROUGH BIHE, GANGUELLA, BAROTSE, THE KALIHARI DESERT,
MASHONALAND, MANICA, GORONGOZA, NYASA, THE SHIRE
HIGHLANDS, TO THE MOUTH OF THE ZAMBESI
ON THE EAST COAST

BY

JAMES JOHNSTON, M.D.

WITH FIFTY-ONE FULL-PAGE PHOTOGRAVURE ILLUSTRATIONS FROM PHOTOGRAPHS
BY THE AUTHOR AND MAP INDICATING ROUTE TRAVERSED

FLEMING H. REVELL COMPANY

NEW YORK CHICAGO

112 FIFTH AVENUE 148-150 MADISON STREET

Copyright,
1893,
FLEMING H. REVELL COMPANY.

The Caxton Press
171, 173 Macdougal Street, New York

PREFACE.

THE author of this narrative of African exploration has been governed by two considerations only in his work: first, the obtaining of absolutely correct information concerning that portion of the "Dark Continent" which was the field of his investigation; second, the presentation of that knowledge in these pages with rigid adherence to the truth. In every instance where disputed questions, whether commercial, political, or religious, are touched upon, he has endeavored to verify his statements by quoting from the writings or sayings of men well known to the reading world. Entirely independent of all denominational, political, or party influences, with no interests to conciliate or ends to serve beyond the acquisition of indubitable facts that would be of value to the world, he has naturally reached results in some regards conflicting with representations made by certain preceding travelers, who have either been less painstaking in the attainment of precise knowledge or—for various reasons—more unable or disinclined to make known, with accuracy, what they had learned. It is not his province or desire to criticise either the methods or motives of others, but he is morally convinced that where the results of his observations differ from the conclusions at which they have arrived, he is right.

Fitting out his expedition himself, indebted to no government, commercial company, or society for its equipment, and responsible to no one but himself for its course or control, he was altogether untrammeled in his work, free from time limitations, and at full liberty to tell the truth, as he saw it. Those advantages but few African explorers have, it must be admitted, hitherto enjoyed.

During a period of twenty months he crossed South Central Africa, traveling four thousand five hundred miles mostly on foot, and alone so far as a white companion is concerned—passing through numerous hostile and savage tribes, traversing areas hitherto reported too pestilential for exploration, surmounting natural obstacles which have been represented as insurmountable, and penetrating regions where no white man had ever gone before. In all that long journey he never once found himself prompted to fire a shot in anger, or compelled to do so in self-defense against a human enemy; while he can say what perhaps no other man who has crossed Africa can—that of the many native carriers who traveled with him he did not lose one by death. He went among the fiercest tribes, not as a conqueror and master, but as a friend, and seeking to leave a trail behind him not of blood and hate, but of peace and good-will.

Inspired in the inception of his undertaking by a belief that black men from Jamaica, by reason of their more ready adaptability to climatic conditions and supposable racial sympathy, could be advantageously employed for the Christianization and civilization of the African savage tribes, he took the only practical means for conclusively determining the probable practicability of the design, by thoroughly informing himself upon the conditions under which they would have to live and labor. This he could only do by personal experience, for the assumedly authoritative reports of precedent travelers were much too contradictory of one another upon important matters, too meager in essential details, and too restricted in their field of exploration, to be accepted as information.

In pursuance of his purpose he not only made a careful study of the native tribes in the vast belt selected by him for exploration, but critically investigated the resources of the country, its availability for development, and the obstacles—where any existed—in the way of its reclamation from savagery.

He saw with the eyes of the agriculturist, the geologist, the naturalist, the hunter, the trader, and the physician, as well as those of the missionary, subordinating all personal bias and preconceptions to an impartial effort at collecting correct data about everything, and under all circumstances. Hence, while we know there is an age of fable in the history of all early explorations in remote and unknown lands, it must recede before increasing light and the growing desire on the part of every honest man to know the business-like truth. The result of the author's investigations cannot but be of value to all who for any reason desire to know South Central Africa *as it is.*

JAMAICA, WEST INDIES,
    October, 1893.

CONTENTS.

CHAPTER I.

FROM LONDON TO CATAMBELLA.

PAGE

Early promptings.—Jamaica.—White men in the tropics.—Purposes of the expedition.—Hearty support.—Departure for Africa.—Lisbon Harbor.—"Stuck fast."—The detective camera.—The Portuguese.—On board the "Cazengo."—Rebels.—St. Thyago.—Barren rock.—St. Thome.—Kabinda.—St. Paul de Loanda.—Bishop Taylor's Mission.—Self-supporting missions.—Circumstances alter cases.—The Liberian Mission.—Pigeon English.—A *quid pro quo*.—Stowing coal.—Arrival at Benguela.—An evil climate.—Adobe.—Catambella.—Delays.—The railway.—Native trade.—Slave caravans.—Bad sanitation... 17

CHAPTER II.

FROM CATAMBELLA TO KWANJULULU.

Toward the rising sun.—A waterless country.—A cold night.—Native foot-tracks.—The Esupwa Pass.—Bad water.—In the Cisangi country.—An outbreak in camp.—Foraging.—Extremes of temperature.—Lost in the forest.—In a game-pit.—Signals of distress.—Safe in camp.—On the great plateau.—Slave shackles.—Native graves.—In dangers oft.—The river Keve.—Utalama.—Indiscretion.—An untimely end.—Bailundu.—Cilumi.—The American mission.—Ekwikwi interviewed.—Trial for witchcraft.—Preparing for war.—Social laws.—Domestic relationships.—Farewell to Cilumi.—Artificial bee-hives.—Carriers.—Arrival at Kwanjululu......................... 36

CHAPTER III.

KWANJULULU AND KOMONDONGO.

An English mission.—The illusion dispelled.—Garanganze.—Five years' work.—Their own superstition best.—*Echoes of Service*.—Vegetable products.—Visit to Komondongo.—The late war.—Cause of the rupture.—The peacemaker.—Burning villages.—Capture of Chindunduma.—The mission station.—Adversities.—Chronic bummers.—Mush and beans.—Courting privations...................... 55

CHAPTER IV.

FROM CISAMBA TO KUTUNDA.

Decide to change my route.—Cisamba.—Collecting carriers.—A surgical operation.—White man's fetich.—Strange comestibles.—Lura-lu-ra-lu.—Native obsequies.—Ocimbombo.—Bacchanalian carousals.—"On show" at Kapoko.—The cornet scare.—"Putting on side."—Sanambello.—Court speeches.—"A nation of the unemployed."—Reflections.—Trouble ahead.—A lucky shot.—Prescribing for the sick.—Fourteen days' delay.—Rumors of war.—Native idiosyncrasies.—By order of the "doctors."—Agricultural prospects.—A quiet week.—White ants.—Kundundu.—Desertions.—A kind-hearted chief... 67

CHAPTER V.

AMONG THE GANGUELLIANS.

My caravan complete.—Face to face with a lion.—A thunderstorm.—Crossing the Kukema.—Nothing for dinner.—A grand concert.—A promising field.—Petty rulers.—Namby-pamby.—Lady missionaries.—Trained nurses.—A wild chief.—Ganguellians.—Hairdressing extraordinary.—Fetich charms.—A fine country.—Iron-smelting.—Palavers and pigs.—The Kwanza River.—A wrinkle in river-crossing.—Native dread of Europeans.—A carved stockade.—A strange phenomenon.—Fever in the camp.—Limping into camp.—In the wilderness.—Rubber regions.—The honey-bird.—Picturesque huts. 88

CHAPTER VI.

FROM VOWELUTWI-ONJAMBA TO THE HUNTER'S PARADISE.

Five hundred natives in our camp.—Daily menu.—Scarcity of food.—Herds of buffalo.—The ombanda-horn.—Soldier ants.—Hostile natives.—Peace by stratagem.—A magnanimous promise.—*In puris naturalibus.*—Caterpillar stew.—Making an impression.—A wholesome awe.—Down with fever.—Extemporized mortars.—A dark outlook.—Carriers on strike.—A complimentary dance.—Rogues all of them.—Nurse and cook by turns.—Swamp villages.—Fail to control the elements.—Exorcising the spirits.—Struggles in the marshes.—Sparsity of villages.—Game in abundance.—Charged by a buffalo.—Has the Bihean a god?—Our rain-maker.—Diviners.—Medicine-men.—Meat and to spare.—A hunter's paradise 109

CHAPTER VII.

ARRIVAL IN THE BAROTSE VALLEY.

Mutiny in camp.—Barotse natives.—Milk for the first time.—The Zambesi at last.—Reception by King Lewanika.—"Yo sho, yo sho, yo sho!"—Salutations.—The royal residence.—"Fail not, at your peril!"—Barotse huts.—A native service.—Lewanika's ambition.—Building the Nalikwanda.—Paying off carriers.—Presented with an ox.—Dining with royalty.—The burden of his heart.—British Protectorate.—Thieves and robbers.—Monsieur Coillard's letter.—The British South African Company.—Concession-hunting.—An emphatic protest.—A letter from King Lewanika................ 134

CHAPTER VIII.

LIFE IN THE BAROTSE VALLEY.

The heroic Frenchman.—A model mission station.—Blighted plans.—A touching story.—Thrilling tales.—Truth first.—Missionary tidings.—Koreans.—Amazing statements.—Futile hopes.—Primitive Methodist party.—Home committees.—Virtually a prisoner.—Marotsi handicrafts.—In the lekhothla.—"A sound of revelry by night."—A perpetual vapor-bath.—A bloodthirsty queen.—Display of fireworks.

—New Year's Day.—First native wedding on the Zambesi.—Amused skepticism.—Ladies take a back seat.—Magic-lantern exhibition.—Silence reigns.—The Mashukulumbwe.—Taking their measure..... 152

CHAPTER IX.

FROM SEFULA TO SESHEKE.

The Sefula Canal.—Haste peculiar to white men.—To be thrown to the crocodiles.—Preparing for the river journey.—Parting injunctions.—A cloud of voracious mosquitoes.—Waist-deep in the swamp.—Afloat on the Zambesi.—Ancestral worship.—An interview with Makwai.—The omande shell.—The great fish-eagle.—Camped at Senanga.—More portentous game.—Memories of the Georgian Bay.—Charming surroundings.—A pleasure trip.—In danger of an upset.—Dragging canoes overland.—Lion stories.—The Falls of Gonya.—Beautiful cascades.—Veldt schoons.—In the rapids.—The aromatic mopani.—A fruitless chase.—A gorgeous sunset.—The graceful zebra 177

CHAPTER X.

FROM SESHEKE TO BAMANGWATO.

At Sesheke.—Working under difficulties.—Indifference of the natives.—Pay for "working book."—Not quite their equal.—Capabilities of the soil.—Monsieur Goy's letter.—Draining and irrigation.—Canoes capsized.—Kazungula.—The French mission.—Isolation and loneliness.—Premonitions of trouble.—Wholesale desertions.—Lost bearings.—A monopolist.—Tropical scenery.—Victoria Falls.—For hours we stand gazing.—The great fissure.—Baboons.—Batokaland.—Return to Kazungula.—Preparations for crossing the desert.—The tsetse-fly belt.—Pandamatenka.—Rough road.—A broken desselboom.—A night among lions.—Program of a day.—No water.—Thirst, thirst, thirst!—Bushmen............................... 198

CHAPTER XI.

FROM PALACHWE TO FORT VICTORIA.

Palachwe.—A terrible epidemic.—Malaria.—Semi-civilization.—Physically losing ground.—Khama and his country.—Total prohibition.

—The Mangwato as a race.—Makalakas.—Darker phases of African life.—McKenzie and Hepburn.—The Matebele.—On the trek again.—My West Indians return.—A monotonous landscape.—Fort Macloutsie.—Hyenas and jackals.—*Multum in parvo*.—Tuli township.—"Show your passport."—A licensed prospector.—Mealies and pumpkins.—Lobengula's impis.—Matipi's kraal.—Whiskey shops.—Syndicates "dead broke."—White men's graves.—"Providential Pass."—A tragic story.—Zimbabwe.—An ancient stronghold.—Fort Victoria.—A hundred miles of sand.................................. 228

CHAPTER XII.

FROM FORT VICTORIA TO INYAMACAMBE.

Fort Charter.—A deserted village.—Chartered companies.—Salisbury at last!—The wealth of Mashonaland.—A vegetable market.—The argument of the upper ten.—British influence.—Missions in Mashonaland.—A lion-hunt.—The parson scores heavily.—By Tete or Sena, which?—Fantastic kopjies.—Termite mounds.—A narrow escape.—Policemen.—"Tie him up till morning."—Umtali.—Massikassi.—Among the Portuguese.—A friend in need.—War in the Humbi country.—Bartering with the natives for food.—Abandoned wagons.—A primitive dug-out.—Courteous natives.—Wading the Kulumadzi.—Gorongoza Mountain.—Digging for water.—Spontaneous combustion.—Baobabs.—Lovely sweet oranges.......................... 259

CHAPTER XIII.

FROM SENA TO BLANTYRE.

River craft.—On the Shiré.—The Wissmann expedition.—Landed at Chiromo.—Trouble with Her Majesty's customs.—"What is to-day?"—The chief of Mbewe.—A defenseless position.—Blantyre.—Might is right.—Misguided men.—Boycotted.—Wild hallucinations.—Courting a martyr's death.—Dr. Ellinwood speaks.—Abortive asceticism.—Faith cure.—Cheap missionaries.—Poor economy.—A foreign tramp.. 287

CONTENTS.

CHAPTER XIV.

FROM NYASA TO CHINDE.

Bush fires.—A strong current and head wind.—Myriads of red ants.—Tampans.—On the back of a hippo.—Lake Nyasa.—Livingstonia.—A storm on the lake.—Anchored at Bandawe.—The Free Church Mission.—"Black ivory."—"Longed to enslave them."—Not soliciting commiseration.—Ungrateful.—Lip "improvers."—"Muavi" ordeal.—Fertile hills of Angoniland.—Liberty of conscience.—Baobab Island.—A choral service.—Return to Blantyre.—Bound for Chinde.—The Indian Ocean 305

CHAPTER XV.

A RETROSPECT.

A summary.—Jamaicans.—Missionaries wanted.—French mission stands alone.—Testimony in favor of West Indian assistants.—Unoccupied fields.—Sparse population.—Interpreters.—Medical missions.—Extravagant waste of ability.—Native doctors.—Conclusion. 325

APPENDIX.

Equipment.—Tents *versus* huts.—Clothing.—Firearms.—Barter goods.—Commissariat.—Medicine.—Tabloids.—Fever.—Insomnia.—Water.—Coolers.—Light.—Photography............................ 339

ILLUSTRATIONS.*

FRONTISPIECE.
CATAMBELLA..*Facing page*	22
OLOMBINGO ROCK MOUNTAINS......................................	28
STOCKADED VILLAGE, CISAMBA......................................	34
CAMP AT CISAMBA..	39
BIHEAN POMBIEROS (HEADMEN).....................................	45
BUILDING MISSION HOUSE, CISAMBA	50
NATIVE WOMEN, CISAMBA..	56
WOMEN POUNDING CORN	61
GANGUELLIAN VILLAGE..	66
GROUP OF GANGUELLIANS	72
CROSSING THE QUITU..	78
EXPEDITION AT KANGAMBA	86
LEWANIKA HOLDING COURT	94
MAROTSI SALUTATIONS...	103
MONSIEUR COILLARD AND NATIVE BOYS...........................	109
LEWANIKA IN WAR DRESS...	114
MISSION STATION, SEFULA...	121
MADAME COILLARD'S GRAVE	127
PRIMITIVE METHODIST PARTY	134
LEWANIKA'S BAND...	140
WILD BATOKA WARRIORS...	146
MACWAI, QUEEN OF BAROTSE, AND SLAVE-GIRLS....................	151
MAROTSI PASTIMES..	156
NATIVE WEDDING, SEFULA...	162

* These illustrations are covered by copyright. All rights reserved.

ILLUSTRATIONS.

Mashukulumbwe Natives.................................*Facing page*	167
On the Zambesi..	172
Falls of Gonya..	176
Horseshoe Falls of Gonya..	181
Zambesi Boatmen..	187
Mission Station, Sesheke.......................................	193
Kazungula Mission Station......................................	199
Victoria Falls (Western Cataract)..............................	205
Victoria Falls (Near the Center)...............................	210
Abrupt Bend and Profile Cliff, Zambesi.........................	216
Pandamatenka..	220
Khama, Chief of Bamangwato.....................................	226
Water-cart—Mangwato..	234
Crossing the Lundi...	240
Zimbabwe Ruins..	247
Bushmen's Drawings...	253
Pug-mill for Brickmaking, Blantyre............................	260
Angoni Slave Warriors..	269
Group of Yaos (Shiré Highlands)................................	276
Livingstonia...	284
Graves at Livingstonia...	290
Mission Station, Bandawe.......................................	298
Native Women, Bandawe..	304
Native Women, Likoma...	310
Nyasa Fleet, Likoma..	315
Katunga (Livingstone's Old Servant) and his Wives..............	323

REALITY VERSUS ROMANCE IN SOUTH CENTRAL AFRICA.

CHAPTER I.

FROM LONDON TO CATAMBELLA.

Early promptings.—Jamaica.—White men in the tropics.—Purposes of the expedition.—Hearty support.—Departure for Africa.—Lisbon Harbor.—"Stuck fast."—The detective camera.—The Portuguese.—On board the "Cazengo."—Rebels.—St. Thyago.—Barren rock.—St. Thome.—Kabinda.—St. Paul de Loanda.—Bishop Taylor's Mission.—Self-supporting missions.—Circumstances alter cases.—The Liberian Mission.—Pigeon English.—A *quid pro quo.*—Stowing coal.—Arrival at Benguela.—An evil climate.—Adobe.—Catambella.—Delays.—The railway.—Native trade.—Slave caravans.—Bad sanitation.

IN early boyhood a deep interest was created in my mind regarding Africa and its people by reading the life and travels of Robert Moffat. Later on the writings of Dr. Livingstone, the story of his lonely and tragic death, and witnessing his funeral in 1874, added fresh stimulus to my purpose of visiting some day the "Dark Continent." I wished to see for myself the actual condition of the African, that I might be the better qualified to plead his cause among English-speaking people, who have, particularly during this century, proven themselves above all other nations the pioneers of civilization, Christianity, and humane government.

Ill-health debarred me from the immediate realization of my hopes, and symptoms of pulmonary trouble compelled me, toward the end of 1874, to seek a more genial climate. This I found in Jamaica, West Indies, where the bulk of the population, though not African, are at least of African descent, and there I lived and labored at my profession until 1890.

My physical strength being then completely restored, the work under my charge firmly established and conducted by a competent staff of assistants, and the long-cherished desire to travel in no way abated, I felt that the time had come when I could leave my work for a year or two.

Meantime, accounts were frequently being received from Central Africa of the privations, hardships, and sufferings of those who were endeavoring to lead the van of light and knowledge into the dark interior—obtaining little or no aid or sympathy from the natives, for whose benefit they had risked so much. Treading the clay, cutting the sticks and grass, and with their own hands building the humble abodes that are to be their homes—white men cannot, in the tropics, do this with impunity and live. The painful fact is all too conclusive from the fearful death-rate among those who have attempted it on the Congo, the West Coast, and elsewhere.

On looking around among the young men of Jamaica connected with our mission, I was strongly impressed with the idea that, having been brought up and trained amid surroundings the most favorable to fitting them for usefulness in their fatherland, as mechanics, builders, and planters, by such services (could their natural lack of "stick-at-it-iveness" and backbone be overcome) they might relieve the white man of manual toil, permitting him to devote his time to the translation and teaching of the native languages.

To put this scheme to the test was now my intention, and although a dark enough program was presented of the probable dangers to be encountered, in the form of malarial climates, deadly fevers, wild beasts, fatigue, hunger, and thirst, volunteers to accompany me were not lacking, of whom I accepted six likely young fellows. On the 11th of February, 1891, I sailed for England, whence, as also from Scotland, the United States, and Canada, I received the heartiest support and financial aid toward the outfits and passages of the colored men; but I preferred to defray my own expenses.

The next few weeks were spent mostly in London, selecting and purchasing the varied paraphernalia and equipment required for camp life in a "foodless and shopless land." Further on I will enumerate, for the information of those who may intend to travel through similar regions, not so much of what articles my outfit consisted, but rather a list of those things actual experience proved to be the most useful. Very many accessories are recommended by outfitters because other travelers have included them in their kits, which on the march are found to be not only useless, but burdensome, and at last must be left behind. Nor are the counsels of those in the field always infallible, as many of them settle down within easy access of the coast and know but little of the requirements for long journeys through the interior. A good rule to follow is to take nothing that one can possibly do without, as the carrier difficulty increases year by year, and the progress of a caravan is often in inverse ratio to the amount of its baggage. "Picnic baskets," "jimcrack notions," and "*multum in parvo*" must give place to the more important well-chosen stores of food, medicines, and medical comforts, on which the health and even the life of the European will in a great measure depend.

Preparations completed, the 17th of April found the Jamaica men and myself at Waterloo Station, surrounded by a host of kind friends who had come to bid us Godspeed and a final farewell. A few hours more brought us alongside the steamship "Trojan," as she lay in Southampton docks. Amid the bustle and confusion of embarking the ship's bell rings—the signal that the time for departure has arrived. The gangway is drawn up, the hawsers slipped, and the vessel stands out to sea.

Benguela, on the west coast of Africa, is our destination by water. And why Benguela? Chiefly because it has the reputation of affording facilities for obtaining carriers, slave routes for the interior starting from that point.

The short run to Lisbon gave no experience worthy of note. A good ship, pleasant company, and a smooth sea—this told, the rest of our life on board a mail steamer can easily be imagined by any one who has crossed the Atlantic; and in these days, who has not?

On the 20th we enter the mouth of the Tagus—Lisbon Harbor. A charming view of the city presents itself as we steam up the river. The weather is all that could be desired, fresh but balmy; air, a delightful change from the bleak winds and drizzling rains we left in Southampton. Mile after mile the city unfolds before us—a grand panorama of splendid buildings, covering the long range of hills on which it is built, rising rank upon rank, tier upon tier, from the water's edge to the highest summits, with a sky overhead beautifully clear and blue. Anything more attractive or more picturesque I have never seen, in any country. Here we must land and tranship to a Portuguese steamer, as the "Trojan" does not call at West Coast ports; and we are transferred to the cranky-looking craft of a tender that is to take us ashore. Three hours are spent in this tub, for the tide is low and she gets stuck fast in the mud. Some of the passengers suggest chartering a couple of the fishermen's punts that are pulling past us; but this idea is voted down as undignified, and we meekly wait for the turn of the tide.

At last we reach the landing-stage—a flight of stone steps leading up to the magnificent square of Terreiro do paco, with its grand Arco da Rua Agusta, an equestrian statue of King Joseph I. in the center.

Stepping ashore, detective camera in hand, hoping to get some snap shots on objects of interest, a diminutive customs officer demands to know what the box contains; but my limited knowledge of Portuguese fails to convince him that I have nothing in it to peddle, when it occurrs to me to show him the reflection of King Joseph on the "finder." This is conclusive, and I pass on to the center of the city. The scene changes. Fewer adjectives will satisfy us now than when describing Lisbon from the steamer's deck. Surely distance lent enchantment to the view: the otherwise fine edifices are ill-kept and dirty, with a general out-at-elbows look, matching the majority of the inhabitants.

But what a lot of little people! A stay of several days in this the Portuguese capital did not remove our first impression, that, if for nothing else, it is at least remarkable for its undersized citizens. But we must not remark on this, as already we see their eyes flash and fists clenched menacingly when the word "English" is whispered in their presence.

The manner of dress is distinctly Spanish, and of a type—especially among the working classes—made familiar to us by Clark's cotton-reel pictures of the bull fight. Gay and loud colors predominate everywhere, and on everything.

Our steamer, the "Cazengo," in which we hope to sail for Benguela, is now in the river, and we embark, only to learn, however, that the government has ordered her detention for three days beyond the advertised date of sailing, as a number of political prisoners who have been concerned in the late revolutionary riots in Oporto are to be sent down to the West Coast. Much against our will, we must yield to the delay. The time passes, and on the fourth day we observe barges being tugged toward us crowded with soldiers, who with fixed bayonets surround the prisoners—a motley crew. The former look like a mixture of the veriest riff-raff of half a dozen different companies of militia—a perfect medley of shapes and sizes: round shoulders, bow legs, and unwashed; scarcely a man standing five

CATAMBELLA

feet eight among them. The majority were smoking cigarettes as they came alongside.

The prisoners seemed jolly enough, hob-nobbing with the "Soldados," shaking hands and embracing all round as they parted; while several had brought their mandolins and guitars, with which to wile away the tedium of the years they anticipated spending in exile. After a great deal of fuss and no little hilarity, they are got on board, about a hundred in all; and now that they feel themselves free, some brass and reed instruments are produced, and we are regaled with selections of republican music.

The next port of call, St. Thyago, we reach in six days. Still no extraordinary incidents to relate; the usual monotonous round of eating, reading, talking, and sleeping goes on, with an occasional game of quoits. It may be of interest to epicures if we mention of what the cuisine à la Portuguese consists. The dinner menu permits of no variation, but may be summed up thus: Seven courses of meat or fowl; sweets, dessert, and coffee, with almost total abstinence from vegetables of any kind. The light table wine "Vinho tinto" is supplied *ad lib.*, but, to the credit of the Portuguese, it must be acknowledged that they are certainly a temperate people as compared with those of more northern climes, for not once during the voyage did we see spirits used, nor any one the least inebriated.

The small island of St. Thyago belongs to Portugal, and, judging from its appearance, we would say it is not likely to be coveted by any other nation. The town is built on an eminence some two hundred feet above sea-level; it has a square and three streets running parallel with one another, and a population of about three thousand. How they live is a mystery, for both hill and plain present a dreary expanse of barren rock and sand, destitute of even a trace of vegetation, with the exception of here and there a hollow where a few parched-looking cocoanut palms struggle for existence.

We visit the marketplace, expecting that samples of whatever the island produces will be seen there. And it is so: a few baskets of beans, some tobacco, and scores of beggars, all extending their dirty hands at once as soon as we appear within the gates. The people are mostly African, of the ordinary type; a few are Portuguese; and there are three Englishmen, employees of the Cable Company.

On the 8th of May we arrive at St. Thome, a beautiful island, also a Portuguese possession. The town resembles somewhat parts on the north side of Jamaica. Here, unlike St. Thyago, the scenery is very rich; the hills are clad to the top with luxuriant verdure, cocoanut and date palms, bread-fruit and avocada pears, puapuas and bananas. This is accounted for probably by the fact that the island is situated within the rain belt—its southern end being on the equator.

We called at Kabinda on the 11th, where we took on forty-two natives to work cargo. This was our first glimpse of the African mainland, which is here very flat and uninteresting, with nothing tropical in its appearance.

Next day we reached St. Paul de Loanda, the chief of the Portuguese settlements on the West Coast. We had a tedious delay here of several days, on account of the many packages to be slowly transferred to lighters, and as slowly towed ashore. No one is in a hurry. Time seems to be of no value to these people. They reverse the old adage and "*never* do to-day what can be put off till to-morrow." The city is said to have a population of six thousand, made up of about four hundred Portuguese, the rest negroes.

Livingstone arrived here with his six Makalolo in May, 1854, and spent long weeks on a sick-bed at the house of his friend, the British commissioner for the Suppression of the Slave Trade. He traveled from Kurmuan, through the Kalahari Desert with its shadeless glare, the deep gloom of forests, and drenching rains, contracting an intermittent fever that almost ended his earthly career ere he reached Loanda—as he said, a "bag of bones."

The buildings look as if they were intended to resist bombardment, so heavy and bare are they, with but few piazzas or porticos to relieve the prison-like walls. The stores have little or no display of goods around the doors, and are destitute of windows. On going ashore we found all the shops shut, and for explanation were informed that it was breakfast-time. It seems to be the rule in Portuguese towns (in Africa, at least) that all places of business be closed once a day, for a couple of hours, to permit the *busy* traders and their assistants to partake of their meals in peace, and at leisure.

Recollecting that Bishop Taylor told me, when I met him in Indianapolis during the previous winter, that he had an important station at Loanda, after a little inquiry I was directed to the mission house, situated on the top of a hill overlooking the town. It stands alone on a sandy mound, built after the bungalow style, about a hundred and fifty yards from the main road. I found the wife of the missionary in charge, with her children, at home; but her husband, who works on the railway during the week, was absent.

Whatever may be said on missionary platforms concerning the feasibility of self-supporting missions in Africa, so far as I have seen or learned it is a grand mistake. The theory may be all right, but practically it is an absolute failure. Actual facts laid bare, and the experience of scores of earnest men now in the field prove, that it is infinitely more difficult for a white man to earn his living in Africa than in any European country—unless, of course, he abandons mission work and confines himself solely to trading. Then he is not likely to have much influence for the furtherance of the gospel among the natives, for his calling would preclude the possibility of this. Certain it is, that a man who must toil the whole week through for the support of his wife and children can have but few opportunities for evangelistic work, which should surely form the primary object in sending missionaries to a land so shrouded in darkness and superstition as Africa.

Mr. P—— does what he can in gathering a few men and boys (women rarely come) on Sunday afternoons in the basement of the house (they have no other meeting-place), and reads and speaks to them in Portuguese, but as yet without any apparent results.

The bishop seems to expect much from the training

of native children as future missionaries to their people. Good enough, if he could by a civilized upbringing change their hearts; but even Christian influences are not sufficient to turn the wayward into paths of rectitude, as many godly parents can testify. They may acquire some knowledge of the three R's, and how to dress in European fashion—the boys developing into idle dudes with unlimited conceit, and their natural antipathy for honest work immeasurably increased; and the girls will be much sought after for wives by the more aristocratic heathen (as has been the experience of missions on the Gaboon and in Sierra Leone, etc.). But is this gain to the kingdom of God? Or is this the work Christ has sent us to do?

Nor am I alone in my conclusions. In the issue for February of this year of *The Regions Beyond*, one who takes a deep and practical interest in African mission work writes:

"Paul said to Timothy, 'Meditate on these things; give thyself wholly to them;' and when he himself, for special reasons, and for a brief time, gave himself to manual labor and tent-making, *it was not in uncivilized Africa!* He had not to learn a barbarous language, or to get acquainted with the thoughts and feelings of a savage people. He was preaching in his mother-tongue, to his fellow-Jews in the familiar synagogue, and living in luxuriously civilized Corinth, where his hosts attended to all his wants, and where he had neither linguistic studies nor translation work nor sickness nor dispensing nor school-teaching nor long journeys to distract him. A very different state of things! Moreover—and this leads to a very important point—there was a good market at hand for the tents he made; and it was no doubt his hosts, not he, who attended to the commercial part of the business.

"There is at present no market on the Congo for anything the soil will grow, hence it is impossible to make money by any form of agriculture, even if a man does waste his time over it. And as to commerce, whether it be the foreign trade in ivory, or the repulsive and time-wasting domestic trade in hippopotamus flesh—which involves the hunting, killing, and cutting up of hippos, the drying of their flesh, and the bartering of it with the natives—or whether it be any other trade, all alike have this grave disadvantage, that even if by their means self-support could to some extent be attained by the missionary, it would immediately put him on a level with other traders, and the people would conclude that self-interest was his motive for dwelling among them. . . .

"The only 'self-support' possible, therefore, in Africa is the mere production for domestic use of a supply of vegetable and animal food on the station. All missionaries who can secure land round their stations go in for this, naturally, as soon as they possibly can, for the sake of health, comfort, and independence.

"But this is not self-support! Without committing the very folly and sin before alluded to of wasting their unspeakably precious time and talents, missionaries cannot raise even this *with their own hands*. Gardening takes much time, even at home. We should not think it wise economy for ministers to spend their days in cultivating potatoes and cabbages, or in feeding pigs and goats, even in England. How much more

OLONBINGO ROCK MOUNTAINS

absurd for missionaries to do it in Africa, where their time and knowledge are *so* precious, where labor under a tropical sun is dangerous to the health and life of white men, where native labor is cheap and abundant, where the people are naked and glad to earn 'cloth' to cover themselves by working for the white man, and where idleness is a vice which we want to cure in them.

"Common sense dictates the employment of the African in the actual work of the garden. They understand better than the missionary their own soil, productions, and climate, and can do the work quickly and easily. The white man must indeed superintend operations himself, or get his wife to do it, in addition to her already onerous domestic duties; but that need not take much time.

"But this, again, is not self-support! 'No pay, no work,' in Africa as in England. The natives have no idea of serving the white man unless he gives them a *quid pro quo*. They will not work for love either of the missionary or of the occupation. But they see and covet many of his European articles—cloth, cutlery, matches, beads, needles, boxes, or what not; and they will work for *these*. How can the missionary better begin to civilize and elevate the poor savages whose spiritual and physical good he has come to seek, than by giving them work which trains them to industry, and wages in the form of the primary necessaries of civilization? But to do this he must receive barter goods from home. These cost money to buy, and still more to transport into Central Africa. . . .

"Missionaries must either be supported by the natives or from home; but in Central Africa self-support is simply *impossible*, if rapid and effective evangelization of the Dark Continent is to be attempted.

"The Liberian Mission of Bishop Taylor is an illustration of this. It is situated on the coast, where steamers call regularly, and among professedly Christian negroes—a very much easier sphere, consequently, than the wholly unevangelized interior, a thousand miles from the coast. Between fifty and sixty missionaries have, at very heavy expense, been sent out since 1887 in connection with this mission, mostly from America. Six of the party died, twenty-seven (including families) withdrew, and nineteen remained last year. These were distributed in sixteen stations, so that a 'station' was for the most part a solitary man, without any helpers or resources. What has been the missionary result of this effort? Some houses have been built by the missionaries' own hands, some vegetable gardens cleared and planted, and some coffee plantations in the same way; but no attempt has been made to learn the native language, to translate the gospel into it, or to evangelize the Kroo people. The missionaries were instructed to preach as they could in 'pigeon English' (which some of the Kroos understand), and to try and teach the children English. No heathen congregations were gathered, no itinerating attempted, and no preaching to the heathen. One who worked three years in this 'mission,' and whose heart was burning to evangelize the Kroo people, found it impossible to get time for the study of the language. He had to build his house, clear and cultivate his garden, to light his fire and cook his food, and even to wash his clothes; for of course he had no means of paying to a native servant even the sixpence a day demanded.

"Is it not, therefore, conspicuously unwise, and the very worst possible economy, to encourage, or even *permit*, the missionary to diminish his already scanty leisure for the real work for which he goes to Africa, by frittering it away in manual labor in order that he may have food to eat?

"We trust that all who have been led to attempt, from right desires, this wrong plan, will do as we did ourselves—for we once tried it—abandon it as a mischievous delusion. 'The laborer is worthy of his hire.' When our Lord began His ministry He laid aside His carpentering. Missionary work in Africa is hard enough in any case—why make it harder? Life there is all too apt to be brief—why waste it while it lasts? And why go the way to shorten it?"

The last five or six days on board the "Cazengo" were anything but agreeable. By some bungling arrangement five hundred tons of coal stowed in the after-hold had to be hoisted on deck and removed in wheelbarrows by the Kabindas to the bunkers for'ard, resulting in our being kept in an atmosphere of coal-dust, which permeated and blackened everything. But on the morning of May 18th Benguela was sighted, and here ended our ocean voyage.

The town stands only a few feet above sea-level, on an unbroken sandy plain. It boasts a first-rate iron pier, with powerful derrick crane, and a tramway for the conveyance of goods to the custom-house and government warehouses adjoining—all spacious and commodious buildings, constructed of imported material, and around which several police sentries are posted, convicts from the East Coast being employed for this purpose.

On landing, I began to realize how terrible was the heat on seeing a fox-terrier belonging to one of the newly arrived passengers being led along the street, when suddenly it wheeled round two or three times, gave a yelp, and rolled over on its back, dead. Fearing a like fatality befalling my bull-dog Gyp, I got her under shade and procured water for her as soon as possible.

The climate of Benguela has an evil reputation, and the odds are very much against the probability of its improving, chiefly because of the low-lying situation of the town, preventing proper drainage and favoring malarial exhalations. Within the past few weeks seven European traders have been cut off by hæmaturic fever. Few white men can live here for any length of time without frequent visits to their mother-country.

The streets are broad and well kept, with a row of trees on each side, mostly sycamores. The houses are built of adobe (sun-dried bricks) laid with mud; the roofs and floors are tiled. A large square forms the business center, where around each door we see crowds of natives who have brought from the interior ivory, wax, india-rubber, etc., receiving in exchange cotton stuffs, guns, gunpowder, beads, and "aguardente" (white rum).

By previous arrangement with my agent, Mr. Kammerman, manager of the Dutch House, I found several carriers waiting to take our personal baggage on to Catambella, a town some sixteen miles north, where our caravan was to be made up for the interior. We started in the evening along a fairly good road but for the deep sand and dust, and arrived at the Dutch House about ten o'clock. But this hasty retreat from Benguela proved ill-advised; for if we were in a hurry the shipping officials were not, and in a couple of days I had to return again to see my goods through, and then found that the greater part had gone on by the "Cazengo" to Mossamedes. Thus I had to wait several days until she returned; then two more were wasted in transferring them from the lighters to the wharf— a bit of business that would have been completed on the Clyde, the Thames, or the Hudson in half an hour.

Mr. Greshoff (also of the Dutch House) kindly took charge of all my papers and had everything passed through the customs without any trouble. But I had still to draw on my almost exhausted stock of patience, for now the packages were in the hands of the dilatory railway company, and although a track to Catambella was commenced six years ago, not more than half the distance is as yet completed. We were not surprised at this, after having had pointed out to us two brass guns lying in the sand near the wharf, for which carriages were ordered in 1790 and are still *expected*.

The navvies employed for the heaviest work in the construction of the railway are native women, many of them toiling along under the scorching sun with pick and shovel, or carrying rails, sleepers, spikes, etc., with babies strapped to their backs.

A large trade with the natives is carried on in Catambella, and during our stay of ten days we had an opportunity of observing its general character. The

products of the far interior are bartered for the most
common quality of cheap and trashy goods it is possible to manufacture—some of the calicoes resembling
cheese-cloth, though not so strong; shoddy blankets;
long flint-lock guns, with gas-pipe barrels, white-pine
stocks painted red, and bound with numerous rings
of tinsel; white rum, etc. The headmen of caravans
receive much-appreciated presents in the shape of dis-
carded military clothing, helmets, tunics, and over-
coats, by way of encouragement to come again. It is
no unusual sight to see those lucky individuals strut-
ting behind their little company as they leave for the
journey homeward—one trigged out in an old pair of
'42 tartan trowsers and a helmet of the London police;
another with a dismantled busby and a footman's
swallow-tailed coat; next a silk tile and the scarlet
tunic of a Highland soldier. Of course, in each case
you must add Africa's national garment—the loin-
cloth!

Every morning, without exception, caravans varying in size up to hundreds of natives come trudging
into the town in long straggling lines, each carrier
bearing a load on his or her shoulder or head of from
forty to eighty pounds weight. The most pitiable
sight it is possible to witness is the long procession,
chiefly women, boys, and girls, limping along, footsore,
with swollen ankles and shoulders chafed by burdens
all too heavy for their emaciated bodies. A large percentage of these are slaves, bought in the interior by
half-breed traders for a few yards of cloth, and return
to their homes no more, being sold on putting down
their loads at the trader's door. I saw a band of sixty

STOCKADED VILLAGE.

such, each with a tin tag round the neck, being marched off to be shipped at Benguela for one of the Portuguese islands. Were *they* slaves? Oh no, only contracted labor. Just so. Or suppose we call them apprentices for life? What's in a name—so long as the letter of the law is evaded? Only this I know: that they were sold to their present owners at from three pounds sterling to six pounds per caput.

Long open sheds are provided in the yards of the houses at which the natives have come to trade, and after a few days these become loathsome in the extreme, from their crowded and unsanitary condition. The death-rate at best on the coast is very high, but add the filthy state of the kintouls, as these inclosures are called, and the mortality is fearful. Not a day passed that we did not see dead bodies, each wrapped in a bit of dirty cloth, tied to a pole and borne on the shoulders of two men to the top of the adjacent hill, where they are thrown over the other side, to be devoured by jackals and hyenas during the night, which is made dismal by their weird howls as they fight over their ghastly quarry. Deceased natives who have friends are carried out of town and buried by the wayside, so that for over a mile of the path to the interior there is scarcely a yard to right or left of the track that has not a grave.

CHAPTER II.

FROM CATAMBELLA TO KWANJULULU.

Toward the rising sun.—A waterless country.—A cold night.—Native foot-tracks.—The Esupwa Pass.—Bad water.—In the Cisangi country.—An outbreak in camp.—Foraging.—Extremes of temperature.—Lost in the forest.—In a game-pit.—Signals of distress.—Safe in camp.—On the great plateau.—Slave shackles.—Native graves.—In dangers oft.—The river Keve.—Utalama.—Indiscretion.—An untimely end.—Bailundu.—Cilumi.—The American mission.—Ekwikwi interviewed.—Trial for witchcraft.—Preparing for war.—Social laws.—Domestic relationships.—Farewell to Cilumi.—Artificial beehives.—Carriers.—Arrival at Kwanjululu.

FOR several days before starting much has to be done in the way of repacking and making up loads to the required weight—sixty pounds per man.

But at last, on the 29th of May, we are ready, and at three o'clock in the afternoon turn our faces to the east and set out on the march toward the Indian Ocean. How very far away it seems to us now, and how many weary steps must be taken ere that goal is reached and the great continent crossed! But it will be done if health and life are granted us. I take the lead myself, with two of the Jamaicans, the other four bringing up the rear; all of us feeling "very fit," and delighted to escape from the pestilential and fever-stricken coast.

Our path lies along the usual caravan route to Bihe. We have six extra men to carry water and other provisions through the waterless country between here and the Esupwa Pass. By six o'clock we camp for the night, making a short march of eight miles; but it is a start.

By the time my tent is pitched the food-boxes have arrived, and we set about preparing supper, gipsy fashion, but with a keen relish for our frugal repast. By 8 P.M. all is quiet, a score of camp-fires blazing, and around each the prostrate figures of several men with a little grass for a bed, and no covering but the canopy of heaven and their meager loin-cloths, there being neither sufficient wood nor grass to build huts. The dew is heavy and the night cold, so that the poor fellows have but a comfortless bivouac. By daybreak all are astir. There is time only for a hasty cup of coffee with a few biscuits, or the remains of last night's supper, wherewith to fortify the inner man for the road. The carriers eat nothing in the morning, but each man, seizing his load, cold and shivering, breaks into a half-trot, and follows the lead along the narrow track, that winds and twists, now up the rugged face of a hill, and anon through the long grass of the valleys. These tracks are mere footpaths, seldom over twelve or fourteen inches in width, but in many places worn into deep ruts by the rains and generations of native traffic; and woe betide the ankles of the pedestrian if he wears low shoes with sharp heels. Their general direction is as straight as the configuration of the country will permit; but in detail they turn and bend in the most tortuous fashion, without any apparent reason. A stone or stump is sufficient to switch the African out of his course, and on no account will he step over a fallen tree, be it ever so small, if by making a detour he can get round it; in a short time the white ants eat the tree, but the new path has been made, grass grows on the old, and so it remains for all time.

The country between Catambella and the Esupwa Pass—two days' march—is the most uninteresting and dreary waste imaginable. Not a drop of water is to be had, and the land yields nothing but a few isolated bobs of rough, reedy grass; and although we get an extensive view of hills and plains, there is nothing to relieve the eye, only the vast stretch of stunted scrub, with here and there a puny tree with gnarled trunk and shadeless foliage. But on the 30th we camped by the Esupwa River, and had a delightful swim in its beautiful clear waters, the natives warning us to keep a sharp lookout for alligators, as they abound here. Numerous long-tailed black monkeys grinned at us from the trees as we performed our ablutions. This is a charming spot. I wonder if we shall come across many more like it?

Next day we commenced the ascent of the Esupwa Mountain—a stiff pull over immense boulders of rocks. The pass reminds me very forcibly of a bit of Scottish Highland scenery. We are now getting up to the great Central African plateau, and in a day or two expect to reach an altitude of five thousand feet above sea-level.

Reached the camping-ground about noon. We have not seen a village, and only one human habitation, since leaving the coast. We had to wait until four o'clock for dinner, as the only means of obtaining water was by digging a deep hole in a dry river-bed, and waiting for a muddy pool to form, to be dipped up in cupfuls. What a change from yesterday! But by boiling and allowing it to settle, we collect sufficient

CAMP AT CISAMBA

See page 65

for our immediate use. These long fasts become very trying, especially when, after a long march, we get into camp weary and hungry about 2 p.m., having had nothing but a few ounces of food at daybreak, and now to wait until water is found and food cooked! To eat biscuits by the way would cause thirst, and often without the means of allaying it. This brings us down to one meal a day, as, by the time dinner is over, it is getting dark, and after a chat round the camp-fire, rehearsing the experiences of the day and the prospects for to-morrow, we are glad to roll ourselves in our blankets and go to sleep.

Another day and we arrive in the Cisangi country, where, near a small village, we camp. We purchased some sweet potatoes, the poorest I have ever seen; also corn on the cob, the longest about four inches; but when we look at the poor sandy soil, we wonder how it yields anything at all.

The last of the loads had only just come in, when I heard loud shrieks proceeding from some distance behind my tent. Hastening to the spot, I found a band of my carriers, who, presuming on the fact of their being with a white man, were attacking and doing their best to plunder a small native caravan bound for the coast. At first I could not comprehend what all the row was about, until the excited strangers directed my attention to several men retreating toward the camp, each carrying some article he had seized. Then I took in the situation. Right before my eyes two burly fellows were helping themselves to small bags of meal, carried by some little girls, who were screaming piteously and begging to have their food spared. I made signs—not knowing the language—for the robbers to desist, but in vain; they pretended not to notice, and my only alternative was to make them feel. Laying hold of a stick that was handy, I applied it with some vigor across the shoulders of the cowardly villains, when they speedily dropped the meal and made off. In a very short time, by means of the same stick, I succeeded in restoring all the spoil, and walked with the scared little company until they were a safe distance from my men. None can regret more than I do the necessity for such drastic measures being resorted to; yet it is imperative that a clear understanding be arrived at between the leader of an expedition and his men on the question of plunder; neglecting to define it emphatically at the start would probably mean the ruin of the undertaking, as has been the experience of some we could name, besides being the cause of great loss of life.

The small defenceless party come from the far interior and belong to a powerful tribe lying right in our route. In a few weeks they return from the coast, pass on ahead of us, and report the assault of the Bihenans to their people. The former have nothing to fear in this case, as they do not travel beyond their own country; but the injured natives sound their slogan as the white man approaches their territory, and they lay wait for him. If he refused to defend the weak and wronged, or winked at the depredations of his men, he must now fight or die—and perhaps both. I am persuaded that many of the disasters that have befallen large expeditions through various parts of Central Africa might have been averted had the explorer in charge rigorously punished the natural predisposition of the African to steal from the tribe through whose country he is passing. Of course it is called foraging, but it means in many instances that hundreds of men are set free to take what they want by force from the villagers, who in turn appeal to the white men for redress. These, not knowing the extent of the pillage, hand over a bit of cloth, a few beads or handkerchiefs—compensation altogether inadequate: result, a passage at arms and probably losses on both sides.

June 2d. I find it difficult to start the carriers in the morning before the sun is up, the cold is so severe. They huddle together round the fires, and when at last they are roused to make a move, with one hand they steady their load, and with the other grab a firebrand, and trot off blowing upon it to keep up the glow and so supply a little warmth to their fingers. The extremes of temperature between night and day are now very trying to those of us who have warm clothes. What must it be to their naked bodies! At 6 A.M. to-day the thermometer in my tent registered 38° F., and yesterday, at noon, in the shade, over 90° F.

Water still very scarce—not a drop to be had except by digging; and so impure, that boiling, precipitating with alum, and filtering were not enough to prevent it bringing on a sharp attack of dysentery when about a mile from camp. All the afternoon and night of the 4th I was completely prostrated—the most acute twelve hours of suffering I ever endured.

June 5th. Feeling very weak, but thankful to be sufficiently recovered to take the road, four men carrying me a good part of the way in a hammock. Our path led through thick bush; there were no villages in sight, and we were impressed with the apparent sparsely populated condition of the country.

We were quite out of fresh meat, and after a frugal meal of desiccated soup and manioc I took my gun and went out—unwisely, alone—in search of something for the pot. I shot a few pigeons, and, seeing a good many at some distance, but very wild, kept following hither and thither, until I got turned round and lost my bearings, forgetting the direction of the camp. The sun having set, it got dark very quickly, and in a short time I had to face the awkward position of finding myself lost in the forest. I wandered up and down for hours, endeavoring to strike some track that might lead me out; but in vain. It was now pitch dark. I sat down, tired of hopelessly struggling among the bushes; but, having on neither coat nor vest, and without matches to light a fire, I felt chilly, and determined to make one more effort to obtain sight or sound of camp. I climbed several trees, hoping to get a glimpse of the camp-fires; but no, there was nothing to be seen but the black outline of the trees against the sky. The welcome stars began to appear, and soon the southern cross was in view; and, having an idea that I ought to turn north, I set out once more, but had not gone far when I entered a deep ravine and encountered a swamp with long reedy grass towering high above my head. I pushed on, holding my gun horizontally, to keep the spear-grass from cutting my face. Suddenly my feet went from under me, and I was precipitated into a deep game-pit. The branches of trees with which its mouth had been covered broke the fall considerably; but an angry snarl from below announced that I was not alone in the trap. I felt for my sheath-knife in prospect of an encounter, but a coarse fur brushing past my face intimated that the animal, whatever it was, had no such pugnacious intent, but, being equally scared, took advantage of my shoulder to effect its escape. The hole was narrow and I managed to scramble out by butting my feet against the opposite side. The struggle in the pit, however, took away the last vestige of strength I possessed, and to go farther was impossible.

I discharged the remaining cartridges in the forlorn hope that the shots might be heard by some of my people. Breathless with anxiety and fatigue, I listened, when, to my unspeakable relief, after a few minutes I heard, though at a great distance, the answer of a native gun; and soon the shouts of my men, getting more and more distinct, told me that I would sleep in my tent that night and not in the woods, as a short time before seemed inevitable.

Next day brought us through a more thickly populated and better cultivated district than we have seen since starting. I was much interested in several peculiar-looking mountains, seemingly solid blocks of granite without a vestige of grass or herbage, and no crags, fissures, or jagged rocks. One in particular was round and smooth, like a gigantic inverted basin. We camped at the base of the Olombingo range, so called because of its rocky peaks, resembling, when viewed at a certain angle, the horns of an animal.

For several days now our path leads over a series

of mountains, including the Elonga (or plate, from the hollowed-out shape of its summit), on the top of which both boiling-point thermometer and aneroid indicated an altitude of seventy-two hundred feet. From this point the view of hills and valleys is really very fine— the atmosphere so clear, and no forests intervening. The immense landscape of rolling country is limited only by the extent of our vision.

I noticed by the pathway a great many blocks of wood, from a foot to eighteen inches long and about five inches wide, with an oblong hole cut in each. These, I was informed by the natives, were the articles used by slave-traders with which to fetter their captive carriers during the night. The feet are passed through the hole and a wooden peg driven between the ankles.

We passed by the wayside the grave of a pombiero, or headman of one of these caravans, where the natives had with grim satire erected a monument to his memory, by stringing some twenty of these shackles on a pole and sticking it up at the head of the mound where the tyrant was buried, that the passer-by might read the suggestive epitaph. Numerous bleaching skulls a little way from the track tell how the slaves whom death has set free are disposed of. But the headman of an ordinary caravan is generally buried in a very respectful manner, his hat, umbrella, cooking-pot, and powder-barrel being invariably placed on the grave. Over all a rude hut is built, open at the sides, while near by a rough seat is erected, lest the spirit of the departed should get tired wandering up and down—as they suppose it does—and, returning to the spot, it

BIHEAN POMBIEROS (HEADMEN)

might be gratified by this mark of consideration for its comfort on the part of the relatives or friends, and so refrain from haunting or troubling them.

On the 8th, soon after starting, we were accosted by four blacks, whom we recognized as Portuguese soldiers. They were armed with Snider rifles, bayonets, and cartridge-belts, and announced to us that an officer and his wife were on their way to Bihe; but most of their carriers having deserted, leaving their loads in the bush, these worthies had orders to get men where and how they could, to fill the vacant situations. While making these explanations they kept casting furtive and admiring glances on some of my carcadores (porters), ultimately expressing their opinion that some of them would serve their purpose. But, pointing to my Winchester and Webley, I emphatically assured them that to touch a single individual in my caravan would bring about the funeral of more than one Portuguese soldier before the sun set. At this the cowardly quartet sneaked off, allowing our carriers to pass without further molestation; but later in the day we learned that no sooner were we out of sight than they intercepted a party of natives, seized and bound twelve men, marching them off at the point of the bayonet. The whole district seems terror-stricken because of these marauders. We passed several villages where we had hoped to obtain food, but the inhabitants had fled.

Two days more bring us to the Bailundu country. The ground being white with hoar-frost in the early morning, it is very difficult for the first hour or two to urge the men along; they want to stop every few minutes to make a fire, while some sit down to cry over and hug their cold feet.

On the 10th we reached the Keve River. Some of us were ferried across in a native bark canoe, others waded over. It is said by some travelers that this stream is likely in the future to prove a great waterway into the interior from Novo Rodondo. The wisdom or otherwise of the suggestion may be judged from the fact that the body of water is comparatively small, navigable for most of the year only by canoes, and its elevation five thousand feet above the sea—a pretty steep climb for steamers in that short distance. But what would they come here for, anyhow?

Another few miles and we reach Utalama, the village where poor Morris and Gall died and lie buried a stone's-throw from the path, the graves inclosed by a palisade of sticks. Thoughts of deepest gratitude to God rose in my heart for the good health of our party thus far; but as I gazed on those lonely mounds I found myself in a melancholy reverie, having learned, since coming to Africa, the painful circumstances connected with their death—circumstances reflecting anything but credit on those who had charge of the party, and proving the indiscretion of permitting a man like Mr. Morris, just out of a London counting-house, to tramp all day in the glaring heat of Africa, living on the coarsest fare and sleeping sometimes in the open at night, as we gather from his own diary:

"It was late before we reached camp. Only one tent was pitched, into which the three sisters retired, and we brethren just lay round about, wrapped up in our rugs on the bare ground, some of us—I among them

—putting up our umbrellas over our heads to keep off the night dew, which falls very heavily."

The privations suffered were from no lack of means, but from sheer mismanagement on the part of those who were responsible for the conveyance of this new party to the interior. For Mr. Morris was a gentleman of high standing and repute, an eminently successful Christian worker at Walthamstow, and connected with a lucrative mercantile business. Selling out his share, he with Mrs. Morris started for Africa at their own expense. But they never reached their destination. Mr. Morris was stricken by the fever, and Mr. Gall about the same time, their deaths occurring within four hours of each other.

For some days previous to his death Mr. Morris lay in a semi-conscious condition. Night and day his heroic wife was by his side; but who shall tell of the anguish of mind she must have endured as she watched her husband shortly before he died? "Wringing his face at the memory of his poor children left behind, 'I cannot, no, I cannot leave them!' he burst forth. 'My precious girls—my boy, my boy!'"*

Some may seek to moralize, and quote Scripture for their comfort, on the premature end of two valuable lives; but the harrowing details as related by eyewitnesses of the tragic scene haunt us like a horrible dream, and satisfy us that this mournful event might have been averted had the leader been possessed of as much common sense as sentiment.

June 11th. A number of our carriers belong to this district, and refuse to lift their loads this morning,

* From *Echoes of Service*.

wishing, as they say, to spend the day with their friends. I was successful, however, by dint of coaxing and threats, in inducing half a dozen men to start with me for Cilumi, a station of the American mission some eighteen miles distant, and to the left of our route.

Leaving the Jamaica men in charge of the camp, with instructions to advance next morning, we set out and arrived at the mission compound by noon. The missionaries, the Revs. Stover, Woodside, and Cotton, extended to me a hearty welcome. Nothing could have exceeded the kindness of these good friends, and I was easily persuaded to prolong my stay for a couple of days.

This mission—an oasis in the desert—was founded about twelve years ago, and there are now twenty-four converts in church-membership; but the influence of these men, their wives, and Miss Clark, a young Canadian lady who assists in school-teaching, cannot be calculated by figures.

The marked improvement in the social condition of the natives in the neighborhood, as compared with those we have met hitherto, testify that, if slowly, yet surely, the power for good of a mission such as this, conducted on practical common sense as well as Christian principles, must in due course become manifest both in the lives and homes of the people among whom it is established.

It may be said that the results seem small considering the large staff of laborers, and the many years that have passed since the work was organized. Yes, if it were true, as is asserted again and again, that the African earnestly reiterates the Macedonian cry, "Come over and help us;" and that already "Ethiopia stretches out her hands unto God." *If* he calls for missionaries at all, it is because he expects them to bring him cloth, beads, guns, and gunpowder; but he is not particularly anxious for the gospel, for he is ignorant of its import and meaning, and in his heathen condition wants nothing that does not add to his sensual gratification. Anything else he must be taught; and this means slow, uphill, and often discouraging work. Only in the field is it possible to know a tithe of the hindrances and barriers to the progress of missions in Central Africa, requiring, as they do, unlimited patience, strong faith, and steady plodding toil on the part of those who would succeed.

I accompanied Mr. Woodside on a visit to Ekwikwi, king of Bailundu, at his "ombala" or capital. The royal village is situated on the top of a hill, commanding a good view of the surrounding country. A hole in the palisades about twenty inches wide and five feet high forms the grand entrance to the courtyard, which at night is used as a cattle-pen. Here we found his majesty, seated on a stone placed against the fence. At a distance of some thirty feet, and in a semicircle, squatted a large number of minor chiefs, counselors, and headmen. In the center sat a man who was being tried for his life under an indictment for witchcraft; and by his side an aged chief, who had espoused the culprit's cause, was, at the time we entered, eloquently pleading the innocence of his client. The speaker stopped short as we appeared, and waited until the ceremony of being "presented at court" had ended. The king greeted us cheerfully, graciously accepting a present of cloth, a bit of soap, and a box of matches; and we took seats, by his request and favor, on stones close to "the bench." The advocate then proceeded with the case, while Ekwikwi kept up a running fire of interrogations at Mr. Woodside, concerning the stranger. "Who is he?" "Where from?" "Whither bound?" etc., etc.

The king has a shrewd and not unintelligent face. He is probably about sixty years of age, and rejoices in a harem of over fifty wives, most of them being captives from distant tribes, brought home as booty during his periodical raids on districts which he thinks ought to pay him tribute and don't! Only a short time ago, he returned from one of these campaigns bringing back some sixty slaves and large herds of cattle.

While sitting in the court we observed the young men busy making cartridges, forming a case by deftly rolling paper round a stick, filling it with gunpowder, and inserting iron slugs at the end—suggestive of coming trouble to some unsuspecting community.

There was nothing very royal in the king's attire, however, his only habiliments consisting of a ragged loin-cloth and a dirty red night-cap on his head; but he possesses a real court dress of which he is very proud, and dons it only on state occasions. It was made for him by one of the ladies at Cilumi, of gay furniture chintz, fixed up with flounces and a train.

Several boys and girls from the ombala attend the mission school, and on inquiring if the fathers of the children sought in any way to hinder them from being educated, I was surprised to learn that they have, as a

BUILDING MISSION HOUSE, CISAMBA

rule, little or no voice in the matter. We are accustomed in England and America to picture the native African as sitting under his own "vine and fig tree" with his happy family circle around him; and the brilliant perorations on antislavery platforms referring to the "ruthless rending asunder," and so on, are familiar to us all. So far as I can learn, neither our preconceived ideas nor the allusion apply, to this part of Africa at least.

The terrible record of "man's inhumanity to man" in the slave-trade is much deeper and more far-reaching in its cruelties than the "severing of family ties"— ties, in most cases, less than nominal. For that matter, they think nothing of selling one another when it suits them; and when, by the vigilance of British gunboats, the slave traffic on the East and West Coasts, as carried on by Arabs and half-breed Portuguese, is put down, by far the worst form of slavery will still remain untouched, as it exists to-day among the tribes of the distant interior.

In reference to the social laws that obtain in Bihe, it may be said that a father is scarcely acknowledged as a relative of his own child, and can exercise no control over it. Nor can the child, on the other hand, make any claim on its father, except it be the child of a slave wife; then it is the property of the father, just as the mother is.

When a man wishes to marry a free woman, he applies to her eldest brother, and, if accepted, seals the engagement by paying four yards of calico. On the day of the marriage some sixteen yards more have to be laid down. At the close of the wedding-feast he takes home the bride to his own village, and he can retain his wife only by paying tribute to the brother, of a fowl or handkerchief every new moon; failing this, she must be returned, and the cloth paid is forfeited. The offspring of this union belong not to the father but to the uncle, who alone has the right to dispose of them or their services. Should he get into debt, he can pass them over to his creditors as surety, or they may be sold to liquidate his liabilities. If it happens that the wife fails to work in the field or cook the "mush" to her sire's satisfaction, he may dismiss her; and if he can make good his complaint before a court of the headmen of the village, he gets back the cloth he paid for her and looks around for a better mate.

At 6 A.M. on the 13th we reluctantly bid farewell to Cilumi, and strike out briskly, knowing that my caravan is by this time a long way ahead, and it must be overtaken, if possible, by noon, so as to select the camping-ground for to-night.

Here, as all through the forests of Angola, are to be found many artificial beehives, made from the stout bark of a tree four or five feet long and from twelve to fifteen inches in diameter. To remove this bark, the natives make two incisions around the trunk and a third longitudinally, when the elasticity of the bark permits of its being peeled off and assuming its original form. The edges are then drawn together by means of pegs and withes, and the ends closed in by weaving grass over them, leaving a small hole for the entrance and exit of the bees. These hives are then placed in a horizontal position high up among the branches of the trees; and from them is obtained most of the wax exported from Benguela and Loanda.

A sharp five hours' march brings us to a stream, where we find the loads are all laid down, while the carriers fill their water-gourds and rest a bit. At our approach Frater reports all correct, and each man, shouldering his load, falls in Indian file, as usual, along the track; which in this part of the country must be very old, for it is worn in some places fourteen inches deep and about nine wide, causing many a hard knock on my internal *malleoli* from the heel of the opposite shoe, as hour by hour we thread the narrow ditch; and, like horses, we strike worst when tired.

Four more marches. To-day a counterpart of yesterday—nothing of importance occurring, except that on the fourth day we traveled twenty-five miles, and reached Kwanjululu at about 3 P.M. Here we must pay off the men who have brought us thus far—three hundred and twelve miles from Benguela—and remain for some time to collect a new set of carriers for our next stage inland.

These delays in changing carriers are very vexing, and a severe tax on patience; but the traveler is entirely at their mercy, and must simply wait their pleasure. A sufficient number being engaged does not by any means imply a start forthwith. No; they have to go to their villages, taking the loads with them, and for a couple of weeks they will think and talk about the road; another ten days for the women to pound their meal; yet another week for a big farewell beer-drink; then we move off ten or twelve miles along the intended route and form camp as a preliminary notice that we can wait no longer. During the next week or two they will come in twos and threes until the most have turned up; then another move is made.

But perhaps in the meantime rumors of inter-tribal wars from countries through which we have to pass frighten the whole crowd, and they lay down the loads and desert to a man.

CHAPTER III.

KWANJULULU AND KOMONDONGO.

An English mission.—The illusion dispelled.—Garanganze.—Five years' work.—Their own superstition best.—*Echoes of Service.*—Vegetable products.—Visit to Komondongo.—The late war.—Cause of the rupture.—The peacemaker.—Burning villages.—Capture of Chindunduma.—The mission station.—Adversities.—Chronic bummers.—Mush and beans.—Courting privations.

KWANJULULU is the headquarters of the English Brethren Mission, and is situated in the territory of Bihe, within a day's march of the American mission stations, Komondongo and Cisamba.

This entering a district already occupied by the American Mission has been unfortunate, and the cause of no little friction. Surely there is room enough in Africa for different societies to organize mission centers without treading on one another's toes! God forbid that Africa should ever know the jangling and rivalry of the sects so prevalent in more enlightened lands.

The Kwanjululu Mission is superintended by a Mr. F. S. Arnot. My preconceived ideas in favor of this mission have received such a shock, as week by week its actual condition has been laid bare, that I would prefer to draw a veil of silence over all I have seen and heard here; but I am impelled, from no other motive than my interest in missions generally, to plead for a reformation in such quarters, *lest* the day come when the enthusiasm aroused at home by the flaming and high-colored reports of grand conquests of the gospel will suffer reaction. The supporters of this enterprise have been led to contribute large sums of money toward what may be truthfully designated a huge farce, and, when the manner in which they have been hoodwinked is brought to light, disastrous reflections will be cast upon the noblest enterprise of the Church of God at the present day—foreign missions.

Whatever Kwanjululu may be as a transport depot, its influence as a Christian mission is almost *nil*. But few natives attend the meetings, and next to no evangelistic work is being done. Not a single gospel meeting was held for three successive Sundays in last month, nor came there a solitary hearer from outside the compound. On Sundays, at the usual time for morning service the missionaries meet for mutual edification and "breaking of bread"; but as this is the most suitable hour of the day for getting the natives together, the opportunity is lost. While at the other station, Garanganze, Mr. F——, one of the mission staff, who has just come out from that district, tells me that but little spiritual work has been accomplished there, the time being occupied chiefly in making gardens, hunting for food, waiting on King Msidi, and personally conducting the transit of supplies from Kwanjululu. Thus Mr. T——, one of their best men, has spent twenty-one months on the road, out of the two years he has been in the mission.

Mr. S——, in charge of the Garanganze branch, writes:

NATIVE WOMEN, GESAHHA

"It is now nearly three years since we came here, and how very little seems to have been done! If we add the two years that Brother Arnot was here, it makes *five* years. What a length of time to have been living in the country and yet many of the natives scarcely know our object in living among them! It is true, and we thank God for it, that those who are in the habit of coming to our meetings are beginning to understand more clearly what we are here for; but the great majority seem to think we have some personal interest in living among them.

"A few days ago a man who had heard something about the white man's country said, 'You must have committed crimes at home, or you would not live here.' Some might think that all that is necessary is to tell them you have come 'to teach people the Word of God' and they would understand at once. But is it so? Far from it. You must first tell them who *God* is, where His *Word* comes from, how it is that *we* are so interested in them that we come to live with them. When you remember that before any of these things can be told them it is necessary to learn a language altogether different from your own, without the aid of vocabulary or grammar, you *begin* to understand to some extent how so much time passes away without any or with very few results to show. Even after you fairly master the language and tell them distinctly that you are here to teach them about God and His precious Word, you are sometimes greeted with 'buvella' or 'buramba,' the Yeke and Luba words meaning 'nonsense, untruthfulness,' etc.

"Again, you sit down with a man and try to teach

him something about right and wrong, and after you have finished he goes away without feeling his responsibility to do what you tell him is right and leave off doing that which you have sought to show him is wrong. Perhaps the conclusion he comes to is that their superstitions are far better than ours. He looks around, and he sees Va-yeke, Va-lamba, Va-luba, Va-lunda, Va-sanga, and a host of others, with their peculiar beliefs of right and wrong, and when he hears us he looks upon us as one more among the rest, and cannot at all see that he is responsible to take heed to what *we* say. Of course we tell him that the Word of God is for all people, but to *tell* him is not to *convince* him."

Would that all the reports from the Brethren Mission were as honest as this! Then there would be nothing to gainsay, for results are not in the power of man to control; but he may, if he will, control his pen and refrain from idle embellishments, exaggerated and fictitious stories of success, that are without foundation.

From the head of the Kwanjululu depot we received several letters extolling the agricultural capabilities of the district; also in the *Echoes of Service* we read that every kind of vegetable product is grown in abundance, including wheat, yams, potatoes, cabbages, strawberries, etc. The fact is that the crop of wheat referred to was raised on a spot of land previously used as a cattle-pen, and made up by large quantities of earth carried from a neighboring marsh. Scarcely a fair criterion by which to judge the productiveness of the soil! At this season of the year it would be hard to find a handful of vegetation in any of the mission gardens; only during the brief period of the wet season can any vegetables be grown, and then only by the free use of fertilizers. But the extravagant accounts of the land as a source of food-supply for white men were as disappointing as the Christian work we expected to find, and as misleading as many other statements we had to deplore.

On the 22d of June we set out to visit the American mission at Komondongo. About half-way stands the Portuguese fort, Silva Porto. I called on the "capitan" in command to present my compliments and show my passport, and found him very polite and agreeable. He conducted me round the premises, where everything was neat, trim, and ship-shape. The fort is garrisoned by a force of some two hundred slave soldiers armed with Snider rifles. In the armory stand four field-pieces, including a "Krupp" and a "Nordenfeldt."

Soon after leaving the fort we struck the wagon road made by the Boers during their visit to suppress the late native rebellion. And now we travel mile after mile through a country desolate enough at best; but since every village and human habitation on the road to within a short distance of Komondongo has been burned to the ground, leaving nothing but charred palisades and the ruined huts, the prospect is anything but inviting.

The cause of the rupture was, briefly, as follows: Portugal has long claimed sovereignty over Bihe, and until lately was content that her authority remained nominal. Early last year a few of her soldiers, under Captain Conceiro, were ordered inland, but were refused permission by the king of Bihe to pass through his country. The king protested that an agreement had been made between him and the Portuguese government that black soldiers should never be quartered in Bihe—that only white people were welcome to his country. The natives, who had never felt the force of European arms, refused to be included among the vassals of the Portuguese, and assembled in large numbers to resist what they deemed an invasion of their territory, promptly moving against the captain, who, having but a small company of black soldiers with him, wisely retired, to wait for reinforcements.

In the meantime, Señor Silva Porto, the representative of the Portuguese, who had lived at what is now the fort (and from whom it obtains its name) for upward of forty years on amicable terms with the natives, did his best to allay the fears of the chief, but failed. This pseudo-insurrection having been taken up by the imperial government, and his previous success in controlling the Biheans ignored, so distressed Porto that he concluded life was for him no longer worth living. Going to his magazine and arranging a dozen kegs of gunpowder, he wrapped himself in the flag of his country, lay down on the explosives, applied a lighted fuse, and in a few seconds was blown through the roof, expiring shortly after.

Portugal, still determined to punish the rebels, sent Captain Piva with a company of black soldiers and a force of Boers from Caconda with fifty wagons to the scene of action. Why engage Boers for this purpose? it may be asked. The Portuguese know, and do not hesitate to say, that while their demoralized blacks under strict supervision answer very well as police,

WOMEN POUNDING CORN

without the presence of a white force to stiffen their courage they cannot be depended upon in a hard fight. A regiment of white troops would only complicate matters, from their lack of experience in such warfare, entailing also the transport of supplies; but Boers being a people born and brought up, it may almost be said, in wagons, inured to hardship, expert shots, and well acquainted with the guerrilla tactics of native fights, it was decided to employ them, stipulating that each man take his wagon, carry stores, etc., for the government, and provide his own. The Boers, knowing that the natives, with their uncertain flint-locks and cowardice, could make no stand against their superior weapons and skill, looked upon the whole business as a pleasant picnic with one pound terling a day per man.

Mr. Saunders, of Komondongo, apprehensive of coming trouble and anxious to avert it, if possible, visited the military camp and requested an interview with the officer in command. This granted, he inquired if there were any messages he could carry to the natives, but received the curt reply, "No; we want the chief Chindunduma."

The foolish Biheans, meanwhile, were preparing for war, and, as a preliminary step to attacking the white men, brought out their fetich-doctor to put "something" in the river Kakema, that ran between them and the Portuguese camp, which would have the effect of causing instant death to the enemy should they have the temerity to cross the water.

To accomplish this, the "potent spell" was put in a gun and with much ceremony fired into the river. This the Boers took as a signal for attack, and rushed up, firing on them, dropping eleven of the naked warriors dead on the bank, the remainder beating a hasty retreat. A few days after, the Biheans attacked a small party who were engaged in clearing a road for the wagons; but the Boers responded with such deadly effect that a panic seized the assailants and they fled east to the Ganguellas. The burning of villages now began, and every human abode over a great track of country, including the "ombala," was sacrificed to the flames; the latter is said to have had a population of ten thousand inhabitants.

A truce for nine days was now declared, and within this period it was required that the chief be found and given up; failing this on the expiry of the few days' grace, the whole of Bihe would be destroyed by fire.

Mr. Saunders lost no time in dispatching messengers to all the minor chiefs holding the roads of exit from the country, that they might be guarded and so prevent the escape of Chindunduma. Then, calling a council of the headmen, he placed the serious state of affairs before them, thus obtaining their help. For eight days the country round was scoured by the missionary and hundreds of natives, but in vain. On the ninth day, however, when hope was about giving place to despair, the man so much wanted was discovered cringed up in an isolated hut armed with a Martini rifle. Mr. Saunders entered and explained his business, whereupon the old man offered no resistance, but, surrendering, was handed over to the authorities that same night, and is now a state prisoner on one of the little islands on the West Coast.

Missionaries sometimes meddle unwisely in political disturbances; but in this case it was well, for thereby much bloodshed was averted and an immense territory saved from entire devastation.

By sunset I reached Komondongo, tired and weary; but the hearty greeting of the Rev. Mr. Saunders and the kindly welcome of his good wife dispelled all thought of fatigue. Once inside the mission house, I could easily have imagined myself in a genuine New England farmhouse, but for the cane-mat floors and the black faces of the servant-boys peering round corners to get a glimpse of the stranger.

This station was formed some eleven years ago, but the mission here and the one at Bailundu have passed through seasons of bitter trial and persecution, principally through the prejudice and jealousy of half-breed traders, who poisoned the minds of the king and natives, until the terrible crisis in May, 1884, when Ekwikwi, bribed by gifts and alarmed by false reports, ordered the expulsion of the missionaries. The whole party were compelled, with such few effects as they could carry, to seek the coast, suffering hardships and exposed to dangers by the way, ill provided as they were for such a journey, that can scarcely be described. But through the negotiations of Mr. Walters (a member of the mission) with the Portuguese governor, general letters of commendation in behalf of the Americans were addressed to the native chiefs, resulting in the two kings expressing their regret for what had taken place, and, promising to listen no more to stories against the white teachers, begged them to return.

What I have written concerning the Bailundu station applies with equal truth here as regards the success of the work. There is not only sowing, but *reaping*, though long deferred, has at last begun to cheer the workers. Twice on Sunday the large meeting-house was well filled with attentive hearers, both men and women, besides a well-attended Sunday-school, held between the services.

Mr. Saunders hopes in the near future to commence an industrial school, for he realizes the danger of educating the native lads without teaching them also the dignity of labor; but the extreme poverty of the soil in all these districts is the great drawback of farming. I observe that the natives generally select for their gardens patches shaded by trees, or moist low-lying spots near brooks, but avoid the higher levels. Still, it would be a great achievement if the young men and boys could be induced to work in the fields, for at present manual labor—indeed, every form of hard work—falls to the lot of the women alone, while the men try to amuse themselves and kill time hunting, visiting their friends, making a mat, a basket, or doing a little sewing; but as a rule they are chronic bummers and inveterate idlers, not even caring to mind the babies. These poor unfortunates, when only a few weeks old, are carried by their mothers to the field, strapped on their backs with a bit of rough bark cloth; and there they remain the livelong day, with the exception of intervals for refreshment, exposed to the fiery rays of the sun; and whether they sleep or laugh or cry, their little heads go bump, bump, bump, with every stroke of the toiler's short double-handled hoe.

A story I heard at Cisamba serves to illustrate the position of native African women. A native caravan bound for the coast reached a river, and, the water being pretty deep, some difficulty was experienced in crossing, when one of the men called to his wife and commanded her to carry him over on her shoulders. To this she obediently complied, and accomplished her task successfully. The husband, on being remonstrated with by a white man, asked, in astonishment, "Then whose wife should carry me over if my own don't?"

The old men teach the young that to plant a shrub or a tree would only insure their death before it came to maturity; thus it will be seen that agriculture is handicapped from various causes, and white men, if they wish to live here, must depend chiefly on imported food-stuffs for many a long day to come.

Europeans may *exist* on native fare for a short time, but though some poor white mortals whom we have met lately boast that they *thrive* upon "mush and beans," their cadaverous countenances, scaly skin, pimples, and sores that refuse to heal, testify to the contrary, indicating that their blood is impoverished, their constitutions being ruined, and in a shorter time than they think the penalty of their folly will have to be paid.

I have tried this native "mush," but will be hard pressed by hunger before I get reconciled to it. It is only necessary to explain how mush is made to convince an ordinary intellect that it must be an indigestible mess. An earthen pot is placed on the fire three quarters full of water, into which, when hot, meal is thrown in handfuls, until it becomes thick, when it is at once taken from the fire, vigorously stirred, and the scalded meal compound doled out. The native takes it down by the pound into his cast-iron stomach, but the white man retires after eating a few ounces, to be kept awake half the night by pyrosis, particularly if prepared from manioc meal.

"But it is expensive to import English food, and we must remember we are using the Lord's money." Do you thereby imply that the Lord sets more value on money than on the lives of his servants? It cannot be! Is it not written, "No good thing will He withhold from them that walk uprightly"? And surely that should include the missionary, if he deserve the name. Those who leave the comforts of home to spend their lives in a land like this, were they even supplied with every luxury that money could buy, will find plenty of unavoidable opportunities for self-denial and self-sacrifice without courting privation and suffering.

GANGUELLAN VILLAGE

CHAPTER IV.

FROM CISAMBA TO KUTUNDA.

Decide to change my route.—Cisamba.—Collecting carriers.—A surgical operation.—White man's fetich.—Strange comestibles.—Lu-ra-lu-ra-lu.—Native obsequies.—Ocimbombo.—Bacchanalian carousals.—"On show" at Kapoko.—The cornet scare.—"Putting on side."—Sanambello.—Court speeches.—"A nation of the unemployed."—Reflections.—Trouble ahead.—A lucky shot.—Prescribing for the sick.—Fourteen days' delay.—Rumors of war.—Native idiosyncrasies.—By order of the "doctors."—Agricultural prospects.—A quiet week.—White ants.—Kundundu.—Desertions.—A kind-hearted chief.

AUGUST 1st. Six weeks since the last entry in my journal, and yet the prospects of a start eastward seem darker than ever; the fair promises of obtaining carriers remain unfulfilled; hopes and expectations raised one day, only to be blighted the next. Seeing the scarcity of men, I have sent back to the coast a number of my packages for shipment to England, along with several boxes left at Catambella for the same reason. Still, bearers have to be found for fifty loads, all of which I deem necessary to the safety and progress of the expedition.

For some months past Mr. A—— has been collecting natives to take on a party of Brethren as far as Nana Kundundu, and is still booking every man he can pick up. I being a stranger, and not knowing the Umbundu language, the odds are against me; the only alternative now is to look elsewhere for the means of conveying my trade cloth, beads, provisions, etc., so as to enable me to proceed on my journey; but move on I must, or die of *ennui*.

The 3d of August found me at Cisamba, thirty miles northeast of Kwanjululu, my camp pitched in the forest near one of the mission stations of the American Board of Commissioners for Foreign Missions, in charge of the Rev. W. T. Currie of Canada, where a variety of circumstances which need not be detailed here determined a change in my route inland.

I had intended going through the Katanga country and striking east to the Lakes, purposing to visit, so far as my limited time would allow, those parts of South Central Africa of most interest to the friends of missions. But as there is only one station on this route, viz., the Brethren Mission at Garanganze, and having met two of their party just returned from that country, who had been five months on the road, seeing but little worthy of note by the way, traversing for weeks together vast plains of burning white sand, I felt that to me it would mean five months wasted. So I decided to steer a course farther south, in the direction of the Barotse Valley, visit the French Evangelical Mission on the Zambesi, from thence pushing on to Nyasa as the way might open up. In the meantime, I set to work in earnest to acquire what I could of the Umbundu language, as an interpreter to accompany me was not to be had. Thus a further delay of several weeks was unavoidable.

Within a few days, through the aid of Mr. Currie, a number of headmen from the surrounding villages were brought together and commissioned to collect carriers as speedily as possible.

I did not think it advisable to leave any of the Jamaicans at the Kwanjululu mission, there being a plethora of missionaries on that station, and the cry is, "Still they come;" besides, several of them are specially adapted to do the work for which the colored men were intended.

At Cisamba, however, it was far otherwise. We found Mr. Currie toiling bravely, though almost single-handed, having only the help of a few native lads in erecting a dwelling for himself and his colleague, the Rev. W. Lee, who was then on his way up from the coast with his young wife, while the buildings were yet far from ready.

My men were heartily welcomed, and they set to work with a vigor and a will that left Mr. Currie free to attend to the many duties which had otherwise to be suspended—such as visiting among the villages and aiding with medicine the many sick people who came every day for relief. In this department I was glad to be of service, and had thereby an opportunity of observing the class of diseases to which the natives of the district are subject.

Many interesting cases appeared, among them an old man with a large ulcer on the leg, that had resisted every remedy—seemingly a hopeless case. On examination, I found extensive necrosis of the *tibia*, and proposed to remove the dead portion of bone; but as chloroform has never been administered in this part of the country, and the patient being far advanced in life, we realized that there was no small risk. We placed him, however, on a table in the open yard, and in a few minutes had him under the influence of the sense-stealing vapor, while a wondering crowd of natives stood around, marveling at the strange proceeding, and conjecturing among themselves what kind of fetich this could be that made a man submit to having his leg cut and gouged without a murmur or remonstrance. In a short time the wound was dressed, and, the effects of the anæsthetic passing off, the astonished Sekulo sat up, amid the shouts of surprise and greetings of his friends.

The month spent at Cisamba has been in every way pleasant and profitable. Daily contact with the people has given me to understand a good deal of their manners and customs. I visited several villages in the surrounding districts, and while crossing a plain on one of these excursions observed hundreds of women and children wandering about among the young grass and weeds that were just springing up after the annual fires. They were most of the time in a stooping posture, as if looking for something, and were gathering the object of their search into calabashes and baskets.

Leaving the path and approaching a group, I heard them making a peculiar noise by protruding the tongue and moving it rapidly between the lips from side to side, meanwhile keeping up a high-pitched monotone in a minor key, like "lu-ra-lu-ra-lu." My curiosity was excited. What was it all about? They were harvesting the August crop of caterpillars, which they dry in the sun, stew, and eat as a relish with their cornmeal mush, considering them a great delicacy. But why keep up that peculiar cry? Well, the insects being of the same color as the grass, it was difficult to see them; but no sooner did the harvesters bend to their work and commence the "lu-ra-lu" than there was an instant commotion among the green blades, the creeping things standing up on their hind legs and swaying their bodies to and fro, when they were easily captured.

The tastes of the Ovimbundu are not confined to caterpillars as a relish, but grasshoppers, rats, mice, and every kind of hawk or buzzard may be included among their luxuries—anything in the form of flesh, no matter what. Whether dead from disease or killed by themselves, it makes no difference—horse, mule, or dog, if even buried and the place of interment discovered, it may be a few days late—all the same, it is meat. The idea expressed by the word "nasty" has no equivalent in their vocabulary.

I was interested in watching the movements of a funeral procession passing within a short distance of my tent. The body was carried in a hammock decorated with gayly colored cloth and suspended from a pole carried between two men, and followed by a crowd of natives yelling and shouting at the top of their voices, while gun-firing and beating of drums added to the unearthly uproar. The bearers of the corpse ran hither and thither among the people, while the witch-doctor danced around it, gesticulating in the most frenzied manner, every few steps calling a halt, pretending to interrogate the dead as to the probable cause of death, or as to who had put this fetich upon him that he died. Should the men controlling the hammock with its burden stop suddenly opposite any individual in particular, it is taken as a sure indication that this is the guilty party, who will have to pay cloth, sheep, or pigs as an atonement. But in this case, after performing for about an hour, off they went with a rush to the burying-ground; so it was probably decided that the deceased had swallowed his own fetich, and he was buried forthwith.

The disposal of dead bodies by placing them in trees signifies that the deceased was a stranger from another tribe; and this method is resorted to in event of relations coming to inquire for the departed. Should any doubt arise as to his demise, they are directed to his elevated resting-place, where they may identify the body for themselves. In the evening, the village where the death took place will be filled with people, an ox killed and a big feast spread, a portion of the meat being laid aside for a peace-offering to the spirit, and the horns of the animal stuck on a pole by the grave, together with the earthly belongings of the departed. Then for several days there will be a great beer-drinking, when young and old get drunk, and the nights are spent in dancing, singing, and drum-thumping.

These beer or "ocimbombo" carousals are not confined to funerals, for at this season of the year they form the chief occupation of the natives; so much so, that it is especially difficult to induce carriers to take the road while these revelings are in progress. The liquor is made from corn soaked in water until it begins to sprout, then dried and pounded into meal, boiled to the consistency of thin gruel, and allowed to stand until it ferments, when it has a sourish taste with a peculiar flavor, from the presence of a juice obtained from the

GROUP OF GANGUELLIANS

umbundi root and added at the time of boiling. The greater part of the year's crop is consumed in this way.

While passing the village of Kolombambi a short time ago, I had an opportunity of seeing one of these orgies in full blast. Over five hundred natives of all ages and both sexes were assembled within the stockade; calabashes of the intoxicating beverage were circulating freely; the drummers were pounding on the goatskins as if for their lives, about forty women accompanying their wild chants by rhythmically shaking gourds containing small hard seeds, the crowd joining in the choruses between times, giving vent to the most hideous and demoniacal yells. Hundreds of men and women all but nude presented every phase of intoxication from mere talkativeness to maudlin and pugnacious drunkenness, shuffling and swaying their bodies in gestures too indecent to describe. I turned away from the sickening sight, convinced that whether rum is introduced as an article of trade into Africa or not, the savage already knows too well how to manufacture drink for his own debaucheries.

In the course of our perambulations about Bihe we were led to remark on the many forms that superstition assumes among the Biheans. One in particular we met at cross-paths near villages and in the vicinity of native dwellings, in the shape of a miniature conical hut of grass about two feet high, with a door proportionately small, and built by the public sorcerer. Sometimes it contains a little roughly carved wooden image, but more often only a few bits of broken pottery, eggshells, or hair. Its special function is not very clearly defined, but it is supposed to scare hostile neighbors, insure the safe return of the warriors who go forth on fighting and plundering expeditions, and also to protect their families during their absence.

September 8th. At last we make a move, although the loads are not all lifted; but even the carriers who are engaged don't seem to believe the traveler is ready to start until they see his flag move on to the first camp. Seeing this is expected, we have gratified them, for here we are at Kopoko, eight miles from Cisamba, with our headmen, thirty carriers, and two Jamaicans, Frater and Jonathan (the others remaining to assist Mr. Currie), expecting that the remaining loads will be forwarded in a few days, although how long we are destined to sit in this the first camp on the road, I cannot tell.

My tent is pitched by the side of a forest, in sight of a number of villages; consequently the last peg had scarcely been driven when we were besieged by throngs of natives, one and all taking a critical interest in everything they see about the white man's belongings, amused and frightened by turns, and expressing their amazement by ejaculations of "Eh! Eh!" when shown the mechanism of a rifle or revolver; but the marvel of marvels was my little American magic lamp. The next best show was dinner, laid on the camp-table in the tent; when I proceeded to eat, with a rush they crowded round the door, mothers lifting up their children to have a look at the, to them, strange performance of eating with a knife and fork. Every movement during the meal was watched with unabated interest to the end. This over, and desiring still further to please the citizens of Kopoko (as I am in want of more porters, and among my audience are many relatives and friends of the men now in camp, *en route* with me), I got out my cornet. Its glitter caught every eye, and the crowd pressed closer than was agreeable, to examine it; but at the first shrill blast I was alone, with only a few of the older men. Such a stampede! They tumbled over one another in the desperate effort to escape from a sound that resembled nothing they had ever heard before. When at a safe distance, they peered from behind trees, and, seeing the Sekulos still sitting near unhurt, and even laughing, they took courage and ventured back again, resuming the squatting position. To quiet their nerves they passed the snuff-boxes, for they all take snuff, men and women; and as the sun went down children were sent off to the huts to bring several baskets of yams and meal, manifesting in this way their desire to reciprocate our friendliness. This experience is quite bearable and even amusing at first, but when it comes to be repeated day after day, with scarcely a variation, one gets heartsick and faint at the very sight of approaching visitors.

I went on a visit to the chief of Kopoko by the express wish of my headmen; they were anxious that I should make a good impression on the great man (more for their own glorification than mine), and directed the order of march. I must not walk, but be carried in a tipoia, although the distance was not over a mile. My trumpeter or spokesman takes the lead, and behind, a native carrying my camp-chair, followed by another with the cloth to be presented to his majesty; in the rear, a retinue of the favored individuals who have been invited to attend the interview. On reaching the

palace (a round mud hut) we found the chief busy with
a needle and thread mending his loin-cloth; but on seeing us approach, he dropped it and hurried half across
the yard to greet us. Kananene, for that is his name,
appears to be about fifty years of age, quiet and unassuming in his manner as compared to most African
chiefs; but there is something foxy and sneaking in
his face that I mistrust, although I am told he fills his
place at the ombala with credit, and seeks the peace
and welfare of the country, avoiding raids, war, and
strife, and expresses a desire that missionaries should
come and teach his people, although these petty chiefs
have in reality very little control over their subjects
and country.

We were seated amid the clapping of hands and
"*kalungas*" of the guests and courtiers, who filed in and
squatted in a circle around us. My speaker, Sanambello, proceeded with the palaver (it is not considered
dignified in these formal or business interviews that
two chiefs should address each other except through
a second party) by a long harangue about how far I
had come to see the country; that I had shown kindness to the people by paying them well for any service
they had rendered me, giving them medicine, etc.; that
now I was about to travel farther into the interior and
required carriers to take on my trade cloth and other
goods; closing with a grand peroration of flattering
eulogisms to Kananene. Now the prime-minister takes
his turn. His face, like several others we have met
during our journey, is terribly disfigured by the burst-
ing of one of those wretched trade guns supplied to
the natives by the traders at the coast. He replies at

great length, stating that I had been long enough at Cisamba for them to hear of me, and that they had no doubt I would deal fairly with and protect any men who might venture into the countries beyond with me; also, that the chief would visit my camp in a few days and talk over matters. Oh, if only he knew how sick and tired I am of sitting in the forest day after day, he would have ordered his men to get ready at once, instead of saying, "In a few days we will talk about it;" but the innate greed of the African suggests this further delay in the hope of more pelf. Some of his wives appeared, carrying large gourds of beer for my men, who have an enormous capacity in this direction. A few minutes suffice to see the vessels empty. The word "Twendi" ("we go") is passed, and without more ceremony we take our leave and return to camp, where from dawn until dark there is no room to stir for the giggling, jabbering crowd of the "unemployed" occupying every available space round the tent.

Time hangs heavy on the hands of the native African. Now and again a man of some importance in the community honors me with a call and presents himself with many ceremonious salutations. I try to attend when he speaks, and can just make out sufficient from his harangue to know who he is, where he comes from, and that he wants medicine, a knife, a needle and thread, or some such trifle. But the setting of the sun generally brings relief, as all natives have a great horror of being out after dark. This is by far the most thickly populated district we have come across as yet, and offers a splendid center for mission work.

September 13th. Sunday, or "Calimingo," as the

natives call it. I explain as best I can to the people as they arrive that this is the day of rest from palavers, entertainments, buying and selling, when they retire, assuring me, at the same time, for my comfort, that they will come back to-morrow—which promise I doubt not they will keep to the letter, although they are by no means proverbial for sticking to their word. At any rate, we have one quiet, restful day, although when I reflect on my position and the prospects of accomplishing this undertaking, the future looks so dark that an overwhelming sadness oppresses me. My thoughts wander back to the little island of the west where my loved ones dwell, and where I have spent so many happy years of toil among a people who have to own this as their fatherland. I think of the crowds as they assemble at the various stations of the mission, from mountain hamlets and luxuriant glens, where in rich profusion grow the orange trees, the cocoanut palms, coffee and bananas, while the balmy air is laden with the perfume of spices—so cleanly and comfortably attired, leaving behind for the time their cottage homes of peace and plenty, to gather in the house of prayer, to sing as only they can sing, and pray with earnestness and simplicity of faith, and listen to the Word of God. It is to them, indeed, a message of love and good tidings.

Such are the scenes which pass rapidly before my mental eye, until the first impulse is to give up this struggle and return. But the thought that what the Jamaican is to-day these poor benighted and degraded people around me might be had they the same opportunities, confirms my determination to proceed as far

CROSSING THE QUITU

and to see as much of their condition as I can; earnestly hoping that my experience be of service to others who may follow, and that the journey will in some way add its quota to the opening up of this dark, sin-blighted land.

September 14th. Early this morning one of my tin boxes already given out was brought back. The carrier on receiving it had taken it to his village, as is the custom, to have his carrying-sticks tied on. In the meantime he had committed some crime, for which he had to remain and be tried. This circumstance was far from amusing to me, particularly as I saw in the faces of several of my men evidences of displeasure at the way in which the culprit was being dealt with by the headmen of the village; and I dreaded the probability of their wishing to stay to attend the trial, thus delaying me indefinitely. A dispute forthwith arose, and for a full hour the babble of voices was enough to drive one to distraction. Sitting at my tent door in anything but a calm or peaceful state of mind, though hardly restraining the strong inclination to drive the whole gang from the camp, I espied a large hawk soaring over our heads at about forty yards. My rifle was lying close by; instantly raising it to my shoulder, I fired. Ere the crowd had time to recover from the alarm caused by the sudden shot, the bird dropped dead in their midst. The uproar was immense, and the previous squabble was too insignificant to be thought of now. Here was a bird every feather of which is prized by the men as a talisman of strength and courage, and by the women as possessing certain undefined charms which enter into their fetiches. For the rest of the day all other topics were forgotten; again and again they mimicked the picking up of the rifle, and how the bird fell with a thud; to every new arrival the whole story was related, and they were satisfied there would be plenty of meat on the road if they traveled with me. Let us hope they will not be disappointed.

At noon Kananene appeared according to promise, carried in a tipoia, in full dress, having donned, besides his loin-cloth, a long black coat with military epaulets. He was no sooner seated than he asked for something to drink. Having no spirits, I mixed a little chlorodyne in water and gave it him, which he evidently appreciated. I tried to interest him in the usual way, and presented him with a box of matches on his departure. In the evening his secretary came to the camp with several men offering their services as carriers. I closed the various duties of the day by prescribing for eighteen sick people; several of them were cases of fever, but the majority skin disease very difficult to diagnose, as the problem is to decide whether the incrustations are from within or without.

I was surprised at the extraordinary prevalence of goiter, some of enormous size, affecting chiefly women and children. I should say it is quite within the mark to put the percentage at forty-five. They have to thank Dr. Lowe, Professor Simpson, and the directors of the Edinburgh Medical Missionary Society for the benefit they received from the medicines; for had it not been for the liberal supply of drugs presented me by that noble institution, I might have had to refuse aid to many poor sufferers I have helped since leaving the coast, besides replenishing the stock of several missionaries short of quinine, rousers, etc.

September 22d. We have been here now fourteen days, and during this time have tasted to the full the bitterness of collecting carriers among these wretched people—one day rationing and booking a number of men, the next canceling as many. I had been told that when a native takes rations and ties his stick on a load, he rarely, if ever, retracts; this is sheer nonsense, as the Bihean (and subsequent experience of months with a hundred of them gave me no reason to alter my opinion) is influenced by neither conscience nor principle. His actions are controlled by the basest of motives, selfishness and superstition coming out ahead every time. We were to have started on the 17th, but the child of one of the headmen fell sick, and the cause had to be inquired into by the tedious process of consulting the fetich-doctor. Another headman came to say that his men refused to go because news had reached them of war in the Ganguella country, through which we have to pass, about four or five days' march from here.

This may be true, as I understand the Portuguese are fighting among the tribes east of the Kukema River; but as I do not intend to side with either party, and my carriers know it, this is a paltry excuse. They are arrant cowards, every man Jack of them. Around the camp-fire they vie with each other in boasting of their bravery and prowess, but, like big overgrown children, run at the first appearance of danger. I promise to go on ahead each day to see that the coast is clear for them; and after a long palaver they consent to start to-morrow. The vexing repetition of this sort of thing day after day is enough to drive one mad, seeing that several of my loads are still to be lifted, and the rainy season approaching, when the lowlands *en route* will be flooded.

But I resent the idea of my plans being defeated by a people exhibiting the most despicable traits of character ever heard of. Oh, how they enjoy treading on the white man when they think he is cornered, or in any way under obligation to them! Some will come, have their names put down, and just by the way suggest that they have a little debt that hinders their starting right away, but that a piece of cloth would square matters. We are not caught, however, and they return no more. The result would have been the same had they got the cloth, but my chagrin would have been greater. Yesterday, my chief "pombiero," Sanambello, whom I trust most—which is not saying much—arrived with his men and their loads, telling me the others would come on to-day. For several days we have had two women pounding corn for our own use, so that we have now a good supply. I decided to go on to Ciyuka to-morrow—eight miles—and sent a notice to that effect to those in the rear.

September 23d. Hiring a dozen women to carry the unlifted loads, we started for Ciyuka, arriving there at 11 A.M. I pitched my tent near a small stream, and stacked the loads with an awning over them, as there is every indication of rain. I lost no time in paying a visit to the chief, Ohosi, and found him in a small hut within a skerm of brush, but outside the ombala, as he is sick, and the spirits of departed chiefs gave him no chance to get better while in his own house; hence the isolation by order of the doctors. He is the youngest petty ruler I have seen—probably about thirty-five; of slim build, rather delicate-looking, and genial in his manner. He received us most cordially, with of course the usual ceremony. He was told the purpose of our visit, viz., to get young men to join our caravan as far as the Barotse. He replied that he would do whatever lay in his power to get men, as several of his people had received medicines from me at Kopoko, that had done them good. He was glad I had come so near his village, for no doubt I would be able to take away his sickness, though his own medical advisers had failed. I gave him a present of cloth and departed. In the evening he called for his medicine, when I was glad to find his malady one, as a rule, quite amenable to treatment. His sickness may yet prove fortunate for us, as, if relieved, gratitude may induce him to render the aid we need. Next morning he sent us a fine black goat and a basket of meal; abundance of yams and sweet potatoes have been brought from the villages for sale.

The elevation of Ciyuka is four thousand feet, and the country generally is a great improvement on Bihe. Sugar-cane, mealies, cassava, pumpkins, yams, and sweet potatoes seem to thrive well; but neither here nor anywhere else since leaving Catambella have we seen bananas or plantains. Attempts have been made by the American missionaries to introduce them; but though planted, some of them for five or six years, they have as yet yielded no fruit. (In the islands of the West Indies each sucker yields a bunch of fruit within twelve months from the time of planting.) Every care has been taken during the winter months to keep out the frost by wrapping each plant in grass; still, the leaves and center shoots are exposed and get blighted by the black frosts of July and August, and are thus prevented from ever reaching maturity in these regions.

We are not annoyed by crowds of natives here, the chief having forbidden their entering our camp, except on business—a happy contrast to the miserable time we had at Kopoko. Here we are not in such a hurry to advance; I should almost enjoy a couple of weeks' stay, but there is something wanting. Week in and week out I see no white face, and the longing becomes intense to have some one with whom to talk and consult over matters. Prison-life could scarcely be worse than this monotony, for there, at least, we would have something to do; here, the chief employment is hunting up carriers, and this must be equivalent to the treadmill. Even the companionship of books is denied me, having had to send most of them back, to lessen the weight or number of my loads.

The white ants are a constant source of trouble; they are everywhere; there is nothing they will not destroy if within their reach. Last night they succeeded in cutting the bottom out of my camera case, and made a hole eight inches square in the tarpaulin that serves as a ground-sheet for my tent. Only by moving every article at least once a day, or placing the goods high above the floor, can anything be preserved from these pests. Fortunately, there are no grass lice or ticks, as in the West Indies.

Two carriers came in for loads, and there is prospect

of more to-morrow. But this "to-morrow" is a most tantalizing word from the lips of a native, as it simply implies some future time; so I won't "throw up my hat" yet awhile. I am feeling thoroughly broken up to-night from worry and anxiety.

Sunday, 27th. Most of the men have gone to neighboring villages. There seems to be a big beer-drink on, for the drums have been going at a great rate ever since daylight. No missionary influence here; but there is a big population, and it is certainly a promising field for mission work. The chief is in warm sympathy with the mission at Cisamba, and speaks of Mr. Currie as his friend; although nowhere have we as yet seen a native man or woman giving evidence of having anything like a true conception of the Christian's God —not even among those who have been in the habit of visiting the mission station for years. With them Jehovah takes a second place to their god Kundundu. The former name they will use in addressing man, as a sort of complimentary term, but the latter never; and Suku (God) they often apply as a pet name to their boys. Until a thorough system of evangelistic work, by itinerating from village to village, is adopted, there is little to be hoped for from the casual visits of the natives to the mission stations on Sundays toward breaking down the prejudices of centuries.

September 28th. Three new men took loads this morning. The chief, who, by the way, has almost recovered from his sickness, takes a kindly interest in all that concerns us, spending the most of each day in camp, and, strange to say, seems to be above begging. He turned up with six more carriers and a pombiero, so that I begin to feel almost happy at this rift in the dark cloud and brightening of my prospects. But by noon the future became blacker than ever. I was informed by Sanambello that eighteen loads had been brought back, and that the carriers had deserted, including nine engaged at Cisamba and the five from Kopoko.

Kananene is at the root of this; his men would not have abandoned their loads without permission. It is evident that my suspicions of his being a cunning and two-faced rogue were not uncharitable; and unless we get the others away from the vicinity of their villages, this will not be the end of the desertions. But I will not linger over the recital of the terrible heart-burnings that have fallen to our lot in this the commencement of our journey, as it has been the experience of almost every traveler who has sought to penetrate the unfrequented regions of Central Africa. On expressing to Ohosi, who was standing by when the loads came in, my purpose of striking camp and marching on another stage above, he promptly turned round to a band of his young men who were near, and ordered each one to take a load and follow me to Kutunda—nine miles. In a couple of hours we were on the road, escorted for several miles by the chief, whom I shall ever remember with feelings of respect and gratitude; he has truly been a friend in need.

We reached the camping-ground late in the afternoon. Leaving Frater in charge, I went off with two of the headmen; when sent alone I find that they get into a village, beer is on the tapis, and business has to yield to pleasure. We were fortunate enough to

EXPEDITION AT KANGAMBA

happen upon a village where I found several fellows who carried for me from the coast to Bihe; they readily engaged, and now, to my unbounded satisfaction, every load has a carrier. I have promised to stay a day or two to give them time to pound their corn.

It is no easy matter to keep the women at work who are employed to pound corn for us. I have been released from that onerous task to-day, however, by a man putting in an appearance early in the morning with two of his wives and asking me to hire them a few days on the pestles at half a yard of calico each. At the same time he promised to stay by and do the driving himself gratis. The bargain was struck, and so far he has not deserted his post, and we have quite a heap of meal as the result.

CHAPTER V.

AMONG THE GANGUELLIANS.

My caravan complete.—Face to face with a lion.—A thunderstorm.—Crossing the Kukema.—Nothing for dinner.—A grand concert.—A promising field.—Petty rulers.—Namby-pamby.—Lady missionaries. — Trained nurses.—A wild chief.—Ganguellians.—Hairdressing extraordinary.—Fetich charms.—A fine country.—Iron-smelting.—Palavers and pigs.—The Kwanza River.—A wrinkle in river-crossing.—Native dread of Europeans.—A carved stockade.—A strange phenomenon.—Fever in the camp.—Limping into camp.—In the wilderness.—Rubber regions.—The honey-bird.—Picturesque huts.

OCTOBER 1st. Thank God, my caravan is complete—ninety-seven persons all told, including fifty carriers, eight pombieros, and thirty-six youths carrying meal and salt and dried fish for the men. By daybreak this morning, and with a heart lighter than it has been at any time during the last three months, I gladly took the lead, and marched out of Kutunda; the men, too, seemed in good spirits, for all along the line they sang in noisy chorus, as they trotted on with their sixty- to eighty-pound loads on their shoulders. I had walked for about an hour at a brisk pace a stone's-throw ahead of the flag, through a forest, my mind full of the pleasure of at last effecting a fair start, when my reflections were rudely interrupted, and I was involuntarily brought to a halt by the sudden apparition, right in the path, about fifty yards ahead, of a full-grown male lion, leisurely watching our approach. Having nothing in my hand but a stick, I had no desire to see the distance between us shortened. My gun-bearer was some distance behind, but he had taken in the situation, and in a few seconds the "Express" was in my hands. Still, too late, as the shaggy brute skulked off into the long grass with a surly growl before I could draw upon him; but his appearance had a salutary effect upon the men, who, from fear, kept well together, and prevented straggling. We made but a short march of eight miles, considering it judicious not to allow the carriers to feel the weight of their loads too early in the journey.

The flag stopped at Kondole, where we found a number of ready-made huts, which had been occupied the night before by a party of natives bringing ivory and rubber from the interior, and bound for the coast. A heavy thunderstorm broke over us about 9 P.M. and continued to rage furiously until 2 A.M., torrents of rain falling all the time. The huts of the men were too frail to resist the wind, most of the grass thatch being swept off, leaving the bare poles and the occupants exposed to the full fury of the blast. Happily, it was not cold.

October 2d. Every one feeling very comfortless, their bits of cloth being soaked by the rain. There was no delay in getting started, for all wanted exercise. Our tortuous path lay mostly through forest, now and again crossing a savanna, where the young grass was springing. Nothing remarkable about the topography of the country, except that the great ant-hills, for which the Cisamba district is notable, abound here; some of them are eighteen feet high and have a diameter at the base of thirty feet. We reached the Kukema River at 9.30 A.M., and several hours being occupied in ferrying our people across, we decided to go no farther to-day, especially as the ombala of Ongandu was close by, surrounded and shaded by beautiful trees, called by the natives "ulembi."

The chief, Cipopa, invited us to stay in his village, promising to provide huts for the men. Notwithstanding my very strong objections, for many reasons, against camping in a strange village, I was so favorably impressed with this man's appearance and manner, that I accepted his hospitality, and forthwith had my goods stacked and tent pitched inside the stockade. All was snug, and I was just having an audience with the king, when Frater whispered in my ear the commonplace remark that there was nothing for dinner but desiccated soup. This stuff tastes to me now very much like desiccated glue, and I decided to go and look for something more palatable.

Two young natives volunteered to take me where game was to be found. Following my guides, after walking about five miles we came to a valley opening out to a vast plain; and sure enough, right before us, about six hundred yards, were four oryx and two Lechwe antelopes peacefully browsing on the young grass. Although we lay flat on the ground, the grass was too short to cover us, and in an instant they sighted us and were off. For two hours we tried every stratagem to get within three hundred yards of them, but in vain; every attempt to circumvent them failed. It was of no use; there was nothing to hide us from their keen sight. At last I thought of attempting a long shot, for

I was hungry, having eaten nothing since 5.30 A.M., and it was now 4 P.M. But alas for my dinner! Though I adjusted the sight carefully, took steady aim, and fired several times, the bullets dropped far short of the game. This was mysterious until I examined one of the remaining cartridges, and found that the firm from whom I obtained the ammunition had cruelly made up about half the order with *stale* stock, practically worthless, the firing-pin breaking through the rotten caps at every shot. The powder was decomposed and clogged in the shell, and the brass green with corrosion. Disappointed, we turned back, and got to the ombala just as it was getting dark. I found a large pig tied up by my tent, and the chief with his suite squatted round, waiting my return, to proceed with the palaver and presentation, which was duly performed with all the honors—clapping of hands and speeches.

The pig did not live long; a portion of the pork was reserved, and the balance given to the headman for distribution. The pig business over, and while dinner was preparing, I entertained the villagers by exhibiting my curios. I produced the cornet and began to play "'Way down upon the Swanee River"; but there was such a rush for the "boxes" and "front seats," that a free fight was imminent. I feared the tent might come to grief, for already several had been sent sprawling by tripping on the ropes, so I was obliged to play the national anthem and bring the concert to a close. But more hearty shouts of applause, ringing laughter, and expressions of simple delight I have never heard; and I feel happy that in spite of my weariness I may have been able to inspire these people with a measure of confidence toward white men, for their experience of Europeans, being confined to half-breed Portuguese hitherto, has had the very opposite effect.

About eight o'clock one of the old men of the village came out to where the loads were piled up, and in a loud voice proclaimed that the "ocindele" (white man) was the guest and friend of the chief; and should any one dare to disturb the stranger, his loads or people, the transgressor would feel the full force of Cipopa's wrath.

Next morning, by daylight, the chief came to see us off, and begged me to intercede in behalf of his son, who had been captured by the king of a country that lies in our route. I promised to hear the case and do what I could to have his boy set at liberty. With many adieux we parted, firmly convinced that, so far as we can judge from what we see during the brief periods of our sojourn among these Ganguellians, no more inviting or more needy fields exist anywhere. The degrading effects of contact with the half-caste traders have not been felt here as in Bihe; nor do they travel as the Biheans do, hence are still comparatively free from the vices of the coast. The prospect is all the more promising in that Ganguella is composed of detached confederations under the jurisdiction of petty rulers, allowing more independence to the people; also, perhaps, because of the weakness of these small communities, war and bloodshed is less frequent than under the government of autocratic chiefs, who maintain their claims over immense territory by sheer force of arms, and gratify their pride of savage power by a reign of terror and cruelty.

In no country on the continent where such potentates wield their baneful sway has mission work made the slightest headway—not even, in some instances, where a quarter of a century has been spent in unremitting effort by missionaries resident among them; while in communities where liberty of conscience is allowed, genuine conversions have taken place within a few years of commencement of the mission. Wholesale conversions in totally new fields have been reported within a few months, but investigation has generally revealed the fact that a chief or some individual in authority has taken the initiative in outwardly acquiescing with the white man's teachings, when their people necessarily follow suit. But a profession of Christianity under such circumstances by no means warrants their being called converts.

Not every one, however, who may choose to volunteer for such a work need expect to succeed. If his labors have been unsuccessful at home they will be more so here, where the hindrances to be overcome are infinitely greater. A special fitness or adaptability is required of the man who would be a pioneer of missions in Africa; he must possess indomitable zeal, strong, unwavering faith, good education, sound judgment, practical common sense, ready wit, and tact in dealing with the natives—in a word, every inch "a man." We have already met too many namby-pamby, useless volunteers posing as missionaries in this country; wasting time and money, accomplishing nothing, mentally and physically incapacitated for grappling with the innumerable difficulties which present themselves at every turn, in the shape of superstition, profound ignorance, and yet unlimited conceit in the superiority of their religious beliefs over that of their teacher.

We cannot see eye to eye with those who advocate the sending out of young unmarried ladies to Central Africa, except to well-established stations, their position being so misunderstood by the natives. India and China offer ready spheres for lady missionaries, married or otherwise, where the women already civilized can and do appreciate their coming. Mrs. Searle, who has had experience at Benguela, gives it as her opinion that the white women can render most efficient aid in the kitchen, and says: "If a girl can't or won't cook, she won't do for Africa, however good a linguist or theologian she may be." In no case have we seen native women as house-servants in Central African missionary homes; not even where these have been established twelve or fourteen years. The work of the culinary department is deputed to boys, as no native woman will submit to a domestic training. They consider themselves wronged and robbed of their rights as women if taken from field work.

The digestion is so often disordered, the system weakened, and the appetite rendered uncertain by fever, that we might almost say the life—certainly the health and consequent usefulness—of the missionary depends in a great measure on the quality and preparation of his meals; and surely this is a department that can most properly be superintended by the missionary's wife. Then, it may be asked, Is there not a wide field of usefulness open to single ladies as trained nurses? To this we would reply that many trained nurses go out, to find that all the ideas they had formed on the

subject of nursing were based on the supposition that the home-life of the native African bore some resemblance to that of the poorer classes at home. They soon discover, however, that the domestic arrangements of the native hut offer no facilities for the services of a trained nurse. Thus years spent in a hospital, mechanically obeying and carrying out the doctor's directions concerning the patients, is so much time wasted when Central Africa is to be the goal for future service; for, although skill in dressing, bandaging, etc., is acquired, a far more effectual preparation for usefulness would be obtained by attending for a few months the out-patient consulting-room of a city physician. There, practical, if elementary, information would be gained on the diagnosis of ordinary diseases and their treatment, so as to intelligently apply the simple remedies the medicine-chest contains to the relief of suffering natives, who, as a rule, either come or are carried to the mission station. Nor would this simple course be beyond the reach of the missionary's fiancé. Opportunities for dressing a wound or putting a few stitches in a cut will occur, such as may be better done by the deft and gentle fingers of a woman; but is there anything in such emergencies that the missionary's wife, if she be worthy of the name, would not be able to meet?

By 11 A.M. we arrived at Okambokoakwengi. A number of headmen from the ombala came around our camp, but squatted at some distance; evidently a reconnoitering party, and, as I afterward learned, sent by the king to see if I looked dangerous, before he should venture on a visit. Their report must have been favorable, for in the afternoon Cipi himself put in an appearance, his face and body streaked all over with the fetich white clay, as a protection against the evil spells he feared might possess him in our camp. My pombieros could not coax him to come nearer than twenty yards of where I was seated; and having occasion to rise from my chair, he jumped up, dropped his blanket, and would have escaped, but that the crowd around him was too dense. He kept looking about in the most uneasy and suspicious manner, as if dreading some impending danger. Meanwhile, his spokesman was reciting an address, at the close of which a fine goat and a basket of meal were produced for my acceptance. Sanambello replied for me, saying that I was pleased with the gift and would visit the chief in the evening at his village. At this Cipi joined his people in a great hand-clapping, with shouts of "ewa, ewa" ("yes, yes"); and forthwith about a hundred and fifty of his soldiers executed a war-dance for my special benefit, and before we parted Cipi and I were the best of friends.

We are now in the Ganguella country, and have been ever since crossing the Kukema. Here we have an entirely new language and different class of natives, far finer specimens of humanity than the Biheans, so far as physique is concerned; particularly the men, who are, as a rule, fine stalwart fellows, and in point of physiognomy would compare favorably with the negroes of either the United States or the West Indies. As they are too independent a people to engage as carriers, and seldom cross the Kukema on the west or the Kwanza on the east, their supply of cloth is very,

very scanty, their clothing being confined to a bit of leopard or antelope skin. Few amulets, anklets, or other adornments are worn, but their heads display the prevailing fashion; and there the skill of the native tonsorial artist is exhibited.

So intricate and fanciful are some of the patterns that they must be seen to really understand what they are like. In some cases the decorations are all on one side of the head, where the hair is allowed to grow long for the barber's manipulations; the other side is shaved. Others have the hair cut off both sides of the head, leaving a ridge of long hair on the top, running from the forehead to the nape of the neck, the effect produced suggesting a fireman's helmet. But there are dudes who spend an hour or two every day in the hands of the hairdresser, and affect something more elaborate still: he may have isolated tufts of long hair, like the headgear of the clown in a pantomime; but the main part of the scalp is shorn close, and then with a sharp knife geometrical figures, squares, crescents, and diamonds are scraped out, like the plan of a flower-garden. The head-arrangements of the women are not a whit behind the men in grotesqueness of style or design; but they spend less time over it, one great dressing sufficing for months, and even years: plaits with three or four white or red beads strung on the end of each; rolls, horns, screws large and small, according to taste, with cowry shells woven in, as fancy may suggest. For example, see the woman sitting in the center of the "Group of Ganguellians" (from a snap shot at my tentdoor).

The Ganguellians seem to have less faith in charms

than the natives farther west, for I have noticed very few of them worn, as is customary among the Umbundu. Almost every one of my carriers and headmen have their favorite charm suspended by a string around the neck or waist, in the form of sundry bits of wood, points of horns, shells, or an assortment of such knick-knacks as have passed through the hands of the fetich-doctor, with the assurance that they will ward off every ill that might otherwise befall them. Others pin their faith to a collection of rubbish tied up in a dirty little bag. All come under the name of "Ombanda"—patent medicine, a panacea for every ill; so that in this respect they quite equal some of their more civilized, though little less gullible, white brethren.

Sanambello carries an eland horn filled with a variety of trash, each article supposed to have its own special virtue. This he carefully sticks in the ground near his hut on reaching camp; and it is not removed, nor is any one allowed to touch it, until the flag moves on again. Only on such a journey as this with the Bihean can one fully know how almost their every action is governed by their belief in Kundundu. When twitted about it they only laugh and say, "Ah no, we don't expect you to believe in this; it is something beyond the intellect of a white man."

Another march of thirteen miles brought us to the Kwanza River. Nothing remarkable by the way; in fact, so far as each day's journey is concerned, it is only the monotonous tramp, tramp, over a rolling country, with an occasional lift in the tipoia when tired or feverish, and when there are men to spare. Now an open plain; then a small forest; anon a rivulet; rarely a river; no plants or trees that by their appearance would suggest our being in the tropics; no fruit of any kind except a nauseous sort of wild berry. Near the villages small plots of corn and manioc are cultivated; but the soil in Ganguella, between the Kukema and Kwanza, is by a long way the richest soil we have come across. With proper attention good crops of cereals and vegetables as yet unknown to the natives could be raised.

This district is noted for the excellence of its iron. During the coldest months of the year the miners and blacksmiths turn out and camp near the pits, working night and day until they have manufactured a supply of hoes, spear and arrow heads, axes, hatchets, knives, snuff-spoons, etc., sufficient to meet the demand. I examined several holes from which ore had been dug. They were about ten feet in diameter and eight feet deep. Close by were the small sheds, with broken clay furnaces and crucibles scattered around among the coke and slag, where the ore had been smelted and the metal transformed into implements of labor or weapons of war. The bellows or blast employed is a simple contrivance, but it serves the purpose. Those I have seen consist of two hollowed-out disks of wood, ten inches in diameter, resembling a large wooden ladle, with a tubular cylindrical handle a foot long; round the edge of the disks goatskins are bound with rawhide, forming a sack about fifteen inches long; this is gathered at the top and tied tightly round sticks, that serve as handles. The two wooden tubes are made to converge into a clay muzzle, which is connected with the fire; and by the alternate and rapid movement of the sticks a strong current of air is produced. The metal is said to be tempered by means of ox grease and salt.

We camped on the bank of the river, near Kongovia, the capital. In two hours the thirty huts required for the accommodation of my people for the night were built, there being an abundance of long grass. In the afternoon we had a similar experience to that of yesterday, the chief Liwika coming up with a large retinue of men, all unarmed, however, but approaching very warily, as if in doubt as to what the nature of their reception would be. A pig, three large calabashes of beer, that made the eyes of my men twinkle, and a basket of meal were the gifts he brought. The palaver and speech-making lasted an hour and a half, and by this time we had made such an impression on the old man that he ordered the pig to be taken away, considering that I deserved nothing smaller than an ox, which would be sent to-morrow, the herd being away in the forest. I demurred about accepting so large a present, and expressed doubt as to whether I should be able to make him an adequate return; but he gave me a receipt in full, in the presence of all, native fashion. Taking a piece of stick the length of an ordinary penholder, he broke it in two pieces, throwing one over each shoulder.

Next morning Liwika called round to say that he was off with his men to fetch the animal; but as big thunder-clouds had gathered, would I be so good as to keep off the rain until he returned? Not comprehending his meaning, I turned to Sanambello, who assured him the matter should have my immediate attention;

and away they went. When the request of the chief was explained to me I wished it would rain so that Liwika might learn that it was not in the power of even white men to control the elements; but the storm which threatened all day did not break until after the ox was brought home and the chief safely housed in the ombala; so I suppose he felt himself under extra obligation to me for having kept off the rain, as, in addition to the ox, he sent a large goat.

October 7th. Liwika's kindness has unfortunately been the means of delaying us three whole days, for what with libations of beer and abundance of meat for my men, threats and coaxing were alike unavailing in getting them to move; but by six o'clock this morning we were all at the river-side ready to be ferried across. The Kwanza is about ninety yards wide here, and fourteen feet deep in the center. It flows at the rate of three miles an hour in a northwest direction toward its destination, near Loanda. There were five dug-out canoes placed at our service by the chief, and manned by his own men. They seem to have no idea of a paddle with a broad end, but laboriously propel their craft with a long round pole, using each end alternately to the right and left. I went over first, and was amused watching the carriers with their loads being brought across. Many of them venturing on a big river for the first time, they did not dare to look up, but lay down flat in the bottom of the canoe, hiding their faces in their hands. The older men sat up and gravely looked around, for they knew a trick which was a certain preventive, in their opinion, against any calamity befalling them while on the river. This was to take a bunch of grass between their teeth and keep their mouths firmly closed until they reached the land.

I observed fishermen busy at work with nets and lines catching some good-sized fish, which they killed by biting them on the back at the junction of the body with the head, their teeth being well adapted for the purpose, as they have both the upper and lower incisors filed to a V shape and fitting between each other like the teeth of a rat-trap. The hooks they use are not barbed, but are merely bits of strong wire bent and pointed; so they have to depend for success in landing the fish on the dexterity with which they can tighten the line when they feel a nibble at the bait.

In two hours and a half we reached Mowanda, the chief of which is named Likalula. I went to see his highness, but on entering the village learned that he had been told some days ago that a caravan with a white man was approaching, and he had fled. It is hard to divine the cause of the mortal dread these Ganguellians entertain of white men; their ideas can only be formed from stories they have heard, or their intercourse with half-breed Portuguese, for I am not aware of any European having gone into the interior through this route—certainly no Britisher or American.

Suspecting that he might not be far away, I told the natives who were sitting round that I wished the chief no harm, but had called in passing to salute him and make his acquaintance, and intended waiting there until he turned up.

This appears to be the private inclosure of the chief, and the dozen particularly neat and tidy huts are for

MAROTSE SALUTATIONS

the accommodation of his harem, the occupants of which are conspicuous by their absence, having one and all escaped with their lord. A great deal of time and labor has been spent in cutting and carving in a variety of designs each separate pole composing the high stockade, until they look like three hundred yards of old-fashioned turned bedposts. But a former chief, I understand, must get the credit of these pleasing features of the ombala, as this man is a feeble-minded, cowardly, and superstitious fellow, who never misses an opportunity of enriching himself by plundering those who are too weak to resist him.

In about an hour Likalula's men produced him, literally covered from head to foot with white clay. Our interview was short, as he was trembling with fear. I made him a present of cloth and invited him to visit the camp. We must remain in this district for two or three days to pound corn, as for the next eight or ten marches there will be no meal to be had. Next day the chief came to us with a great deal of pomp, but we did not take to him, nor did his people seem to show him the usual respect. A vest-pocket would hold all the habiliments he wore. With an air of generosity he told me that for one of my repeating rifles he would give a big goat. Little did he know that not for fifty of his big goats would we have parted with a rifle in the vicinity of such men as Likalula; at the mere suggestion we laughed so heartily that he quitted our company.

About noon a strange phenomenon appeared. The mercury stood at 100° F. in the shade, a strong wind arose, and darkness came on as from an eclipse of the sun; when suddenly a shower of hail-stones, each as large as a marble, began to fall, and continued for fifteen minutes, until the ground was well covered. Some of the carriers happened to be returning from the villages, and fairly yelled as the hail peppered their naked bodies; but they did not seem much surprised, so I concluded that it was no rare occurrence here.

The road before us must be a very hungry one, judging from the quantity of meal and small dried fish being tied up. By the evening of the 18th the men had finished their preparations, and seemed so satisfied with themselves that speech-making, song-singing (if the dreadful braying and unmelodious recitations could be called such), and general hilarity continued round the camp-fire far into the night.

October 11th. We got a good start this morning by daybreak. Our path lay mostly through forest. We crossed on an improvised bridge the river Varia, about forty feet wide, flowing to the northwest to join the Kwanza; and twenty-three hours later another stream, the Hondo, not quite so large, but flowing in the same direction. We passed only one village on the way—a distance of fifteen miles. My heels are badly blistered; this is unfortunate, as there will be no more delays probably for a week or two, so that they will have no rest, and several of the carriers having fever, there are none to spare for the tipoia. I must make the best of it by bandaging, and cutting out pieces of my shoes, being only too glad to be going forward. We halted for the night at Kawangu. At present there is no chief, the last having died about a month ago. We saw his hat, calabashes, and pots piled on the grave, with all the remains of his hut forming a heap near by, every care being taken to see that none of his belongings were left inside the ombala, thus removing, as far as possible, the necessity for nocturnal visits of his spirit to claim them.

October 16th. For the last five days we have not seen a single village or native hut, every day toiling through deep white sand, across plains with scarcely a weed, far less grass, to shade the fiery path, the hot sand blistering our feet until we could scarcely limp into camp. For two days we had the Hondo in sight on our right. Traveling east-southeast, we crossed a small stream called the Quitu on the 14th. We have seen none of the large ant-hills since crossing the Kwanza.

We got on the path to-day by 6 A.M. The morning was cloudy and cool; but oh, the sand! It seems to get deeper and stiffer every day. Not a sign of life; the country through which we are passing is the most desert-like we have seen yet, and that means desolation indeed. Sand, sand, sand everywhere, with a few patches of shrubs here and there, but rarely a root of grass. We crossed a small brook, the Mongovie, which flows south to join the Quitu, and camped at Kambimbia. We were surprised in the evening by the appearance in camp of a man accompanied by two boys bringing baskets of a manioc meal, which is the only product of the soil in these parts, and a large gourd of beer or mead made from wild honey. He turned out to be the chief of this wilderness, and his is the only village for many miles around. He was made happy with four yards of calico.

October 17th. Rain detained us in camp until 7 A.M. Soon after starting we entered a forest, and began the assent of a hill called the Coia. At the summit the boiling-point thermometer and aneroid registered an altitude of five thousand feet, or about eight hundred feet above the surrounding country. For about ten miles we followed the ridge of the hill, which stretches northward in a great plateau, and southward sloping abruptly down to an immense and densely wooded valley, forming an unbroken expanse of foliage as far as the eye can reach. The trees are tall, but few of them exceed eighteen inches in diameter. Rubber and wild honey are found plentifully all through this district.

The gathering of honey is not the work of bees only, as every camp is infested with a small fly, about half the size of the ordinary house-fly; these are most assiduous in collecting and storing a honey whiter and sweeter than that of the bee. They find their way into the hollow trunks of timber where bees cannot enter, having access through holes made by the boring-worm. Our daily meeting with the honey-bird served to remove any skepticism I may have had in reference to this cunning little creature. It is not much larger than a canary, and as soon as man makes his appearance hops from branch to branch, making repeated flights toward the traveler, and then flying off in the direction in which it appears to wish attention attracted, with a sustained chic-en, chic-en, chic-churr, churr, returning again and again, until its importunity is rewarded by some one accepting its invitation to follow to the spot, where is stored the—to it—inaccessible treasure. It makes a great fuss, flying round and round, leaving no doubt as to the whereabouts of its find. Sometimes there is no opening to be seen, when the native proceeds to tap upon the trunk with the head of his hatchet, until he locates the hive. He then obtains the honey by making a fire at the root of the tree (in the case of fly-honey this is, of course, unnecessary), and under cover of the smoke with his hatchet secures the prize. Then is revealed the reason for the excitement of our tiny guide, who now comes in for its share of the pickings. To the taste, bee honey is harsh in flavor, and looks like molasses.

Rubber has to be dug for with hoes, only a small plant showing above ground, the roots, from which alone it is obtained, running along for many yards, about six inches below the surface, varying in size from a quarter-inch to an inch and a half. These roots are beaten with wooden mallets and boiled in water; when the rubber dissolves out it is collected and formed into balls, mixed a good deal with the woody fiber.

We were happy in finding a suitable camping-ground (the small village of Vowelutwi-Onjamba) and a stream of water just as we emerged from the forest; and we were down to the level of this morning's camp, forty-two hundred feet. The sand is so loose and deep, and the plain, stretching eastward, so void of vegetation, that I am continually imagining myself by some sea-beach. The huts of the village near by are built in an entirely different style to any we have seen in other parts of Ganguella. They cannot, of course, use mud, for there is none to be had, and stone is out of the question—we have not seen a pebble since leaving

Bihe; but they tie up small bundles of grass tightly, and weave them together in a perpendicular position, like a basket, to form the walls. The roofs are also of grass, resembling in outline the shape of a Chinaman's hat, the eaves coming down to within four feet of the ground. The mode of carrying loads, too, is not seen among the tribes west. Take water, for example: instead of the gourd being poised on the head, it is placed in a large basket or net slung on the back, and the weight borne by a band of plaited bark-cloth across the forehead, in the same way as New Haven fishwives carry their creels. The practice of filing the teeth to a sharp point prevails here, as all through Ganguella.

We purpose resting to-morrow, to give the lads of the caravan a chance to pick up a bit, the feet of a good many being played out from the burning sand. Several of them are very young, and are the slaves of the men whose meal they carry.

October 18th, Sunday. In camp all day; but it is a question with me whether the day is not better spent on the road than in camp. From daylight to dark there has been nothing but noise and carousal, drinking fermented honey beer to excess. When we travel on Sunday one's mind has at least the rest and quiet of the path, and at the end of the march the men are too tired for revelry.

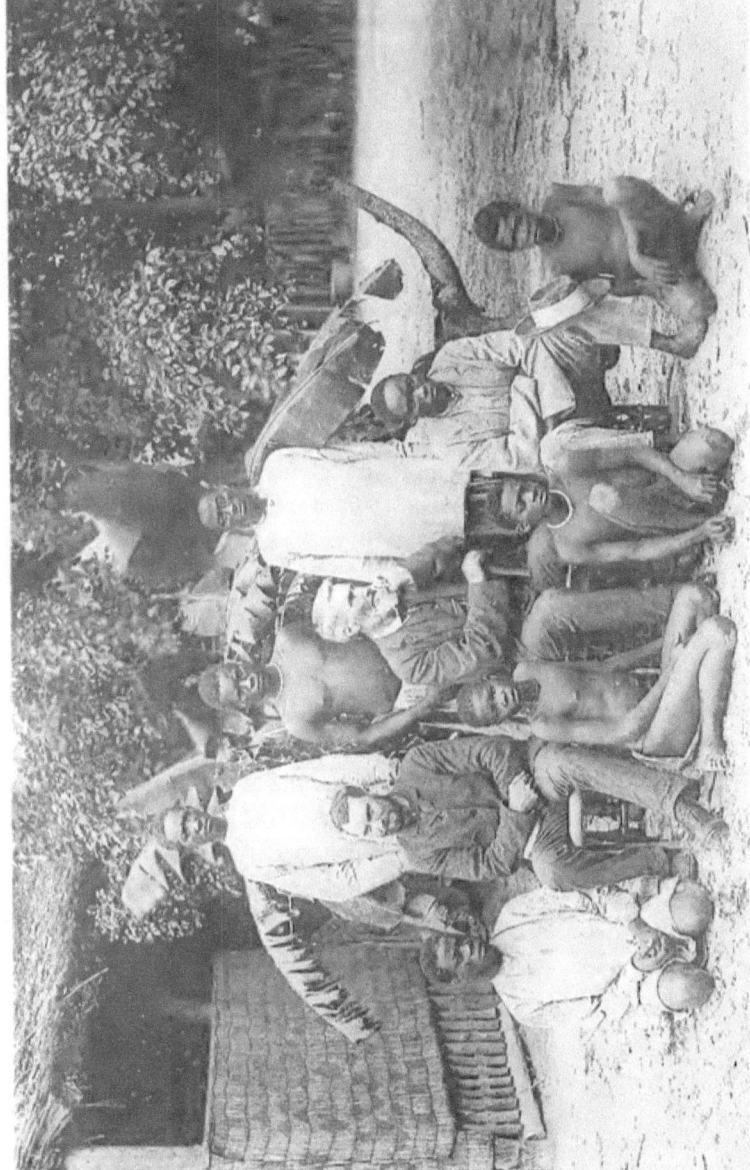

MR. WADDELL.   MONSIEUR COILLARD AND BOYS.

CHAPTER VI.

FROM VOWELUTWI-ONJAMBA TO THE HUNTER'S PARADISE.

Five hundred natives in our camp.—Daily menu.—Scarcity of food.—Herds of buffalo.—The ombanda-horn.—Soldier ants.—Hostile natives.—Peace by stratagem.—A magnanimous promise.—*In puris naturalibus*.—Caterpillar stew.—Making an impression.—A wholesome awe.—Down with fever.—Extemporized mortars.—A dark outlook.—Carriers on strike.—A complimentary dance.—Rogues all of them.—Nurse and cook by turns.—Swamp villages.—Fail to control the elements.—Exorcising the spirits.—Struggles in the marshes.—Sparsity of villages.—Game in abundance.—Charged by a buffalo.—Has the Bihean a god?—Our rain-maker.—Diviners.—Medicine-men.—Meat and to spare.—A hunter's paradise.

OCTOBER 19th. We had started about half an hour, when we came upon three native caravans, bound inland for rubber. The headmen stated that they had been waiting our arrival for two days, and wished to travel with us, as there were more rumors of war three days ahead; and they thought it would be discreet to follow in the white man's train, which now, including these natives, numbers five hundred persons. The route is very hilly; so many steep ascents to climb compelled us to make the march short. The only village we have seen to-day is a small one opposite the camp, Kambata. The chief, with a dozen of his men, gave us a call in the evening, bringing the usual gourd of beer, and a goat; the latter very acceptable, as it is now over a week since we have tasted meat. Meal and tea alone, day after day, with hard marches, was beginning to tell upon me. My diet these days is, as a rule, exceedingly simple. On getting into camp at noon I have some water boiled and poured over a teaspoonful of cocoa, which, with a couple of crackers, constitutes my lunch. At sundown or dinner-time a dish of porridge is made, part of which I eat with some wild honey, followed by a cup of tea; and the balance, with a cup of coffee, serves for breakfast next morning, before getting on the track. Scarcity of men compelled me to leave a good deal of my provisions behind, and we miss many things, such as condensed milk, and flour for bread.

This is still the Ganguella country, but I notice something peculiar to-day in the appearance of the natives. They differ from any we have seen hitherto. The language is the same, with its oft-repeated *z*; but the men are smaller, and most of them have beards three to six inches long, high foreheads, thin lips, and wear the hair long all round the head in fine plaits, profusely greased, but not cut or carved, as is the general custom among the Ganguellians. In fact, they resemble very closely some types of Hindoos. I was sorry they came when the light was gone, so that I could not get a photograph of them.

Another stiff march of six hours brought us to the Kwandu district, where there is a small town. Food is getting very scarce; the carriers could get very little meal where we stopped two days ago. These long marches don't pay, as we have to rest a day, several of the men being sick and footsore.

In the forenoon we crossed a stream called the

Kwangu, flowing swiftly to the south, only four yards wide but nearly nine feet deep. At the foot of the hill where we are camped to-night flows the Kwandu, having its rise in a swamp about a mile to the west of us, and deriving its name from the district. It travels east-southeast to join the Chobe. In the evening I went down to the marsh and shot a brace of fine fat ducks—a great treat. Probably we are getting near the game country. Although there are only three or four villages in the whole district, it boasts of two chiefs, both of whom came to visit us, and each brought a goat and "ovasangu" (canary seed) meal, the only species of grain the soil will produce. It is of a dark color, and tastes a little like rye. One chief was the happy possessor of four coats, presents from passing traders; and he evidently thought it the proper thing to don them all on this special occasion, while six of his men were rigged out with one coat among the lot, two of them considering one sleeve each, if properly adjusted, quite sufficient.

October 24th. For two days we have followed the north bank of the Kwandu. We sighted several herds of buffalo, high, shaggy-maned brutes; but as they also sighted us, it was easy for them to keep at a safe distance, for there was not a single shrub to hide us. They scampered away, stopping now and again to have a look at us, the bull always keeping a bit in the rear, between the cows and danger. Yesterday the mercury reached 105° F. at 1 P.M. in my tent; but to-day we have been chiefly in forest, which, though hilly, has afforded us a welcome shade. About 8 A.M. the Kwandu took a turn to the south-southeast, while we kept on east-southeast and came upon the sponge where the Kwandu River has its rise. We had a tough struggle getting through. Some of the men, being heavily laden, sank into the black, foul-smelling mud up to the waist. One of the carriers knocked off a toe-nail, and came for some medicine to dress it. I gave him a bandage with some carbolic ointment, directing him how to apply it; but before he proceeded to follow my instructions, he produced his ombanda-horn, stuck the small end in the ground near him, put a live coal inside, which from some stuff the horn contained sent up a dense smoke, and while it was ascending he made haste to fix up the injured toe. When it gets well my treatment will come in for a very small share of the credit, but faith in his fetich-horn will be confirmed.

October 26th. We were unceremoniously driven out of camp this morning, long before daybreak, by an army of soldier or driver ants. They swarmed into every hut in millions—no mean foe to the naked carriers, and from which there is no escape but in flight. The enormous mandibles of these ferocious warriors are very strong, and shaped like reaping-hooks; when once they get a hold there is no let go, but, doubling their bodies under them so as to obtain a purchase, they pull with all their might, and unless killed fetch the bit of flesh every time. We see them frequently in the path hurrying along in close phalanx, flanked by their generals and officers on either side, attacking viciously everything animate or inanimate that comes in their way. They are dreaded and given a wide berth by both man and beast.

Monsieur Coillard, who has had special facilities for

studying their habits in the Barotse Valley, writes: "One sees them busy in innumerable battalions, ranked and disciplined, winding along like a broad black ribbon of watered silk. Whence come they? Where are they going? Nothing can stop them, nor can any object change their route. If it is inanimate, they turn it aside and pass on; if it is living, they assail it venomously, crowding one on top of the other to the attack, while the main army passes on, business-like and silent. Is the obstacle a trench or a stream of water? Then they form themselves at its edge into a compact mass. Is this a deliberating assembly? Probably, for soon the mass stirs and moves on, crosses the trench or stream, and continues in its incessant and mysterious march. A multitude of these soldiers are sacrificed for the common good, and these legions, which know not what it is to be beaten, pass over the corpses of these, victims to their determination. Woe to him who puts his foot on that black ribbon! He has not yet seen what he has done, when thousands of these choleric fighters cover him from head to foot and force their *tenailles* into the flesh. It is enough to drive one mad.

"The most redoubtable carnivora can do nothing against these tiny enemies. They bellow, low, and roar when attacked by them, and then run away. Even the 'lord of creation,' who destroys and annihilates on sea and land the most savage cetaceans and mammifers, is quite powerless before this insect. So much the worse for his dignity; he has to take off in the field all his clothes, and rub himself down as well as he can. But at night the martyrdom is complete. I do not like to think of a person down with fever in a room that these ants have invaded. To coat a man with grease, tie him hand and foot, and throw him as a prey to these implacable carnivora, is a favorite form of execution resorted to by the Marotsi when they desire to specially torture their victim."

We are now traveling southeast by south, the Kwangu on our left, with its marshy banks stretching out on either side for over a hundred yards. Rain fell heavily yesterday, making the road a little cooler and the sand firmer; and a small leafy bush covering the ground gives the face of the country a slightly improved appearance. We met a party of natives, several of whom had received spear and arrow wounds while defending their ivory from an attack made by the tribe among whom we intend to camp to-night, at Cinjinji. They warned us to go no farther, as the savages were gathered in great force and were getting ready for us; that our little band would only be a mouthful for them; and so on. The Biheans were terribly scared, but we pressed on, and by noon got into the dreaded camp, so lately vacated by the unfortunate native traders.

We had just got the loads stacked when a crowd of men came along to look at us. They are the first we have seen in five days. The villages are not in sight, but cannot be a great way off. These men are of the regular Ganguellian type, but evidently in a very bad humor, and, being elated by success in their last fight, seem eager for another. Taking precaution to repair the temporary stockade around the camp, I served out cartridges, gunpowder, and lead, and ordered every man who carried a gun to have it by him in case of an attack.

LEWANIKA IN WAR DRESS

Meantime, the natives were disappearing in twos and threes until we were alone. Now we feared the worst. "They have gone for their weapons," said Sanambello. His surmise was correct, for in less than an hour over two hundred men, armed with bows and arrows, spears and hatchets, came dancing inside the stockade and halted at my tent door, where I was sitting mending my shoes. Their gesticulations and bawling beggar description; but I went on with my work, until several spears came so uncomfortably near my face that I jumped up, drew my revolver (a regulation 450), while Sanambello remarked, "Now see how the white man's guns shoot!" I fired several shots at a tree a few yards off, and as the bullets made the bark fly they were silent and drew back a little. Then, taking a Winchester, I fired half a dozen rounds as quickly as I could over their heads, and paused, telling Sanambello to let them know that I was not half through yet, and that they should have the remaining shots unless they cleared out of my camp forthwith. The words were scarcely uttered before they made off, tumbling over one another in their haste to get at a safe distance from such infernal machines. My men fairly yelled and roared with laughter when the bloodless battle was ended and the warriors had fled.

But we were now in danger of a night attack; and to try and avert this I gave Sanambello a handsome piece of figured calico and a jackknife for the chief, with the message that I would spare their lives and do them no injury provided they left their weapons behind and came in a respectful and proper manner to my camp for palaver. These conditions of peace were

accepted. Quite a number came back, and with them
several women carrying presents of rubber, meal, and
fowls from the chief, who thus indicated that he wished
to make peace. I treated them to a lick of coarse salt
each, which they seemed greatly to relish.

We arrived at Kangamba (altitude, 3750 feet), rain
falling heavily as we halted. As it did not begin to
fall until we had reached the camping-ground, some of
the carriers, as they came in wet, were grumbling because I had kept off the rain until under shelter myself,
and allowed it to come while most of the caravan was
still on the track. I disputed the point with Sanambello, but he simply remarked that he had seen me
with his own eyes take out my ombanda (a compass)
on the road. This was conclusive, and I had to take
the blame. Here, also, we found the natives in a very
sulky mood; but as they had come off second best in
their skirmish with the native caravan already referred
to, they did not seem so keen for a fight as the Cinjinjis.
We added fresh thorn-bush to the skerm and put sentries on for the night to guard against a surprise.

There seems to be a large population here; crowds
have been coming and going all the afternoon. Most
of them were all but nude, particularly the women; an
ordinary trade handkerchief would provide all the garb
they seem to require for half a dozen. As a rule, both
sexes have good figures, and are quite up to the average
height, although the lazy life of the men is not conducive to muscular development. They are expert basket-makers, and we saw some really beautiful specimens
of this handicraft, perfectly water-tight, the smaller sizes
being used as drinking-vessels. The trade or barter

goods in demand here are iron and copper wire for anklets and armlets, the limbs of some of the women being loaded with them; red white-eye beads, gunpowder, salt, and tobacco, the latter being in universal use as snuff by both men and women, every one wearing round their neck a flat iron spatula, with which they shovel it into their capacious nostrils.

The carriers are short of meal again. I cannot understand how they have stowed away such sackfuls as they were provided with a few days ago. We must stop here for two or three days to enable them to refill. For the last ten days the employment of the boys of the caravan on getting into camp has been to go off into the woods to gather a species of large black-and-yellow-colored hairy caterpillar, generally bringing in a dozen or more basketfuls, which are stewed in clay pots, and served round to be eaten with their mush. The insects are about three inches long, and, as may be imagined, make a repulsive-looking dish; but this is the tasty bit of the native repast, and is to them what *pâte de foie gras* is to a modern epicure. The carriers at mealtime sit round in groups, their dish in the center heaped with a sodden stiff paste of scalded meal. Each man helps himself with his fingers, kneads each lump into the form of a cone, and dips it into the savory stew before passing it to his mouth. They seldom have more than one meal a day, but I could not venture to state how many pounds of this mush they will put out of sight at their evening sitting; after which the fires are stirred, fresh fuel added, pipes and snuff-boxes are in requisition, and they settle down to entertain one another by relating tales of "love and war."

Smoking assumes many forms in Africa. A few carry their own individual pipe, but usually there is but one among a dozen or more men, each tribe having its own peculiar style of family hookah. Some, like the bushmen, make a new pipe every time they want a smoke, by twisting up a leaf into a cone and filling it with crushed tobacco, which they light with a fire coal, and apply the mouth to the small end, passing it to their neighbor after two or three whiffs. Others mix a little earth with saliva and mold it into a bowl, making an opening at one side with a straw; then, drying it by the fire and passing a long hollow reed through the orifice, they load up and proceed with their inhalations. All the natives I have seen at this operation take the smoke right into their lungs, and seem to enjoy the fit of coughing that follows. But the form of pipe in most general use has a receptacle for water, through which the smoke is drawn. An eland or koodoo horn has a hole cut in the side halfway between the base and the point; into this a reed is inserted, on the end of which a clay bowl is fixed and filled with tobacco or bang (*cannabis nativa*), and occasionally both; water is poured in until it rises above the node, when it is ready for business, placing the mouth over the open base of the horn and inspiring the fumes.

But the most objectionable form of smoking is that of bang, or dagga. It is more used than tobacco among the Batokas, Mashonas, Inhambanes, and those toward the East Coast and Lake regions. Its intoxicating and injurious effects compare very closely with the sensations produced by the use of opium. After filling the lungs, the head is thrown back, and the surplus smoke emitted in a dense cloud; the mouth is filled with water, and this squirted right and left with the fumes from the lungs. They are now in a hysterical condition, giving themselves up to coughing, laughing, shouting, and incoherent mutterings. Natives addicted to the use of this weed become in a short time imbecile, emaciated, and helpless. The Portuguese are so strongly convinced of the evils resulting to the votaries of bang that slaves discovered indulging in it are punished as for any other crime.

On the morning of the 29th the chief appeared, gorgeously arrayed in leopard-skins, with a large band of men at his heels armed with assegais. Quickly buckling on my revolver, I ordered them to quit the camp and leave their weapons outside if they wished to talk with me. They obeyed, and returned, when I gave the chief a seat, and, my headmen having gathered round, proceeded to make myself agreeable, taking care to show them my repeaters and Express rifles, drawing special attention to the size of the bullets, and to the fact that some of them were explosive. The great man became very civil, and after passing a few compliments took his departure, returning, however, in the afternoon with a fat goat, meal, and beer. In return I gave him a blanket and some cloth, which pleased him, and we parted friends.

Our route now lies south-southeast instead of east-southeast (as it has been ever since crossing the Kwanza), following the Kwangu on its east bank. The surrounding country gradually improves in appearance as we advance, grass being more abundant, although still trudging through sand; but there seems but little of any other soil on the great central African plateau. Game is more plentiful, scarcely a day passing without our seeing herds of buffalo and antelope, but always in the open, where the absence of cover denies us the opportunity of a shot, much as we want meat.

Arriving at Metua, we have now to build a skerm around each camp, not only as a protection against wild animals, but to break the rush of a charge from hostile tribes. There are two entrances, which are built up at night, and at each, during the day, the men stick their fetich-horns in the path to awe the natives; but an exhibition of the quick-firing rifles has a greater effect upon the Ganguellians than any number of horns, for thus far I have not seen a tithe of the outward signs of superstition with them that exists among my own men. They have a wholesome dread of the guns, which they say go "bam, bam, bam!"

November 2d. I have to record my first real attack of African fever. For some days back I have been dreading the results of camping so often and traveling so long among these marshes. The heat of yesterday was intense. I got into camp very exhausted, and sat by the fire for some time, feeling chilly, then sought warmth in my tent, wrapping myself in several blankets; but the ague took hold of me in earnest, and continued until near midnight, while my mind was harassed by the saddest thoughts and most melancholy forebodings. This was followed by the hot stage, finding relief only in the next stage, when perspiration began to flow copiously and continued until daybreak,

MISSION STATION, SEFULA

See page 152

when I got up, drank a cup of coffee, but could not look at my cold porridge. I sounded the bugle and aroused the camp, and in half an hour more got on the path, feeling very weak and shaky. My poor dog Gyp refuses her food, and looks as if she would not follow us much farther. I am grieved for this; she has been good company, running along at our heels all the day, and keeping faithful watch over the loads at night. The burning sand and heavy swamps have lately proved very trying to her, and sometimes she will not arrive in camp until hours after the last man is in.

We met a large caravan in charge of half-caste Portuguese coming from the Barotse, laden with rubber and over one hundred tusks of ivory, varying in size from three to six feet in length; they had also about two hundred and forty head of cattle. They have been twenty-four days since crossing the Zambesi, having had to follow the marshes and windings of the stream, so as to find grass for the stock. At 7 A.M. we entered a dense jungle, with scarcely any visible path. Rain had fallen during the night, so that the bush was heavy with water; and, having to lead the way, in a few minutes I was drenched to the skin, and remained so until we got into camp at noon, by the swamp where the river Kusivi has its origin.

On the 4th we reached Kalumbwi, and here again we have to delay a couple of days to prepare meal, as another uninhabited country of forest and jungle lies before us. The men succeeded in borrowing only one wooden mortar in which to pound their corn; and as I have promised but two days for this purpose, several of them have gone into the forest to extemporize a few, so as to expedite the work. These are produced more speedily than one would imagine, as they are neither hewn nor dug out, like those in ordinary use. A tree with a thick, soft, yielding bark, eight or ten inches in diameter, is selected and felled. From it a log about three feet six inches is cut, when they proceed at one end to dexterously fold back the bark, as in rolling up a coat-sleeve, for fourteen inches, when the denuded wood is carefully chopped square off, leaving a smooth surface; the bark is then returned to its original position. Next a stick four or five feet in length and two and a half inches thick is peeled, the ends rounded, and a very serviceable, if not durable, mortar and pestle is ready for use.

Villages have been more frequent than west of Kangamba; but though we are thereby better supplied with food, the denser population is far from being an unalloyed blessing to us, for, if there is beer to be had, my men are constantly framing excuses to stop over a day or two, until I begin to realize that my own small stock of groceries is all but exhausted, though we are yet many marches from our destination. The men are making fresh demands for rations, although they have already received more than was agreed upon at starting. I offered to divide among them, as a gift, twenty-four pounds of beads; but they coolly told me it was not enough, they must have two yards of cloth each besides. On declining to accede to their unjust demands, I was told to make myself comfortable—which meant that they intended to pit their patience against mine. This is easy enough for them, as anywhere is home to the African while there is something to eat; so very likely they will get the best of it in the end, but not to-day. I observed several of the women wearing pieces of wood about three inches long and half an inch thick through the lobe of the right ear, while many of both sexes have their heads closely thatched all round with red beads. Cloth is in little demand among them, but an empty jam or sardine tin, or, better still, a brass cartridge shell, which they use as snuff-boxes, will buy a basket of manioc meal.

In the afternoon the chief of Kalumbwi paid the usual visit, followed by a tremendous crowd of natives. He went first to the headmen and asked them to walk with him to my tent. Like his people, he was all but naked, and made no attempt to act the grandee, like most chiefs. He is a handsome, well-built savage, and far less repulsive in his nakedness than the half-draped, half-civilized natives of the west, with their greasy shirts and dirty loin-cloths. I entertained him as best I could, while he expressed no end of pleasure at everything I had to show him. On leaving, he hinted that as I was the first white man he had ever seen, he would send his people that night to do me honor. What form this "honor" was to take remained a mystery until nearly eleven o'clock, when I was roused by a terrific noise close to my tent. Jumping up, I rushed out, to find a high fire blazing, spears, battle-axes, bows and arrows, etc., stuck in the ground at one side, while some two hundred young men and women danced in a circle round the fire, as if their very lives depended on the vigor with which they capered and wriggled their bodies. For music, they had five big drums beaten with the open hand, producing a noise that was positively deafening. I earnestly hoped they would not prolong the demonstration past midnight; but as the hours went by the unearthly din only grew more wild and more unbearable. The monotonous and discordant choruses on the same high-pitched key over and over again, interspersed with howls and yells, made up a pandemonium which to endure was to put one's sanity to a severe test. At 8 A.M., when I suppose they considered I had been honored sufficiently for one night, they ceased, and came to know how I had enjoyed it; at the same time promising that if I would give them each some salt they would repeat the little treat the following night. Needless to say, there was no salt distributed, and my reply is not recorded here; but they did not return.

The carriers sent their spokesman to-day with the message that they had decided to accept my gift of beads, provided I added the two yards of cloth; otherwise they intended to stay here until their demands were complied with. Hoping to get square with them when pay-day comes, I let them have the stuff. Their threat to remain here indefinitely only shows the unreasonableness of their character, as, if they have means to buy food while in camp, they can find it to provide for the road; but they are rogues, without a single exception. On the journey I have tried to put confidence in five or six men, who appeared to be honest, intrusting them with cloth to buy food for my Jamaicans; but in each case I found they were thieves. If any one of them offered to do anything for us on the road, it was only that they might have an excuse for extorting three times the value of the service rendered. I heartily indorse every word that Professor Drummond has written concerning the average African carrier.

On the morning of the 9th we started once more, skirting the marsh of the Kusivi River for some hours. Both Jamaica men are suffering from fever, and struggling along with great difficulty; for some three weeks Frater has scarcely been a day without it, although the heavy doses of quinine he is taking make the intervals longer now. When the two are down I have to be nurse and cook by turns. I think it is pretty clearly proven that the West Indian is quite as liable to malarial fever as the European, if not more so. We made a short march and brought up at Kalomo (altitude, 3550 feet).

November 10th. We made an early start to-day, but had only gone seven miles when rain began to fall heavily, and we had to stop and stack the loads near the village of Kusivi. As there was no sign of the weather clearing, I gave orders to build huts for the night. I was surprised to see a number of men come round the camp with hoes on their shoulders, and was told that all through the eastern part of Ganguella the men work in the fields along with the women, during the planting season. The land here is of a reddish color, and the swamps by the river—in many places stretching out for half a mile on either side—yield a fair crop of Kaffir-corn. Most of the villages are built right in the center of the marsh, partly for the purpose of watching their patches of grain, but chiefly to be less accessible to their enemies. Being surrounded by water, the huts are built on piles some six or eight feet above the ground. A rough ladder, which they draw up at night, is used to reach the platform at the entrance of each hut.

Monday, November 14th. For the last four days we have been traveling mostly in the forest, with heavy rains every day. Yesterday morning dawned with thick fog and drizzling rain, and two of the headmen came to say that unless I would promise to keep off the rain the men refused to leave camp. A few minutes later it began to clear up, when they picked up their loads, shouting vociferously, and telling me I had done well; but in less than an hour down came the rain in torrents. Alas for my reputation as rain-doctor! This was too bad! I had just kept it off long enough to get them exposed to it, and then let it come; and for the balance of the day I was in the bad books of the whole caravan.

A path through the forest is very good in hot, dry weather, affording grateful shade; but in the wet season for hours after the rain has ceased there is a perpetual shower-bath from the trees and bushes. For eight miles we trudged along, until every stitch of clothing was drenched through. Frater and Jonathan managed to get into dry clothes on reaching camp, but the man carrying the bag with my extra suit had let it fall into the water while crossing a stream, and the contents were soaked. There was no alternative but to wrap myself in my blanket and wait for the sun to appear and dry them. We have seen no villages or natives for the last three days. Oh, how I long to see a white face! Little did I think, in starting out on this journey, that I would be so depressed with feelings of intense loneliness.

MONS. COILLARD   MADAME COILLARD'S GRAVE

See page 353

This morning broke very gloomy, threatening early rain. I had everything ready by 5.30 A.M., but the carriers would not stir until after six, when, just as we were leaving camp, a boy was seized with an epileptic fit. Then a kind of circus commenced, by the old men performing around the lad with the fetich-horns, exorcising the spirits that were supposed to be troubling him.

At seven o'clock, however, we got off, pushing our way through dense jungle for thirteen miles, until we emerged at the head of the river Cikulwi, which, being about thirty-five feet wide and eight feet deep, we could not ford, and were obliged to halt and improvise a bridge. Pitching camp within a few yards of the river, and cutting down small trees, by night we had fixed up a rough trestle bridge, which, though rather shaky, served our purpose. It was made by placing two trunks of trees, with forked ends, upon each bank; these met and fixed into each other over the bed of the river, and a man crawling along one of the trees lashed the forks together with bark. A few poles were forced into the mud, and acted as supports and braces to the bridge; the fastening of transverse bars ladder-fashion was an easy matter, and the work was completed. It will remain, I suppose, until swept away by the next rains.

November 15th. The caravan crossed on the wooden structure safely; but spanning the stream was by no means the end of our difficulties, for all these rivers on the plains are bounded by far-reaching marshes, and in this case the swamp extended, green but treacherous, and reeking with malaria, for half a mile. Over an hour passed before the last man had reached dry land, though there was no standing still; that only meant to sink deeper. Those with loads every now and again went down to the waist, while only the heads and loads of others were to be seen above the mud, holding on with their hands to clumps of grass until rescued by their companions. This was but one of the many similar struggles we have experienced in the marshes. We entered the thicket again, crossing the Kambuli, a stream about twenty yards wide but only knee-deep, and by noon reached Kalongo, having made a good march of sixteen miles.

On the morning of the 16th we staggered out into the path again, feeling very stiff and tired. We were still in the jungle, and had twelve miles of thick underbrush to contend with, our first opening being at the rise of the Ninda. We passed the grave of a Frenchman, inclosed by a palisade. He had been killed by an "onyani" (wild ox). He had fired on the animal, but only wounded it, and before he could reload, it charged and gored him.

We are now out of the Ganguella country, and on the southern border of Lovale. The landscape is beautiful, rich green grass covering the plains. Still no sign of natives or villages, for which I am rather thankful, as the men make longer marches and travel better when there are no attractions by the way and they know there is no chance of replenishing their meal-bags. Some have run short of food already, and have been digging for edible roots this evening, to eke out their nearly exhausted store. I have kept a sharp lookout all day for a shot at an antelope or a buffalo, as it is now nearly two weeks since my daily allowance of oatmeal has known any variation; even the wild honey is finished; and this fare does not tend to strengthen me for the long, heavy marches. Still, I am thankful to be in very fair health, with the exception of a peculiar vertigo that troubles me every morning, but which passes away after walking a few miles. It may be asked, Why was not better provision made for the journey? Well, I was informed by those who were supposed to know, that five weeks at most would see us at the Barotse. Had we made the journey in that time, there would have been no lack of food; but nine weeks have passed since we left Cisamba, and we are still, I believe, two weeks from the Zambesi. One cannot calculate upon time while having to depend for the conveyance of loads on such fellows as the Biheans.

November 19th. This is the first bright day we have had for a week. We started at six o'clock. The course of the Ninda to-day had many windings, to avoid which we made short cuts through the forest, steering due east. This is the wildest country we have seen. There is plenty of game; we saw several herds of antelope, eland, hartebeest, and onyani. We struck the fresh spoor of elephants at four different places, and at one spot they had, either in a fight or in play, torn up a number of young trees, plowed up the ground, and strewn it with broken branches. There is no chance of getting near game, with a noisy crowd of men whose tongues never seem to weary. A buffalo that was gamboling about on the plain as we passed charged the rear of the straggling caravan, and although most of the men were armed they threw down their guns and loads and hid in the bush. We saw eight large snakes within a mile; three of them were the venomous and deadly green mamba. None of them attempted to show fight, but got out of the way as quickly as they could. While threading my way through the thicket I almost stepped on a huge iguana that was lying right across the path; it made off and scrambled up a tree, when I brought it down with my rifle. It measured four feet three inches from tip to tip. I preserved the skin, and the carriers begged the flesh, considering it a great delicacy.

We reached Kalungalunga early in the day. I bought several good-sized fish for a few beads, so we have a splendid dinner for once. There are several villages in the vicinity, but no meal can be obtained without sending eight miles to the north, causing another delay of several days.

November 23d. After spending three days in last camp, we had only gone six miles when we came upon a village where the natives said they had plenty of dried fish. There is no use trying to get the men past; I am sick of contending with them, yet unwilling to take the law into my own hands and force them, which could easily be done, they are such arrant cowards. If I can only bear with them the few remaining days and get rid of them in peace, I shall be thankful. So here we must camp at Wanambuka for to-night. Were I asked if the Bihean has a god that he worships, I should unhesitatingly reply, "Yes; his god is his belly;" for three parts of his waking hours are taken up with cooking, eating, and talking about food.

November 24th. Rain fell the most of last night,

and did not hold up until half-past eight this morning. The men have given up asking me to control the weather since the day I allowed the rain to come down just after starting. We have a carrier in our company named Cirula, who the Ovimbundu believe possesses wonderful power over the elements, and by 6 A.M. he was out shouting to the clouds and whistling to the rain, while he burned a fetich-powder which he carried with him. After a great effort and much hard work he succeeded in stopping the rain at the hour named; so we struck camp.

The name "fetich-doctor" may be applied to all superstitious pretenders found in Central Africa; but in reality the supposed power over and knowledge of the unseen is appropriated to widely different ends. As all cases of sickness are attributed to some evil spell, or the visitation of some departed relative, friend, or enemy, when a case of illness occurs the "diviner" is applied to first, in order to discover the cause. This is arrived at with much ceremony, and generally in the presence of a number of people, by a wearying program of incantations, accompanied by the sacrifice of a white cock. He feigns to discover a foreign body, in the shape of a claw, or stick, or a piece of iron, generally in the arm, leg, or head of the sufferer. Resort is now made to the "medicine-man," who professes ability to cure all manner of sickness, from whatever cause. He makes no attempt to diagnose a case, but with mysterious words and genuflections he prescribes and administers to the patient pungent decoctions from his stock of dried abominations; and in order that the medicine shall prove efficacious, the patient has often to be removed to an isolated hut. Should the treatment fail to have the desired effect, the skill of the "physician" would not be questioned. The diviner and medicine-man play into each other's hands; and there is yet another iniquitous impostor who must also be considered a partner in this nefarious firm—the sorcerer, or "obeah-man." He is credited with power over spirits to control their actions, or make void their designs by counter-witchery; he affects the crops and increase; and to his ear are intrusted the secret desires of would-be avengers, and by his infernal work persons not wanted are removed.

November 25th. Seeing game so abundant, I determined this morning to start out half an hour ahead, so as to get away from my noisy followers. Accompanied by two headmen, I set out by daybreak, traversing during the first two hours seven miles of plain, and sighting herds of buffaloes and antelopes, which from the absence of cover were unapproachable. We had just entered the forest when I saw three splendid hartebeests, two cows and a bull, grazing quietly at about five hundred yards. Getting down on all-fours, I crept along until I had shortened the distance three hundred yards; the bull, always on the alert, got wind of me, and, facing round, began snorting and stamping with his forefeet. Raising my "Express," I fired and hit him in the chest, when he staggered a few yards and fell. By the time we had skinned and cut up the carcass the carriers arrived, and we were soon under way again. The meat was tender and delicious—a great windfall for us. I reserved a small portion for our own use, and had the rest distributed among the men; but in no instance was there an expression of thankfulness, only a growl that I had not shot two instead of one.

Any one coming to this country to labor in Christian work must be content to look for his encouragement or reward from some other source than from the people he comes to benefit; for the white man, to them, is only a present-giving animal, or an object to be plundered. Respect being gauged by the amount of stuff he distributes, if he has none to give he is despised, and becomes the subject of their sneers and contempt.

All along now we observe with delight the remarkable change in the appearance of the country compared with the sterile plains which lie behind us—immense stretches of luxuriant grass, shaded here and there with patches of palms. We are camped to-night in the forest primeval; very little undergrowth, and magnificent large trees. Any one fond of sport would find here a hunter's paradise, with almost every kind of African game, from duikers to elephants. In the evening three wild oxen came trotting past my tent. I always pitch it in these uninhabited regions some distance from the huts, so as to be away from the noise at night. I picked up my rifle just as a dozen men with guns came rushing out of camp, howling and shouting in full cry after the game. This is their idea of hunting, and the reason why they so seldom bring down anything; so I put up my gun, knowing it was useless to join in such a chase. I heard eighteen shots fired before they returned; result, animals scared a bit.

CHAPTER VII.

ARRIVAL IN THE BAROTSE VALLEY.

Mutiny in camp.—Barotse natives.—Milk for the first time.—The Zambesi at last.—Reception by King Lewanika.—" Yo sho, yo sho, yo sho!"—Salutations.—The royal residence.—" Fail not, at your peril!"—Barotse huts.—A native service.—Lewanika's ambition.—Building the Nalikwanda.—Paying off carriers.—Presented with an ox.—Dining with royalty.—The burden of his heart.—British Protectorate.—Thieves and robbers.—Monsieur Coillard's letter.—The British South African Company.—Concession-hunting.—An emphatic protest.—A letter from King Lewanika.

NOVEMBER 29th. This morning, instead of starting, the carriers, led by two rascals, Bwete and Kesongo (who have been at the root of almost every trouble we have had on the road), conscious that they had exacted from me much more than was due for rations, and fearing I should take it off their pay on getting to the Barotse, refused to take up their loads unless I paid every man, in full, here and now. They strutted about all day, thinking, no doubt, I should be obliged to comply. Calling the headmen together, I told them they could do as they pleased, but that I intended starting for the capital of Barotse to-morrow, alone, if necessary, where men would be found to come back for my loads, and the mutineers would lose all their pay. This had the desired effect, and they promised to start. They cannot do much now, as we are

within three or four days of Lialui, and there accounts will be squared.

On the morrow I sent two men with, as is customary, a letter and presents of cloth to King Lewanika, requesting permission to enter his country. I also sent a letter to Monsieur Coillard, the French missionary.

The natives have their own way of carrying a letter. Having no pocket, and a corner of their loin-cloth not being the best receptacle, they devise a plan to keep the envelope clear of their greasy skins by slipping it into a cleft stick, securing the open end by tying it with bark. When they rest, the free end is stuck in the ground; and they hold it prominently as they travel, the sight of an omakanda (paper that speaks) generally securing for them a measure of protection when passing among strangers, as they recognize the fact that there must be a white man not far off.

Three more marches brought us on the 30th to the thickly populated district of Kanete. None too soon, for my food-supply is at the lowest ebb, my rations for the last two days having been reduced to a few crackers with two ears of roasted mealies. I hope we shall be able to procure a fresh supply of meal here, even if we have to stay a day or two. This is part of the Barotse Valley. The natives are subjects of Lewanika, but most of them are slaves belonging to the headmen of the villages. These people are a mixture of several tribes captured in raids and war; they are of a lower caste and are coarser featured than the Ganguellians. The women make no attempt at hairdressing, plaiting, or ornamenting; a few have beads round their necks, and most of them rings of iron and brass on their arms and ankles. There are no flint-locks among the men, but bows and arrows and assegais. This morning I saw cow's milk for the first time since coming to Africa, brought in large gourds by a native for sale; but as the native does not consider milk fit to use until it has been kept for a week or so and becomes sour and thick, this was the condition of all that was brought to-day; but they promised to bring a gourd of fresh milk to-morrow.

We are convinced, by the apparent abundance of milk, that the breed of cattle as well as the land must be vastly superior to anything of the kind in Bihe or the West Coast; for although there are cattle at all the mission stations, and the time we passed through was the calving season, in no instance did we see other than condensed milk on the table. The education of the Bihean cow has thus far been neglected.

December 2d. For ten miles we followed the western border of the plain, and camped again at the edge of a wood. Several villages are in sight, but the natives are very shy. About 3 P.M. the two men I sent off on the 30th with letters to the king and Monsieur Coillard returned, and, to my dismay and chagrin, said they found no white people, and that the king had forbidden, on pain of death, any white man to enter his country. They could give no reason for having failed to deliver the letter to the king. I will, however, start in the morning and seek the white men, of whom I have heard, and risk the king's interdict. So, leaving Frater in charge, I procured a guide, and, taking Jonathan, set out at daybreak to walk to Lialui, the capital of Barotse. After tramping for an hour and a half we reached the Zambesi. Procuring a canoe, we crossed the famous river, which at this point is about one hundred and fifty yards wide, and called the Mongole drift. Hippopotami were bathing in the cool waters just above the place where we crossed, but I was too preoccupied to take much notice of them. Another hour brought us to the river Kimbo, wide but not deep, so that the guide was able to carry me over on his shoulders. The grassy plains on either side of us abounded with cattle of small size, but in splendid condition, while flocks of wild geese and ducks were everywhere, within easy gunshot. Four hours more and we were at Lialui. To the right, I observed a few huts, where I was told white men lived. Thither I bent my steps, found an English trader and a hunter of doubtful nationality, and was heartily welcomed. I sent back the guide to camp with orders for the caravan to come on in the morning.

Later in the day I went to see Lewanika, whom I found sitting in his "lekhothla," or courtyard, in the center of the town, with a crowd of people kneeling in semicircles before him, near or far according to their rank. The deep, yielding sand is a merciful provision for those who have to remain in this position for hours together. I was graciously received, and could not but feel that at last I was face to face with a real African king, compared with whom the many I had seen were but insignificant. Lewanika was plainly dressed in English clothes, and sat on an ordinary cane-bottom chair; his manner was affable and free. In front of him were his band of drummers and *marimba* players. Each company of men, as they assembled at the evening council, while still at some distance began clapping their hands in unison; and before taking their places raised their hands above their heads and shouted the royal salutation, "Yo sho, yo sho, yo sho!" After kneeling, they continue clapping, and bow their faces to the earth three times. To all this pomp and ceremony, with which the Marotsi have for ages surrounded their sovereign, Lewanika paid no attention (although I understand he is not indifferent to it), but kept up a long conversation with me through an interpreter. He could not quite understand why I had come so far simply to see the country and the people, for he said, "All the white men who come here either want ivory and skins, or liberty to hunt in my territory."

The mode of salutation among the Marotsi is peculiar. They approach a superior clapping the hands and repeating the word "lumela"; but to equals they observe three different grades (see illustration), according to the degree of friendship or relationship existing between them. Those having a slight acquaintance with each other will on meeting lay down their spears or whatever load they may be carrying, and, seizing each other by both hands, elevate them to about the level of their eyes, lowering and raising them three times, silently gazing into each other's face, and conclude the ceremony by squatting down and passing the snuff-box. The second mode of greeting applies to individuals between whom a closer friendship exists; the same dumb show is performed, but in this case the parties kneel. The third form is observed only by near relations, and differs from the second in that each with his right hand seizes the left hand of the other, palm upward, on which he impresses a prolonged kiss, or kisses, according to the warmth of their attachment.

December 4th. Early in the morning a messenger came from the king with his greeting, and to know if I had slept well; at the same time expressing his desire that I should live in his village during my stay in the valley, and stating that a house was already prepared for me. He also sent an invitation to lunch with him at noon. Such kindness and civility from a chief in the interior of Africa I was totally unprepared for, as past experience had led me to look upon them merely as greedy beggars, who never offered the white man a paltry basket of meal without expecting ten times its value in return. There have certainly been exceptions, such as the chiefs at Ciyuka, Kukema, and Kwanza.

Noon found the English trader and myself at the entrance of the reed-mat inclosure within which is the king's residence, surrounded by some twenty large huts, the domiciles of his numerous wives. The entire absence of dirt and rubbish is a pleasing feature of Lialui; but still more praiseworthy is the well-kept and orderly condition of the royal inclosure, reminding one of a military fort in time of peace. Lewanika was sitting at the door of his house conversing with his secretary; but on seeing us he arose and bid us welcome in a very genial manner. The building is after the bungalow style, and is the work of natives trained by Mr. Waddell, a Scotch carpenter at Sefula, Monsieur Coillard's mission station. A narrow veranda runs along the front of the dwelling, and, crossing the threshold, we enter the sitting-room, where only white people besides the king are admitted. The walls of this room are composed of reed mats, beautifully woven, in various designs, with the beaten bark of trees, dyed in several colors—the work of his wives.

December 5th. No sign of my caravan yet; they seem determined to follow their own sweet wills to the very last. I went to the king and laid the matter before him, when he immediately dispatched a messenger with the order that they put in an appearance at once, with the result that before night they were all here, and very much frightened. I never saw such a change in the demeanor of any company of men. Just like the cowardly knaves! Now they know that they have incurred the king's displeasure, for he had told his messenger to say they were to fail not, at their peril. They have had a big scare. "It's a long lane that has no turning."

All day there has been held in the "lekhothla" the great native festival of the month—the dance of the new moon. From early morning the drums have been going hard, and as I passed through the council-yard at noon the dance was at its height, performed by some three hundred men, draped almost uniformly in kilts of leopards' tails, and ostrich feathers in their hair. It lasted until sundown. But every night there is a dance for a couple of hours, commencing at ten o'clock, and the drumming continues with brief intervals until daylight; this is for the purpose of driving off the evil spirits that are inclined to disturb the king's slumbers. I now occupy the premises provided by the king, consisting of two large huts, one of which was assigned to Frater and Jonathan. The construction of these huts is peculiar, and deserves more than a passing notice.

They consist of two circular walls, one within the other, made of reeds, and both surfaces plastered over by hand with a mixture of cow-dung and sand, or preferably ant-hills, when obtainable. The floors are made with the same kind of cement, well trodden with the feet, and subsequently smoothed in the same fashion as the walls, a finishing coat being added of bullock's blood, which serves to harden and give a polish to the surface. The roof, made of reeds closely woven together and thatched with grass, and extending beyond the outer wall several feet, forms a shade all round the hut, and, as it rests on both walls, forms an inner and outer compartment, perfectly light-tight, having no windows, and I might say "air-tight" too. The inside or sleeping-room is stiflingly hot and close, so that I prefer to sleep in the outer section. In the largest dwellings the door is only about four feet high by two and a half wide. The privacy of each family is secured by inclosing their yard with a tall reed fence. Our huts are nearly new, consequently the smell is very strong; but we are getting used to it.

December 6th, Sunday. The chief's secretary, Sajika, who has been educated in Basutoland, had a service in the village, reading a portion of Scripture and singing some hymns with the boys who are under the tuition of Monsieur Coillard at Sefula; but in the evening the drums beat and the dance goes on as on other nights, loudly and fiercely, until two o'clock in the morning. There is a manifest struggle going on here between light and darkness; so far, the latter is in the ascendency.

I spent three hours of the afternoon with the king,

our conversation being interpreted by a black boy, who knows a little English, having been brought up at Cape Colony. Lewanika says he longs for light and knowledge, and wonders why more missionaries do not come to teach him and his people. It must not be imagined by this, however, that he yearns for a knowledge of the gospel. By no means; he wants teachers to instruct his people how to read and write, but especially to train them as carpenters, cabinet-makers, blacksmiths, and for other trades, that they may make furniture and build houses for him. None of his people dare own a chair, or build a square house, or put a wooden door or a window in their hut; the right to possess such luxuries he reserves to himself. But he has a great idea of the ability of the Marotsi to learn the various arts and become wise like Europeans. He is by no means an idler himself, much of his time being spent in wood-carving, with very primitive tools, turning out bowls and other dishes of wonderful symmetry, and exhibiting exceptional skill and taste. At present he is busy with his men building the annual Nalikwanda.

This is a monster canoe, constructed from a number of smaller ones broken up to yield planks for the ungainly craft. It measures a hundred and twenty feet in length by fifteen feet beam, is flat-bottomed, has no keel and no ribs, and will only be used in taking the king in state with his wives to his mountain village, some thirteen miles off, where he spends a couple of months each year during the time when the plain is inundated with water by the overflow of the Zambesi. Ere the waters dry up he returns again, and the boat, that required months of labor from hundreds of men, is used no more; another one is built for the following year. It is manned only by chiefs, and none but the aristocracy are allowed on board. But if the back of this one does not break and slip the whole of them into the water I shall be surprised. Last year they sewed the planks together with bark; now they have got a step further, and are joining the planks by overlaying the seams with boards and nailing them down with four-inch native spikes, and have, like the builders of the ark, "pitched it within and without with pitch."

December 7th. I paid off my caravan this morning. Not a single growl was heard from a man; they were like a flock of frightened sheep, lest I should tell the king of their conduct on the road. I gave to each the full amount agreed upon at Bihe; had they behaved better, they would have received something more. I had only to remember that they had robbed me of at least six weeks of my life, to prevent a fit of generosity seizing me.

To-day the king presented me with a fine fat ox. I had it slaughtered, and sent all but a few pounds of the meat to the sub-chiefs, as we cannot keep it longer than two days. When we have meat for dinner, it is meat alone, for there is not a solitary vegetable to be had except cereals. Yesterday we got a few sweet potatoes, but so small that we could not attempt to peel them; and even these are only to be had once a fortnight, as they are not grown in the valley, and have to be brought a distance of fifteen miles. I hope to get some meal to-morrow, when we shall have the substantial Scotch fare of "porridge and milk." We get abundance of the latter, as the king has had three cows set apart to be milked every day for our special use. Firewood for the "kitchen" is very scarce, every head-load being carried not less than fourteen miles; there is not a bush nearer.

December 9th. Three or four hours each day are spent with Lewanika, discussing every conceivable question relating to black people. He is much interested in Jamaica, and in all I have told him of that country. Nothing could exceed his kindness to us so far. I dined with him yesterday and to-day, in a very good attempt at English style, but for the slave waiters, who in bringing in or removing each dish did so crouching on their knees (no native is allowed to stand in Lewanika's presence), clapping their hands every time they were empty; and when the repast was finished the five slaves knelt in a row at the door and clapped again, thanking him for being pleased to eat the food they had served.

I told him to-day that I wished to visit Monsieur Coillard at his station, eighteen miles off, when he offered me the use of a horse, and men to carry my baggage.

I may mention here that the burden of the conversations I have had with Lewanika, and the reason for his having issued an interdict against white men coming into his country except at his discretion, is what he considers the bad treatment he has received at the hands of the British South African Company. For some years past Lewanika has been writing and sending messages to the English government, asking to be included under "British protectorate," as the chief of Khama and others farther south. To none of his requests did he receive an answer until last year (1890), when an agent of the company was sent up to interview him, and to negotiate for the monopoly of working the mineral resources of his country, giving him to understand that this meant being under "British protectorate," as he had so long desired, and securing his signature to the concession. The agent brought presents which Lewanika accepted, because he was told they were sent to him by the Queen of England. Whereupon, as he himself expresses it, to prove that he was glad that at last his wish was gratified in being under Her Majesty's protection, and that his heart was white toward her, he selected a pair of the finest tusks of ivory in his possession and handed them over to the representative of the company, as a return present to the *Queen.*

But he looked in vain for an acknowledgment from Her Majesty, until he began to suspect that all was not as he had understood it. This feeling was encouraged by traders and others coming to the country, who told him that the English government was in no way responsible for the actions of this company, and that he was not yet under "British protectorate." And his suspicions were confirmed when a book entitled "Zambesia" was published in the interests of the company (June, 1891), which contained the following statement (and was translated for him), page 435:

"Mr. Lochner and the king parted in the most amicable manner, his majesty returning the traveler's present by the gift of two fine tusks of ivory, each considerably over one hundred pounds in weight and over six feet long. These now ornament the board-room of the

British South African Company in their palatial office in St. Swithens' Lane."

Now Lewanika's rage was at white-heat, and he had no name for Englishmen but "thieves and robbers." Unhappily, Monsieur Coillard and his colleague Monsieur Jalla were seriously compromised in the matter, they having acted as interpreters for the agent, fondly hoping that they were doing a service to the king and country, but now judged by the king as abettors in the attempt to sell his country. The following letter, written by Monsieur Coillard to the secretary of the British South African Company, will better explain his unenviable position at that time, and the effects of which remain until now.

SEFULA, BAROTSE VALLEY, UPPER ZAMBESI,
June 5, 1891.

Dr. R. Harris,
   Secretary to the B. S. A. Co., Kimberly:

SIR: This mail will bring you a message from King Lewanika, and Mr. Middleton will remit to you from him through me the £200 paid to the king by Mr. Lochner "as the first annual payment of the Ware Concession."

You are aware that three years ago the king applied for the protectorate of the British government. He was assured of the friendliness of the government, of his request being seriously considered, and that the reply should be conveyed to him at once. That long-expected reply has never come.

Meantime, Mr. F. E. Lochner was last year sent to this country by the B. S. A. Company. That powerful company, with royal charter, introduced to us and recommended to us by persons on whose judgment I could rely, strongly recommended also to King Lewanika by the chief Khama, who escorted it by a special messenger, won at once our confidence. On the strength of the terms of the treaty that "any agreement with the company was to be considered in the light of a treaty or alliance made between the nation (the Barotse) and *the*

WILD BATOKA WARRIORS

Government of Her Britannic Majesty Queen Victoria," the envoy of the company overcame all difficulties, the concession was granted, and the treaty signed.

The Rev. Adolph Jalla and myself were fully satisfied that the transaction was on both parts made in perfect good faith; it is why we gave our support to it. I was anxious to see this unhappy country, a hot-bed of constant intrigues and revolutions, where is so little security for property or life, pass under the protection of a strong but wise and humane government; and in the firm conviction that this great end had been attained, King Lewanika's power strengthened, and the welfare of the people secure, I sincerely rejoiced in the signing of the treaty.

Since then, King Lewanika has not failed to take advice of other men—men who profess to know more of these matters than we do—and the transaction was represented in a very different light. We are accused of having been bribed by the company, of having sold the whole of the country, of having purposely withheld from the king the true nature and full import of the treaty, and, in complicity with the company's representative, of having willfully deceived the king and his people.

This the king, in spite of his personal regard for us, resents bitterly, and the words in which his message is framed give but a faint idea of the state of his mind. All these rumors have spread like fire, and have thrown the natives into the wildest state of excitement.

To this partly may be attributed the shameful treatment which one of the Primitive Methodist missionaries has lately suffered at the hands of the people, under the most trifling pretext.

Now, if the aim of the B. S. A. Company is what it is represented to the king, a mere gigantic mining and land-securing scheme, and if the British Protectorate has been used simply as a blind, I emphatically protest against it, and regret if I have unwittingly been a dupe and an accomplice in such transactions.

The fact that during all the time of his long-protracted sojourn in this country Mr. Lochner was my guest, and that of necessity I served as the only medium in all his intercourse with the king, has greatly compromised me in the eyes of the natives, and caused me to appear to them as being identified with the company. They, of course, give me credit for far more than my share in the business.

Matters having assumed a threatening aspect, and being, as far as our safety and our mission are concerned, in so grave a position, I must decline having in the future any more to do in these matters. Believe me, sir,

Yours truly,
Francis Coillard.

The company of course deny that *their agent treated with Lewanika under the guise of the Queen's representative;* but letters written by him at the French mission station to the king, inclosed in envelopes marked O. H. M. S. (On Her Majesty's Service), and from which we quote, place the matter beyond doubt.

"I am sending to you to ask whether it is possible for you to let me know approximately what date the meeting regarding the establishment of British protection, etc., may be held.

"When I started to come up here it was never thought that there would be any delay or difficulty about the protectorate, as you had written to the government about it, and the government and the company thought everything would be settled on my arrival here.

"Please also to remember always that I should never have come up here if you had not written to the English government for protection.

"If you and your counselors accept the protection of the Queen of England, etc., the company will send traders into your country who will deal fairly with you and your people, the same as is being done now at Khama's town."

Lewanika forwarded an emphatic protest to Her Majesty's Secretary of State in August, 1891, against the concession, and is now looking anxiously for a reply. My excuse for referring to this matter, apart from the personal entreaties of Lewanika himself during my stay at Lialui that I might give publicity to his grievances on returning to Europe, is the following letter, dispatched to me by special runners, overtaking us while on my journey down the Zambesi:

LIALUI, Jan. 16, 1892.

To Dr. Johnston:

King Lewanika hopes you will not forget him and his wishes, but trusts you will use all the complaints and all the desires he has expressed to you verbally to his advantage and that of his people and country. And further, the king commands and authorizes you hereby to make known and to publish all that he has made known to you himself; and further, to publish his determination, and that of his people, that no force must be used by any person or persons to enforce his submission to terms he abhors, and which he did not understand, and which he was led into through ignorance and deceit; and if any force (as is threatened illegally) is so used pending any answer he may receive direct from Her Majesty the Queen and her government, it will be resisted by force, as he will treat it purely as robbery, and the consequences will be upon such attacking forces.

And the king wishes it to be clearly understood that he truly did not know that it was a company to work all the resources of his country; but, on the contrary, he was repeatedly told that it was an embassy from the Queen Victoria of England. But in this they deceived him, and when they asked where were the boundaries of his rule, he did not know it was to mean the country in which they were to have the sole rights of working, but they told him it was to define the extent of his country to be under the protection of the Queen. But as to rights to work resources as written, it was not so; he never gave away the rights to work solely the resources of his country, and in proof of this, all who know his feelings on the subject and are at all acquainted with the king know well that his chief ambition is to be instructed in all such practical knowledge so that he can work the resources of his country by himself and his people; and he intends to do so, as he will not recognize any bond obtained from him by ignorance and deceit. Moreover, he gave his word on the matter, simply as he gave it to Harry Ware, i.e., to seek gold, and, on finding it, to acquaint the king with the fact, when areas of land would be defined where they could work solely; and when he and his people had learned the methods employed, he with his people would work for themselves outside of those areas that had been allotted to the company. He never intended, he did not consent, and he will not consent, to part with the resources of his country. Englishmen he likes, and his political preferences are all in favor of England; but the using of their Queen's name to hide their evil designs he cannot understand. If the Queen really wished his land, his rights, and resources, would she not send direct? A treaty of friendship with the Queen direct does not surely mean that he is to be weakened at all; and if all these industrial rights of his are parted with forever, then what inducement remains to induce them to learn anything of industrial arts? The king says he feels sure that if all these things can be known in England as the words of the king himself, then the English Queen and her people will not permit such deceit, mean advantage of ignorance, to be done in their name and with their approval.

The king says deceit like this is robbery, not friendship, and it must be treated as robbery, and so has fully determined, and his people support him in this. Moreover, those who wish to come to his country must come with sincere feelings toward him and his people, and of supporting the king in maintaining his rights to the resources of his land. He wishes them to come, but on terms of submission to his law, and of agreement to do nothing disadvantageous to him, his people, or his land, or the rights appertaining thereto, either by word or letter, or by deed—such bond or agreement to be in writing, any refusal to be taken as opposing the interests of the king. Apart from this, King Lewanika does not wish it to be understood or thought that by this he closes his land against white people; by no means; but this insures and secures to him people who will help him and teach him, rather than those who only seek to deceive him and try to despoil him of all he possesses of value. The king wishes to cordially welcome all who come willing to teach and to help him and his people to know and understand the works and industries and the knowledge of civilization; he wants secular as well as religious instruction,

MA-WA, QUEEN OF BAROTSE AND SLAVE GIRLS.

i.e., works, trade, religion, and education; and if they are not disinterested teachers, but wish also to benefit themselves whilst benefiting others, the king says it is well, as might be agreed upon; but they must submit to the king, his authority, his rights, and his powers: this is the one bond he will demand of them.

Further, the king says it may be said, on behalf of the company, that he proved his full consent to them about the concession, by giving them two of the finest tusks of ivory seen here for a long time, each weighing one hundred and five pounds. Now he wishes it to be thoroughly understood, and to be published as his own statement, that these tusks were not given with any intention or knowledge of clinching an agreement of which he knew nothing about; but, as they insisted that they were an embassy sent by the Queen, and that the presents they brought him were also sent by the Queen, so he accepted their presents and gave them the two aforesaid tusks as a present to the Queen, as a proof of his friendly feeling toward Her Majesty, and the Queen was to accept his exchange product as proof thereof. Now, these tusks, because of their extraordinary size and beauty, were worth the exceptional price of one pound sterling per pound weight, therefore value £210, or more than the value of the presents they brought to him. All this he wishes to be well known.

Now, in conclusion, the king says he trusts you implicitly; he sees your heart is well toward him, even though you did not care to say much here; the king says a man's heart always speaks true, and you have always shown great sympathy toward him and his affairs. And he says that if he really receives any practical help from you on these matters, you will receive from him and his nation their eternal thanks and gratitude. And the king further says that if God should call him away, nevertheless his son and others may remain and remember all they shall owe to you. He prays you a safe journey and safe and joyful return to your family.

Written at the dictation and by command of

THE KING LEWANIKA.

To Dr. J. Johnston.

CHAPTER VIII.

LIFE IN THE BAROTSE VALLEY.

The heroic Frenchman.—A model mission station.—Blighted plans.—A touching story.—Thrilling tales.—Truth first.—Missionary tidings.—Koreans.—Amazing statements.—Futile hopes.—Primitive Methodist party.—Home committees.—Virtually a prisoner.—Marotsi handicrafts.—In the lekhothla.—"A sound of revelry by night."—A perpetual vapor-bath.—A bloodthirsty queen.—Display of fireworks.—New Year's Day.—First native wedding on the Zambesi.—Amused skepticism.—Ladies take a back seat.—Magic-lantern exhibition.—Silence reigns.—The Mashukulumbwe.—Taking their measure.

DECEMBER 10th. Mounted on a fine black horse and escorted by a guide, also riding, I set out for Sefula. The path lay southward across the plain. We passed numerous marshes swarming with flocks of wild geese and ducks, at times so near that we could have knocked them over with a stone; but here stones are as rare as the "roc-egg." In two hours and a half we reached the mission station. It may be imagined with what delight I grasped the hand of the noble and heroic Frenchman of whom I had heard so much. The warm greeting was mutual. I was introduced to Miss Kiener, a Swiss lady teacher, also to Mr. Waddell, the Scotch carpenter. The station is situated on a beautiful plateau at the extreme end of the low range of hills running along the east side of the great valley. It might well lay claim to the title of a model mission station, it is so fully equipped with every appliance for instructing the natives, not only in divine things, but also how to improve their social condition. So far, however, these privileges have been but poorly appreciated, as the people know it would be little short of a crime to attempt any improvement in their dwellings.

The station contains a fine saw-mill with six span of oxen for the motor power, brick-making machines, smithy with patent forge, miner's workshop, fitted with every tool the mechanic requires, from a brad-awl to a turning-lathe—every building on the station, including the trim little church, displaying skilled workmanship. I was grieved to find Monsieur Coillard in a very low state of health and depressed in spirits. More than ordinary trials and sorrows have fallen to the lot of this faithful servant of God, not only in the dark outlook of the mission's future and the difficulties that beset the cause, dearer than life to him, but in the sore bereavement he sustained, but a few weeks ago, in the death of Madame Coillard, the devoted companion and helpmeet of his thirty years' labors in Africa.

On Sunday I spoke through Monsieur Coillard to a good congregation of the rawest-looking lot of natives I have ever met inside a place of worship. It was no easy matter to speak to such people, for, with the exception of the boys employed or at school on the station, but few, if any, have as yet (after years of unremitting toil) manifested even interest in, far less ability to grasp, the most elementary truths of the gospel. They listen quietly and respectfully, but there it seems to end.

Monsieur Coillard, in describing the present condition of the work, says: "It is now seven years since our expedition crossed the Zambesi and the mission was started —a long time in one's short life; and yet we are still passing through that arduous and uninteresting period of breaking the fallow ground and sowing the seed. We anxiously watch for the appearance of the little cloud and the showers of blessings which it shall bring. Sometimes a little mist in the atmosphere has filled our hearts with hope; then the mist vanished away, and the sun shone in a brazen sky, fiercer and more scorching than ever. 'He that observeth the wind shall not sow, and he that regardeth the clouds shall not reap!' We remembered it. The Lord has given us grace to toil on, plow and sow, and expect against all appearances. We know that the seed is not lost. Silently, secretly, under the clods it germinates, and the first shower shall adorn with verdure our parched ground. The time shall come; therefore we faint not.

"These last three years have been to us more by far than all our missionary life years of toil, trials, and suffering. The social and political state of the country has been greatly disturbed by internal causes, and the advent of the British South Africa Company. Sickness and death have thinned our ranks as quickly as we had the joy of receiving helpers from Europe, at great expense, and we have seen our brightest hopes and our dearest plans blighted and dashed to the ground."

Such is the aspect of the most faithful mission work in *reality*. Of *romance* we have already had far too much from visionaries, who deem it essential to write such accounts for the purpose of keeping up the interest, particularly if they are not guaranteed support, but have to depend upon casual voluntary contributions. In a published letter of one who was stranded in Barotse a few years ago, but ultimately got out to the West Coast by attaching himself to the caravan of a Portuguese trader, we read:

"At one place, among the Bakuti, it was remarkable how the people seemed to open their ears and hearts and gave their time. I spent ten days among them. The first five I went among the villages, having large meetings, at which I told them of Jesus and His love. As I could speak a dialect which many of them understood, I could explain myself quite freely to them. They became very much interested in what they heard me say, and they said among themselves, 'We are only tiring the white man out by coming day after day to our villages; we will go to him.' So, for the last five days, we had all-day meetings—a most extraordinary time, I might say, for Africa. They kept up the discussions among themselves, and before I left at least two of the men stood up in the midst of their tribe, and declared for Jesus before all their friends, in their own simple language. They acknowledged that the things we said to them were true, and they renounced their superstitions and fetich worship. Since then I have heard that they are still longing for a return visit from me, or that some other white teacher should go to their country."

A very touching story, if it were true! But every laborer of experience will bear me out when I state that there is not an authenticated instance on record of a savage genuinely turning to God or renouncing "their superstitions and fetich worship" until he has been many months, and too often years, under instruction. Many earnest men who have toiled long in breaking up the fallow ground have been called away from the sphere of their labor without being permitted to see even the blade, far less the ear, that foretells a probable harvest; and satisfied not to reason why, but to obey.

The mischief created by such communications as the one quoted above is incalculable, giving a totally false conception of the nature of the work, and filling the minds of enthusiastic missionary volunteers with the idea that the Central Africa natives "are ready and waiting to receive the gospel." The actual facts being the very antipodes of such statements, the effect is often to drive the most sanguine to the opposite extreme. Nor are the writers of such articles alone to blame; constant demands are made upon them by their home committees and supporters to provide something specially thrilling for their "quarterly" or "annual" meeting. But as the routine of a well-established mission station seldom furnishes material for "thrilling" tales, some must be made to order. Nor is this merchandise in such missionary reports likely to cease while the feeling exists that was expressed by a wealthy Christian philanthropist, whose name is often to the front with large donations, and who spoke not only for himself, but as representing the monied subscribers to missions, when he said to a friend of mine, "I give only to success." The following extract is from *The Truth*, edited by Dr. James Brooks, of St. Louis, Missouri, bearing upon this subject, though referring to another field:

"It is never pleasant to write of those who have gone to the heathen with the gospel, unless they can be men-

MAKOTSE PASTIMES

tioned in terms of affectionate commendation. But there is danger that the church at home may be misled by false reports of marvelous success; and even if the facts are discouraging, it must not be forgotten that the truth is expedient. It is so delightful to believe that all the missionaries are thoroughly loyal to the Word of God, and wholly devoted to the work of saving the lost, and that pagans and Mohammedans are standing with outstretched hands, eager to receive our Lord Jesus Christ the moment He is presented to them; but such, it is sad enough to say, is not the case. . . . Now comes a letter from Mr. M. C. Fenwick, missionary in Wonsau, Korea, with a request that public use shall be made of it to undeceive Christians in America. He also sends a copy of *The Chinese Recorder and Missionary Journal*, published in Shanghai, and edited by Rev. L. N. Wheeler, D.D. It contains a communication from Mr. Fenwick in reply to the following statement that went the rounds of the religious press in this country: 'Korea presents a striking illustration of the irresistible advance of the kingdom of Christ. One of the most remarkable works of grace known in modern missions is that among the Koreans. Without having heard or seen a missionary, thousands of people have heard of Christ and turned to the service of God. These converts are the fruit of the circulation of copies of the New Testament by the Rev. John Ross, late missionary of the Presbyterian Church of Scotland in Manchuria.'

"Of this marvelous story Mr. Fenwick says: 'It is a grave doubt in the minds of a majority of Protestant missionaries in Korea whether there are fifty Koreans in the whole country who have been "born again." Some are persuaded that there are not even a dozen. Concerning the New Testament that is said to be the translation of the Rev. John Ross, but which is really the production of Koreans, under the direction of a Mr. McIntyre and Mr. Ross, no Korean has yet been found who has any conception of its meaning. There are many words in this production foreign to the Korean languages, and that which is Korean is by no means a translation of the Word of God—not even in the "concept." Some thought perhaps it might be used on the border between China and Korea, but it has been accorded a fair trial there, and failed to find a man who could understand its funny sounds.'

"In the letter just received he more completely exposes the deception too often practiced on the Church in so-called Christian lands, perhaps in the exercise of the Jesuitical principle that the end justifies the means.

"The missionary literature of the day, taken as a whole, is the most deceptive writing I see. . . . A case in point: A missionary in Korea, representing a small committee in ―――― composed of business men united to send the gospel to Korea, made his annual report, truthfully setting forth the actual state of affairs on the field as he found them. The report was promptly rejected, and one of striking cases of interest, conversions, etc., demanded. He complied with the request under protest, but the report was declared to be the proper thing, and given a wide circulation.

"Two years ago a man named ―――― [perhaps it is well to omit the name] returned from this field to America, and has since been spreading his exaggerated stories throughout the churches in the United States. . . . Let me give you an account of his converting work in a village where I afterward lived for six months, as given me by one whom he baptized on the occasion now mentioned. A native who received mission money was directed by Mr. —— to get together at least forty or fifty, and he would be along at such a time. Rather perplexed at the number demanded, the native set to work to gather his friends, but could muster only nine.

"The missionary arrived, and after exhorting at considerable length, asked the natives to remove their hats. 'What for?' said one. 'Oh, never mind,' coaxingly pleaded the native friend; 'take off your hats;' and with the politeness so characteristic of the Easterner, they removed their hats, and then the Rev. Mr. ——, D.D., administered baptism to these nine men, none of whom, with the possible exception of one, he had ever seen.

"The letter contains statements equally amazing and humiliating, but enough has been said to put Christians on their guard against believing *everything* that comes to them from the foreign field. No doubt this habit of story-telling arises from the error, held by nearly all, that it is the mission of the Church to convert the world. Hence it seems to be necessary, in order to arouse and sustain enthusiasm and to procure funds, to tell big tales of wholesale conversions and to represent the heathen as eager to accept the gospel. But 'no lie is of the truth' (1 John ii. 21), and no lie is harmless. It is sure to inflict its own penalty in due time; and the Church cannot continue to act under the delusion that its business is to convert the world, without experiencing some day a dreadful reaction from its futile hopes."

We claim for the lonely and sorely tried workers in the Matebele country, for Monsieur Coillard and his co-workers in the Barotse Valley, and for others we could mention, that, while they have no visible successes to report, but, on the contrary, mourn over the years as they roll by without realizing their desire among the heathen, they are foundation workers, toiling deep down in superstition and gross darkness, and spending their lives almost unknown, amid dangers and discouragement, without a soul to cheer by responding to the message they bring, receiving no sympathy from their surroundings, and hundreds of miles, perhaps, from the nearest fellow-laborer.

There were many weary months of jeopardy and labor to the divers as they toiled fathoms deep beneath the Forth, blasting rocks and building the massive masonry that was to be the foundation of one of the greatest engineering achievements of the age—the Forth Bridge. Had these toilers in mud and stone and flood, whose uninteresting and, to the upper world, invisible work, which was accomplished slowly but surely —in many instances at the sacrifice, and in every case at the peril, of their lives—no honor or recognition on the day when the structure was completed?

It is in such circumstances that these servants of God grapple with untold obstacles, determined that, as far as it is in their power, the groundwork of the future building, which they may not see, shall be well and truly laid. But such are not the men whose services receive full recognition at the hands of their fellows; these workers are often followed by mere surface men, who by their reports elicit the practical sympathy of those who "give only to success."

What we contend for is that the truest and most genuine missions of the present day are those which must be sought out, for rarely are their claims published to the world, except among the few; while, on the other hand, many a man whose mission is superficial resorts to sensational and questionable advertisements of his work.

Let the truth be told, however unpalatable, for no real advantage is gained, in the long run, by false reports, and societies and friends who sustain these missionaries are placed in a wrong position, leading eventually to great disappointment.

Let the truth be told, also, for the sake of those who offer themselves for mission work, that there may be a wholesome sifting of the numerous bands of young men on both sides of the Atlantic who are eager to give up business, etc., to go to the "regions beyond" and preach the gospel; while the solid men would only be strengthened in their purpose to devote their lives to a cause worthy of their best talents and highest attainments.

Camped near Sefula is Mr. B——, representing the English Primitive Methodists, with Mrs. B—— and child, having just arrived here for the second time, expecting to get permission from Lewanika to settle in some part of his country, or be allowed to go through to the Mashukulumbwe for the purpose of organizing a mission center for his society. The king is anything but favorable to the proposition, and far from friendly toward the party; nor is he likely to grant the request; on the contrary, he emphatically declared only to-day that "they had better go back, for they are not wanted." Poor B——! I am sorry for him, but still more so for his wife and delicate little girl, whom he takes about with him in the wagon, trekking these many months exposed to all the privations incidental to such a life in such a country—a most injudicious proceeding, surely, judging from a human standpoint. Are committees at home not aware of the hazard and positive cruelty of committing a whole family to pioneer work where sturdy single men have all they can do to hold their own against the hardships presenting themselves on every hand? While for all this—some three years of suffering and at the expense of thousands of pounds, not to speak of the shattered health of mother and child—simply nothing has been accomplished so far, and even less prospect of doing anything than when they first set out. One cannot but admire their heroism and self-sacrifice; and as they are determined to wait at all costs rather than face the criticisms of the society at home with a report of failure, let us hope the king may yet relent and give them the road. I have urged Mr. B—— in the meantime to send home his sick wife and child.

The saddest feature of the whole is the fact that while Mr. B—— is waiting at Sefula without even a hope of going farther, a map is published in England entitled "Map of Africa Showing all the Protestant Missions Working in the 'Dark Continent.' Prepared from a list of African Missions in 'Africa Rediviva.'" The localities of stations are indicated by white figures on

NATIVE WEDDING, SEFULA

a black ground, and north of the Zambesi, in the center of the Mashukulumbwe country, we find "23." On reference to the list of societies we find this to be the number representing the Primitive Methodist mission. But there is not, and never has been, a mission of any kind in that country; the "23" in this instance only points to where the party referred to above *want* to go.

December 21st. We returned to Lialui on the 14th, and I have been busy every day visiting and prescribing for the sick of the village, including nine of the king's wives. There is a drawback to this doctoring of his people, wishing, as I do, to get away and proceed on my journey; he may detain me longer than is agreeable. However kindly the white traveler may be received and treated by a powerful heathen potentate like Lewanika, he is soon made to realize that his position as a guest is virtually that of a prisoner, for he cannot leave the country, nor dare a porter lift one of his loads, except by the king's permission.

The romance of life among the Marotsi, or any other savage tribe, is of short duration to the European, passing off after the first few days. He is interested in observing their manners and customs—the native smithy, for instance, where during the early hours of the morning blacksmiths are at work smelting iron from the crude ore by means of charcoal and clay crucibles; forging spears, arrow-heads, battle-axes, knives, and snuff-spoons, with the most original and rude appliances, the anvil being a flat stone and the hammer a conical block of iron without a handle. Under a shed is a group of men busy making "karosses" (blankets), by sewing together, with threads prepared from the sinews of antelopes, skins of leopards, jackals, tiger-cats, and other wild animals. I may add that the sewing is not done with an ordinary needle, but by means of a plain spike of iron brought to a fine point at one end by rubbing on a stone, and using it as a shoemaker does his awl, piercing the holes through which the thread is passed, each stitch being made fast by a turn in the loop, as in working a buttonhole. The kaross-maker carries his needle in a wooden sheath, highly ornamented with carving and plaited brass wire, and suspended from his neck. As some karosses have over a hundred yards of seams, containing twelve to fifteen stitches to the inch, the length of time required to complete a blanket may be imagined.

In another corner wood-carvers are hewing, from blocks of wood, bowls, milk-jugs, mush dishes, etc., with various-sized native hatchets, a bent knife-blade serving as a scoop, chipping away morning after morning, for weeks and months, before a single household utensil is completed; but had these vessels been turned in a lathe, the symmetry could scarcely be more perfect.

Here also the basket-maker's art may be seen in perfection, and excelling anything produced by basket-factories of civilized countries, for scarcely would our workers in basketry undertake to weave an impervious vessel from reedy grass, to carry five or six gallons of water.

In the evening, with much pomp and ceremony, preceded by his band of drums and marimbas, his majesty comes out to the lekhothla, where hundreds and sometimes thousands of his subjects are gathered, and kneeling in their usual semicircles round the spot where the

royal mat is spread. A second chair is placed by that
of the king's, and the white guest is invited to sit with
him while court is being held. The business on hand
is perhaps a case of witchcraft, poisoning, or cattle-steal-
ing; or it may be to receive some of the many bands
of natives belonging to distant tribes as far north as
Bangweola and south to Lake Ngami, but who occupy
land supposed to be within Lewanika's dominions, and
by these delegates send the annual tribute he claims.
In this way the opportunity was afforded me of seeing
representatives of several tribes that are but little known
to the civilized world. This over, the king returns to
his wattle-and-daub palace in state, and I to my hut.
Would that it were to spend a quiet night! But not
while ancestral worship is the religion, if religion it may
be called, of the Marotsi nation, can be expected other
than "a sound of revelry by night," their theory being
that, although their ancestors have departed this life,
their spirits still haunt the scenes of their earthly career,
potent to wreak vengeance on those who may have incurred their displeasure. Although Lewanika regularly
visits the tombs of his predecessors to pray to them,
and is liberal in his gifts of oxen as peace-offerings, his
conscience reminds him that some of them did not, to
say the least, receive fair play at his hands on the occasion of their exit from the body, and he dreads their
nocturnal visits; hence the necessity for the drums and
noise to keep them at bay.

For several days a party of Mambundas—a hill tribe
and the recognized sorcerers of the valley—have been
busy tinkling their bells, rattling their gourds, throwing
down the divining-tables, and shaking the witch-baskets

(which contain a collection of trifles such as birds' claws and beaks, splinters of human bones, leopards' claws, bits of iron and strange shells, and from the position of which they pretend to read the will of the gods), in order to discover whether or no the Marotsi are to go to war against the Matebele. In this case it was divined that the gods were sulky, angry with the tribe, and refused to answer. This was a convenient decision, as they were well aware that the Marotsi soldiers were too weak to take the field against the armies of Lobengula, king of the Matebele; and in the event of defeat in battle authorized by the witch-doctors, the latter, of course, would have to bear the brunt.

But their conclusions are rarely so indefinite; generally some poor wretch has to be sacrificed to their whims and conjectures. Nor do they always spare the headmen in giving judgment; even the king is occasionally indicted. An instance of this has in fact taken place since my visit to the Barotse, when Lewanika, after a great astrological inquiry, was pronounced guilty of having been the cause of a violent outbreak of smallpox at the close of last year. Monsieur Coillard relates the circumstance in a letter received recently, as follows:

"'Do you know,' said he (Lewanika), 'that for three days the Mambundas, masters of the black art, have consulted the knuckle-bones. This morning the first chiefs, Gambella at the head, have come to communicate the oracle to me. Ah well! it is I myself that the bones have seized on and pointed out. They accuse me of having brought on the nation the plague of smallpox, and of stopping the rain from falling. If I am cruel, be not astonished.' . . .

BASHUKULOMBWE NATIVES

"Accompanied by Paulus and Jacob, I returned next day to the king, and found him in the lekhothla, and sat down near him. He named new chiefs in place of those the small-pox had mown down—and they are many! On ordinary occasions the ceremony does not lack interest, but Lewanika is anxious and worried. He is absent-minded and throws furtive side-glances. As soon as he was able, he got up and asked me to follow him. But in the great square shed of the lekhothla there was an unaccustomed hubbub. 'They are still here!' the king said to me in parting. I wished to see what went on there, so I made a way in the dense crowd which surrounded the hut. Inside, six or seven old Mambundas squatting on mats were shaking convulsively baskets filled with all kinds of imaginable things. These sages were absorbed in the profound study of each combination, and muttered cabalistic formulæ, while all around them, ranged in a circle, their confrères made a fearful cacophany with rattles made of gourds and baobab fruits, wooden harmonicas, their little bells and tom-toms. The public, packed like sardines, stand with stretched necks, wide-open mouths, and fixed eyes. And all this by the orders of the head chiefs in a full lekhothla, under the very eyes of the king, whom they have charged thus publicly with the misfortunes of the nation! I was looking on this scene and absorbed in dark reflections, when a new message came to call me.

"Lewanika, a prey to great agitation, gave some orders to one of his confidants. Soon after, a loud tumult of voices arose in that public place. The king's man had gathered the crowd, given the message, and wound up by crying, 'Seize them!' Hundreds of voices responded, each one stronger than the other, shouting, 'Seize them! seize them!' They all rushed on the unfortunate Mambundas and fought for the pleasure of strangling them, some pulling their arms, others dragging them by the legs, while still others held on to their necks. It was a frightful confusion, when a second order came commanding the liberation of the culprits, and the king, holding up his hand, said, 'It is enough, they shall be pardoned; but let them know not to take such liberties with royalty again!' The effervescence of the spirits calmed down, and the Mambundas, profiting by a moment of confusion, had already taken advantage of the opportunity to steal away. At another time they would have been unmercifully put to death. Lewanika has used his authority —it is good; but I ask myself, with disquietude, if he has truly realized the peril that menaced him, and if he has not made a mistake over it."

The Barotse Valley is not likely ever to be a place where white men can live. It is a vast expanse of decaying vegetation reeking with malaria; nor could it be otherwise, stagnant water being on every side, to drink of which would be certain fever. The whole valley is annually covered with water to the depth of five to eight feet by the rise of the Zambesi, in the same way as Lower Egypt is flooded by the Nile; when only the villages can be seen, built on mounds (the work of a former chief, Santuru), the only means of transit for several months of the year being canoes. The grass rots when under water, and when the floods cease new grass springs up everywhere immediately, preventing the rotting vegetable matter from drying—resulting in the most offensive exhalations during the wet season, the heat and moisture keeping one in a perpetual vapor-bath. To-day my hands and arms are puckered from perspiration, as if I had spent hours at the wash-tub.

Yesterday Monsieur Coillard came over to conduct service in the lekhothla. About three hundred men were present; women do not attend. He kindly presses me to return to Sefula with him to-day, and I gladly accept his invitation, for I am scarcely a day free from fever here, and begin to feel very much broken down.

Sefula, December 30th. Lewanika arrived here to-day with a great retinue of people, who are building a camp near by, to make preparations for the marriage of his eldest son, which is to take place on New Year's Day. The queen has also arrived, attended by about one hundred and fifty women, with a similar flourish of trumpets. She is the sister of Lewanika, and with him rules the kingdom, having her headquarters at Nalolo, about a day's journey down the river; but she is a much more determined character than her vacillating and pusillanimous brother. Her reign is stained with many a cruel act of murder and bloodshed, avenging herself particularly on those who are in any way the objects of her jealousy. But a short time ago, an aged headman in her village had won for himself, by his kindness and gentle demeanor, far more of the respect and esteem of the people than was agreeable to his sovereign, whose great ambition is that none receive honor but herself. Some one had spoken in her presence of the old man in terms of praise, and forthwith her heart was filled with hate toward him. He was doomed! Next morning she invited him to come to her hut to drink beer, at the same time appointing two young men, armed with spears, to be ready at her signal to kill him. The sign was given, but the venerable face and gray hair so touched even their hearts that they hesitated, when she, uttering a curse on their cowardice, seized a rusty Portuguese saber and thrust him through. Summoning her crier, she ordered him to announce to the town that "the queen had a thorn removed from her foot this morning."

On New Year's Eve the immense crowd of people was treated by Monsieur Coillard to an exhibition of fireworks, which seemed to amaze them greatly. Monsieur Coillard puts himself to no end of trouble to create an interest in the station and draw the people together. To a magic-lantern exhibition or such-like they will come in flocks; but let the church-bell ring and expect to see the same anxiety to fill the building? Alas, no! After waiting until long after the appointed hour for service, we enter, to find but a very, very few, except when there is some other attraction than preaching.

January 1, 1892. Yes, another year is gone, and one that to me has been fraught with the strangest and most varied experiences that have fallen to my lot during my somewhat checkered life. This time last year I was surrounded by all that makes life sweet, in a land where there is light, joy, peace, and love; here, darkness, wretchedness, strife, and hate abound. While writing, I hear the ghoulish yells and wild revel of the natives as they celebrate the opening year. Knowing no joy but in that which panders to their basest passions, love is to them a myth, and peace they have never known, for war and bloodshed is their special delight.

With all my heart I thank God for His mercies to me during the year that is gone, and for His preserving care both by sea and land; and did I know that my loved ones—wife and children—were at this moment well and happy, I could even now be hopeful and joyful; but this is hidden from me, and I fear will be for many months yet to come.

This has been a great day in the Barotse Valley, inasmuch as at Sefula the first marriage, Christian or heathen, has been performed by Monsieur Coillard, in the union of Letia, son of Lewanika, and Makabi, daughter of Katusi, a minor chief. The girl has been for some time in the school at Sefula, and much care has been bestowed and many months spent in the endeavor to wean her from her heathenism; but without success. Still, Letia has made a profession of Christianity, and wished to be married by the missionary. The bridegroom and groomsmen were neatly dressed in suits of tweed; the bride decked out in a dress of yellow luster trimmed with furniture chintz, the material having been brought from Mangwato by Letia and made up with his own hands, Miss Keiner cutting it out and adding the finishing touches.

By 11 A.M. thousands had assembled at the little church, which was tastefully decorated for the occasion with fronds of the fan palm and leaves of the wild plantain. Flowers are scarce in these parts. The most important among the people obtained admission until the building was crammed, while the mass had to be contented with standing room at a distance, or

a peep in at the windows. The ceremony proceeded
without an interruption until the bridegroom promised
to cleave unto this wife only so long as they "both
should live," when an audible titter of amused skepticism passed round among the chiefs, beginning with
his father, who rejoices in the possession of over a
score. And he would be a small chief indeed who
could not boast of at least half a dozen women in his
harem. (Sad to say, the sequel has proven that their
unbelief in Letia's vows had more foundation than our
hopes for his steadfastness, for within a few months he
took to himself a second wife, and has openly returned
to the paganism of his tribe.)

Monsieur Coillard proposed to have a lunch in the
open air for the young people, in European fashion,
as a sort of object-lesson; but it ended in signal failure. First, it was difficult to induce the bride to sit
on a chair, she never having sat at a table in her life,
fas less eaten with the civilized aid of a knife and fork.
Then the queen and the chief wife of the king were
appointed places opposite to him; to this Lewanika
took the strongest and most emphatic objection, declaring that he had never eaten with women, and he
never would. The matter, however, was compromised,
after a great deal of coaxing, by placing his majesty's
chair back from the table a little, making it appear as
if he were not of their party. Then his sister's husband
and his own secretary were invited to chairs; but here
again the great man's dignity was dangerously wounded.
He vowed that no Marotsi should ever *sit* in his presence except on the bare ground, so there was no alternative but to ask them to retire from the festive board

and make themselves comfortable on the sand. Much more of a like nature took place, grieving the missionary to his very soul, and causing him to regret having shown them this kindness; but it proved to me how totally impossible it must ever be to influence for good, civilize, or elevate a people who are tyrannized over by such an arrogant, ignorant autocrat as Lewanika. In the afternoon the natives were treated to a liberal feast, consisting of four fat oxen, mealies, and manioc, at Monsieur Coillard's expense. They formed a procession previous to the feast, bearing the cooked food in baskets, bowls, and gourds; placing all in rows before the king, saluting him in the usual way, clapping their hands, getting down and touching the ground with their foreheads, taking up handfuls of sand and rubbing it on their chests and arms in self-abasement, then uniting in the cry of "Yo sho! Tau Tuna!" ("great lion").

In the evening a magic-lantern exhibition was given in front of the mission house. The audience did not seem to understand photographs of scenery or buildings, however beautiful; but when the picture of a zebra, lion, elephant, or buffalo was thrown upon the screen, they screamed with delight, imitating the cries of the animals represented. At a late hour they dispersed, evidently greatly pleased.

On Saturday measles broke out in the king's camp. I was most of the day walking around with him attending to his favorites. Great crowds gathered for the Sunday services, both morning and evening, because the king and queen were there. A lot of Lewanika's wives marched in and took their places—on the opposite side of the building from him, of course—draped in a profusion of gay-colored cloth, toga fashion, with from six to twelve large ivory rings on each arm, and the indispensable snuff-box hanging by their sides, with which they amused themselves during the service.

January 4th. A blissful stillness pervades the district to-day. Royalty has taken its departure—the queen and her suite to Nalolo in canoes, the king on horseback to Lialui, followed by his satellites, in each case preceded by their respective bands of music (save the mark!). I am not very sorry to see the last of them, for now we shall get a little quiet rest at night. If the "uneasy head that wears a crown" in Africa, purchased as it is in almost every case by deeds of violence and bloodshed, requires this perpetual tum-tumming from dusk to dawn, with impromptu appeals to his good genius that he may sleep, it is at the sacrifice of rest to every civilized being within a mile; for a din more hideous can scarcely be conceived. But such is savage life in the far interior, even among kings.

A band of Mashukulumbwes arrived at Sefula this morning *en route* homeward. They have been on an embassy to the court of Lewanika, carrying tribute, and declaring their desire to live at peace with him, having lost heavily by a raiding party of Marotsi who entered their country last year and captured a great number of slaves and cattle. These are representatives of a wild but little-known tribe—little known beyond the fact that every expedition led by whites who have attempted to visit them came to grief, including Dr. Holub and Mr. Selous, who in each case were obliged to flee for their lives, helpless to resist the midnight attack of hundreds of naked demons in human form, hurling their spears through the tents and huts of the unsuspecting travelers.

I gave each of these interesting embassadors a yard of bright-colored cloth—the first certainly they ever owned, each hanging it from his belt behind like a tail, prancing about and looking over his shoulders to see it fluttering in the wind. Then they all joined in a war-dance. Stopping every now and again and crouching together on the ground, one of their number, creeping stealthily forward, spear in hand, for a short distance, would then make a rush, at a great speed, for fifty yards, rapidly thrusting with his weapon, fencing and fending himself as he retires from the imaginary enemy. We got them calmed down a bit with some food, and grouped them for a photograph, in which it is noticeable that the character of the features is entirely distinct from the usual type of negro. The dressing of the hair, too, is remarkable, particularly in the case of the two chiefs in charge, who have it worked up to a point about four feet long. It is necessary to exercise much patience and tact while endeavoring to get photographs of natives. They are so suspicious, it is hard to persuade them that posing in front of the machine will not in some way bewitch them. But I found the most successful argument was to politely request permission to "take their measure."

One European, who has traveled extensively in Africa, writes: "Photography . . . presents in itself almost insuperable difficulties. In the first place, it is no easy matter to employ photography on a journey of exploration. Fancy, for instance, the conveyance of an apparatus with its appliances in glass bottles, upon the head of a carrier who stumbles and falls at least a dozen times a day! . . . And, even supposing that that difficulty were got over, and that photography could be effectively employed, where is the native of the interior who would allow an apparatus to be set up and stand before it as a subject for the camera?" So far, my experience in this direction proves that in transporting a photographic outfit there is no difficulty whatever, and far less risk of breakages than if traveling in Europe, for damage from rough treatment is the last thing that happens to a load in the hands of an African carrier; they are not "baggage-smashers."

The following instance of their carefulness came under my own notice. A box of window glass, containing a hundred sheets, was intrusted to a native to be carried from Benguela to Cisamba, a distance of about three hundred and thirty miles. While in store at the coast, white ants had got at the straw in which the glass was packed, making a clean sweep of it, and leaving the fragile contents unprotected; but although the journey is one of some twenty-two days, incurring the lifting and laying down of this load perhaps a hundred times, it arrived at its destination without injury to a single pane.

As to the other statement in the extract, my success in photographing this wild tribe, as well as the Ganguellians, Matokas, and others, proves that it is within the bounds of possibility to procure a photograph of even the wildest of Central Africa's natives.

FALLS OF GONYA

CHAPTER IX.

FROM SEFULA TO SESHEKE.

The Sefula Canal.—Haste peculiar to white men.—To be thrown to the crocodiles.—Preparing for the river journey.—Parting injunctions.—A cloud of voracious mosquitoes.—Waist-deep in the swamp.—Afloat on the Zambesi.—Ancestral worship.—An interview with Makwai.—The omande shell.—The great fish-eagle.—Camped at Senanga.—More portentous game.—Memories of the Georgian Bay.—Charming surroundings.—A pleasure trip.—In danger of an upset.—Dragging canoes overland.—Lion stories.—The Falls of Gonyn.—Beautiful cascades.—Veldt schoons.—In the rapids.—The aromatic mopani.—A fruitless chase.—A gorgeous sunset.—The graceful zebra.

MY most pleasant sojourn at Sefula comes to a close. It has been a delightful rest, and I would gladly prolong it were I not still far from my destination, and must now see to getting boatmen for the river journey. The king having sent a canoe for me, I started early in the morning for Lialui. Instead of having to walk some ten miles to the river, as was necessary a short time ago, it is now but a step to the canal, some six miles in length, and connecting a series of small lakes, thus opening a good water-way to the Zambesi. It was cut at the expense of a friend in Scotland, and is a great boon to the mission—a saving of trouble and time that all who visit Sefula cannot fail to appreciate. This route is a long day's journey, owing to the strong current which the paddlers have to contend with, but by no means a tiresome one, as the traveler can, by the active use of his gun, find plenty of sport and lay in a good stock of ducks and geese, as they rise in great flocks at every bend of the river. I bagged seventeen birds to-day, the combined weight of five geese being fifty-seven and a half pounds.

The digging of this canal had another good effect, in this way: Lialui is situated about five miles from the river; and no sooner was the work at Sefula accomplished than Lewanika was roused to see the benefit of it, and at once set thousands of his slaves to work to cut a similar water-way—fifteen feet wide and six deep —not only to the capital, but extending northward a distance of over twenty miles, navigable for large canoes, and tapping one of the most thickly populated districts of the Zambesi Valley.

On the 7th I had a long interview with the king about men and boats. He seems quite willing to do his best, if he could only be impressed with the fact that I am in a hurry. This to him, as to most of his race, is only one of the foolish peculiarities of white men, and he does not hesitate to say so, and seems to think that the responsibility of teaching me that what is not accomplished this month may be the next, rests with him. I presented him with a Winchester rifle, belt, suit of tweed, and one of Jaeger wear, requesting, at the same time, that if he wished our friendship to be maintained he would have the men gathered at once. He promised, and promptly dispatched messengers to the outlying villages to collect them; so now I must simply "wait and murmur not."

While visiting sick natives around the town, my attention was called to a young woman whom a headman had recently added to his harem. The new wife had already become an object of jealousy to his oldest spouse, who thought it best to have her put out of the way; so she ordered a slave to make some bread, and, putting the juice of a poisonous plant into the dough, gave the victim a liberal share for breakfast. The dose was evidently too large, as the stomach rejected most of it; sufficient remained, however, to bring the poor creature near to death. I found her in a comatose condition, administered such antidotes as I thought best, and left. I observed, as I passed out, the would-be murderess and her slave with both hands and feet tied up so tightly that the limbs were fearfully swollen. At my request the thongs were slackened; but I understand they are to be executed by throwing them into the river, where the crocodiles will make short work of them.

A strange superstition which prevails among the Marotsi was brought to my notice to-day by Amba, the king's chief steward, who has been very kind to me in many ways. He came to say good-by, as he was about to leave the capital for a time, giving as his reason, that, having heard of the death in a distant village of one of his children, according to custom he could not come into the king's presence until the next new moon. But it would fill a volume to detail the numerous superstitions, beliefs, and fancies which obtain among these people.

January 14th. I am glad to hear we are likely to get off to-morrow. I have been busy all day making final arrangements—booking canoe-men and unpacking bales of cloth, etc., to adjust them to the new mode of carrying, as some of the goods go by land and the balance in the canoes. We have sixty loads altogether. The men of Barotse do not like porter work, but slaves have no choice. The natives of Bihe carry their loads on the head or shoulder; but these must have it divided into two bundles and suspended from the extreme ends of a stick, six feet long and laid across the shoulder, Chinese fashion. But it would be endless trouble for me to divide up bales of calico in this way, and in the case of the trunks impossible; so they will have to settle the mode of conveyance among themselves. I find no trouble in bringing matters to a focus among these people; the amount of pay for each man has already been fixed, and there is no haggling or backing out at the last. They are under orders, and book without a word.

By ten o'clock next morning all my stuff was lifted and taken down to the canal, where the canoes were drawn up in readiness. Lewanika and a number of his headmen walked with us to say good-by and see us off; also to give final instructions to the men concerning their behavior on the river, winding up with "Remember, if you give any trouble, or cause naka's [doctor's] heart to be sore on the way, you will have to settle with me when you return; so beware!"

It took some time to choose canoes strong enough to shoot the rapids we have to encounter, and to so arrange the men that there should be at least one experienced paddler at the prow of each. But by noon preliminaries were completed—seven canoes, each manned by five paddlers. After much hand-shaking and mutual

HORSESHOE FALLS OF GONYA

interchange of good wishes, the rowers seized their paddles, shouted three times, and away we sped down the stream toward the river, my canoe taking the lead, followed by Jack, a Barotse boy, whom I engaged at Lialui as interpreter. Having been some years at the Cape, he could speak a little English. Then came the two Jamaica men, and also the hunter already referred to as of "doubtful nationality," who, having insulted Letia, the king's son, was under orders to leave the country at once, while the natives were forbidden to render him any assistance whatever. Seeing a fellow-creature in such a strait, I was induced to ask permission of Lewanika to give him a lift down the river in one of my canoes, but had afterward cause to regret having done so.

It was almost dark by the time we reached the mouth of the Sefula Canal, or rather marshy lakes which connect it with the river. This was unfortunate, as in the darkness my headman, who acts as pilot, lost his way several times among the long reeds, running aground, having to back out and search again; until at last we found a narrow opening which we followed, making our way slowly through a perfect cloud of the largest and most voracious mosquitoes I ever encountered. But worse trouble was ahead of us, for the water in the canal was low, and our canoes, being heavily laden, stuck fast in the sand, while still between two and three miles from the mission station, where we intended to camp over Sunday and pick up the supplies left there. The night was now pitch-dark, the long-legged bloodsuckers attacked us unmercifully, and the men were tired. What was to be done? Surrounded on every side by foul-smelling swamps, we knew not how deep, with tall reedy grass stretching far above our heads, the prospect of remaining there all night was doleful in the extreme. Most of the crews had already made off to seek a shelter in the nearest village; and leaving only four men to guard the stuff, I decided to try wading through the marsh, taking Jack with me. I slipped out of the canoe into the water, plunging along for several hundred yards waist-deep, until we felt the ground firm under our feet. By ten o'clock we reached the mission house. Monsieur Coillard had food sent to the men in the boats, and after a refreshing cup of coffee I got off my wet clothes and retired to a comfortable cot, grateful to escape the horrors of a night in the dismal swamp.

January 16th. By daylight all hands went to work and got the canoes over the sandbank and up to the camping-ground, the men taking possession of the huts built by the king's people during his visit for Letia's wedding. I occupied myself all day forming bales of the blankets purchased from Monsieur Coillard for the purpose of paying carriers. In this part of Africa, and for the next eight hundred miles, a porter does not think he is paid, however much calico he receives, unless there is a blanket with it.

I shall never forget the time spent on this station with the veteran missionary, Francis Coillard. If I have seen one mission in Africa that deserves the full sympathy and hearty support of Christians at home more than another, it is this.

By 9 A.M. on the 18th the canoes were loaded and every man in his place, ready for a start. With a final farewell to the kind friends, who accompanied us to the water-side, and a last lingering look at Sefula, we are off full speed down the canal. By 11 A.M. we reached the river. The motion of the rough and unshapely dugouts is anything but pleasant, and an upset sooner or later seems inevitable, particularly as all the men stand to paddle, the steersman at the bow and four astern of the cargo, bending their bodies to each long but steady stroke in perfect rhythm. Sitting on a mat exposed to the scorching sun would be very trying to one's patience but for the interest created by watching the crocodiles as they slide lazily from the banks into the water at our approach, or looking at the numerous hippos that infest the river, bobbing up every few hundred yards, extending their enormous jaws, snorting and blowing, often in dangerous proximity to our fragile bark, sometimes as many as forty to fifty in a herd; but we shoot past, giving them as wide a berth as possible.

There is nothing remarkable in the scenery, as we are still in the Barotse Valley, and the banks are only from four to six feet high; while the vast grassy plains stretch out on either side with scarcely a bush to be seen, although now and again we notice a large tree standing solitary and alone, marking the grave of some ancestral chief. On getting opposite any of these, the boatmen ship their paddles, drop on their knees, clap their hands (Kandele), and, raising their hands above their heads, shout, "Yo sho!" (Shwilela) to these defunct chiefs—the gods of the Marotsi.

At one place, where a very powerful ruler is said to have been buried, they stopped and went ashore, when the headman Limamba requested me to contribute a yard of cloth as a peace-offering. I of course declined, so one of the birds shot in the morning was taken and laid out very solemnly on the ground. Limamba, acting as priest, gathered the crews round him, all kneeling, when he proceeded to implore their genius to be so good as not to be angry with them, as they were starting on a long voyage with a white man; and pleaded that they might go safely and be preserved from the hippos, crocodiles, and rapids. Prostrations and salutations followed, as if in the presence of a living king. They were very wroth with me for withholding the cloth, and threatened to stop; but a little firmness, with counter-threats and some storming, brought them on, and we reached Nalolo, the village of the queen, Makwai, about 3 P.M. We pitched our camp in sight of her town, but by the time my tent was up fever had me down; yet I had to struggle against my sickness, and with an effort walked over to pay a formal call to and salute her majesty, otherwise we should have no firewood. Excusing myself for my brief visit, I returned to camp and turned in as soon as I could.

Next morning we made an early start, but lost a good deal of headway crossing and recrossing the river to avoid the hippos. I find sitting in one place exposed to the scorching rays of the sun and glare from the water for eight or nine hours very trying. The day we left Lialui my underlip got badly blistered; now the blisters are broken and very sore, causing much pain when I touch them. Added to this, the upper lid of my right eye is decorated with the seventh sty I have had since coming to the valley. Still, these are minor sufferings, if the fever would only give us a respite for a while.

Limamba, my boatswain, tries hard every evening to so time our progress that we shall halt at an old camp; but they are generally so very dirty and so infested with vermin that I invariably avoid them. He dislikes being thwarted, and would like to pose as captain, as at home he is a minor chief, and wears round his neck the insignia of his rank—an omande shell. None but chiefs or those of royal blood are permitted to wear this distinguishing badge.

Livingstone refers in his first book (page 300) to the veneration in which the omande shell was held in his day among the Makalolo. He gives a good illustration of the original shell, from the end of which these are obtained, and writes:

"As the last proof of friendship, Shinte came into my tent, though it could scarcely contain more than one person, looked at all the curiosities—the quicksilver, the looking-glass, books, hair-brushes, comb, watch, etc.—with the greatest interest; then, closing the tent so that none of his own people might see the extravagance of which he was about to be guilty, he drew out from his clothing a string of beads and the end of a conical shell, which is considered in regions far from the sea of as great value as the lord-mayor's badge in London. He hung it round my neck, and said, 'There, now, you have a proof of my friendship.' My men informed me that these shells are so highly valued in this quarter as evidences of distinction that for two of them a slave might be bought, and five would be considered a handsome price for an elephant's tusk worth ten pounds."

I may say that these shells are becoming rare, and are more than double the value now than forty years ago. At the present day one will purchase a slave, and two a good tooth of ivory; while it is a recognized law in the Barotse, that, if a condemned man is brought out to be executed, for whatever crime, if any one will hand over their "omande" to the king the culprit is at once set free and becomes the property of whoever pays this ransom. I am pleased at having procured five specimens of these interesting shells, not, however, without a deal of trouble, as the owners were very loath to part with them; but the temptation offered of possessing a red blanket was irresistible.

I shot several ducks, two spur-winged geese, and a beautiful specimen of the great fish-eagle, the outstretched wings of which measured six feet seven inches from tip to tip. This bird resembles the pictures we are familiar with surmounting the "stars and stripes" of the United States—the proud emblem of liberty: black beak, white neck and breast, dark chocolate body, black wings, yellow legs, and enormous black claws. They live entirely on fish, and from the overhanging branches they watch for their prey to come to the surface of the water, when like lightning they swoop down and seize it in their powerful talons, retiring into the bush to enjoy their meal. This bird sometimes secures fish up to eighteen inches in length. When the capture is witnessed by the boatmen they make a bee-line in its direction and rob it of the prize.

In the evening we reached Senanga, the extreme

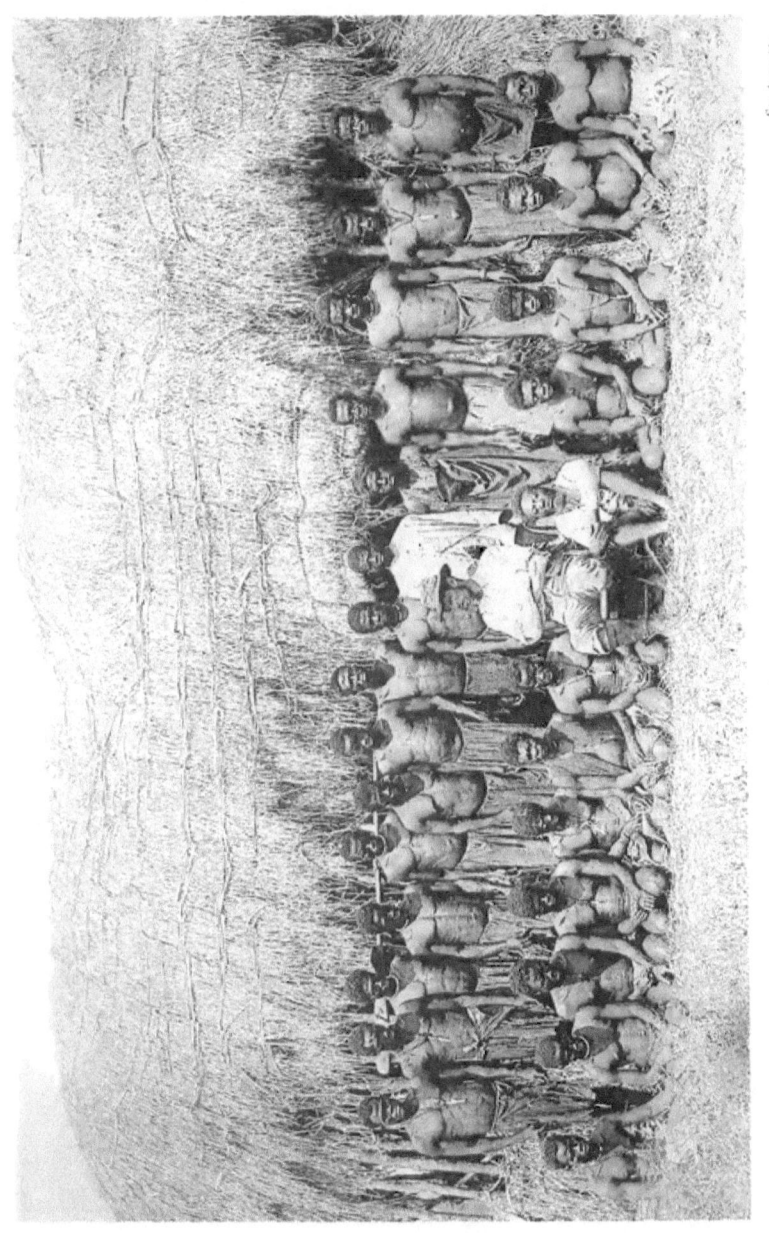

ZAMBESI BOATMEN

southeast end of the Barotse Valley, and we camp at the edge of a forest. It is quite a relief to see trees again after the monotony of seven weeks on the unbroken expanse of grass and reeds. Here we must stop for a few days, as part of my loads, which have come so far by water, must now be taken by carriers overland to Sesheke, which we hope to reach three weeks hence. We were not long in camp when natives brought some sweet milk for sale. Its abundance at Lialui and Sefula has been a great luxury to us, and it will probably be some time ere we meet with such good fortune again, as after leaving Senanga we shall find no more villages until we reach Sesheke. The prominent features of this camp are crocodiles and mosquitoes: the latter fill the air with a buzz like a hive of bees, and their sting is little less severe; while out on the water, at about fifty yards from where I sit, three huge crocodiles are floating like logs on the surface.

January 22d. It has been raining heavily for most of the day. The headman of the overland detachment has arrived with his carriers. This is encouraging, and certainly surprises me not a little—a happy contrast to my troubles with the West Coast natives. Serving out a little gunpowder, caps, lead, and a few pieces of calico completes the arrangements, and they are off; to-morrow, all being well, we do likewise. In the evening I went up the river a mile, and shot thirteen ducks and two geese—the last we shall see of them for some time, as they are seldom seen except in the vicinity of marshes. But we are getting out our belts and rifle cartridges for more portentous game, that we hope to stalk during the next three weeks, as I am told antelopes of almost every variety abound on both banks of the river; but that means, too, that we must keep a sharp lookout for lions and leopards, for where game is plentiful these are generally not far away.

On the 23d we struck camp and pushed off again, the men pulling with plenty of vim after their few days' rest. I noticed the high-water mark of the Zambesi by the débris deposited among the branches of some trees twelve feet above the present level, and indicating the height it will possibly reach in another two months. The scenery is now completely changed; instead of the bald and uninteresting banks on either side, we have a variety of splendid trees with very few breaks. This does not present a tropical appearance, by any means; on the contrary, so far as the vegetation is concerned one might easily imagine one's self on any of our beautiful English or Canadian rivers in midsummer. The many islands brought back to us happy memories of camping days on the Georgian Bay. Nor are the trees so close as to hide the sward, with its crop of rich deep green grass between, at times reminding one of a park in the vicinity of some old English mansion. But the illusion does not last long, for right near us pops up the head of a hippopotamus, with a grunt that startles the boatmen and makes them redouble their energies to get as far and as quickly away from him as possible. While rounding a bend we see the armor-clad crocodiles glide noiselessly out into deep water, casting hungry glances at the naked figures whose approach has disturbed their repose; and in the trees various species of monkeys and baboons are sporting among the branches.

The placid water looks like a lake, and the numerous islands, varying in size from a few feet square to many acres, are all richly clad with vegetation, the larger ones abounding in game. On one of these, called Beta, to our right and on the west bank, we camp for the night. I am simply charmed with my surroundings; and who would not be? Gipsying under the shade of lordly trees like great oaks, which shelter us from the sun by their far-spreading branches; no thorns, jungle, creepers, or underbrush of any kind, but soft, fresh grass, about a foot high. The chief interest, however, is centered in three pots that are steaming over the fire, one containing rice, another cornmeal dumplings, and the third ribs of a pallah buck shot about an hour ago, within three hundred yards of camp. At a little distance the canoe-men are rigging up their lean-to sheds of twigs and grass, while others are cooking their share of the antelope. There are plenty of mosquitoes, and, what is perhaps worse, swarms of the tsetse-fly—the dreaded scourge of domestic animals in Central Africa. The men are not giving me the slightest trouble so far, and, if I may judge from appearances, everything bids fair for the water journey to Kazangulu being little short of a pleasure trip. I would willingly have remained at this lovely spot for another day, but this must not be; so we load up in the morning and launch away.

The river spreading out to nearly a mile in width gave us a great deal of shallow water; twice my canoe was stuck fast on the top of stones—the first we have come across of any size, large or small, in the last six hundred miles. Now we would rather be without them, for, being large boulders hidden under the water, which is dark at this season of the year, we are in constant danger of an upset. We reached Sioma in the afternoon, within a mile and a half of the Falls of Gonya. To avoid the latter we have to get all the canoes taken from the water and dragged overland for a distance of some four miles; but I find that Lewanika has thoughtfully sent on a man to collect natives, so as to have no delay.

The moving of canoes overland at Sioma is made the subject of a picture and description extraordinary in the book "How I Crossed Africa," representing hundreds of men, about forty at each canoe, carrying them on sticks laid underneath, and climbing up a steep hill through dense forest and tropical foliage. This is gross exaggeration from first to last, but only on a par with the rest of this two-volumed book. The same may be said of the writings of several other African travelers who might be named, and whose literature can only rank in the estimation of those who have visited these places, written as it is by these exceedingly imaginative scribblers, among "dime novels" and "penny dreadfuls." I don't believe there is a country under heaven that has been the subject of more romancing and misrepresentation than Africa.

The transferring of the canoes past the falls is, after all, a very commonplace affair. They are not carried, but dragged along the ground by means of bark ropes, and always have been since traveling by the river began, with not more than twelve men to each; and as to the hill, there is nothing imposing about it, being only five or six feet high. Nor is there any forest, unless a solitary tree in every other acre can be made to do duty for the dense jungle so elaborately portrayed by pen and pencil. In the same book we have a sketch of lion-shooting at night, by the light of a bull's-eye lantern in the hand of a boy, reflecting on a pair of monster males, who are represented as standing within twenty yards of the camp, patiently receiving their *coup de grâce*. It also contains the tragic and blood-curdling account of an attack on the author's camp by the Marotsi, when he, with but a handful of men, defended the honor of the Portuguese flag against hundreds of natives, killing seventeen of the assailants. This thrilling story is also untrue, and without the slightest foundation. I feel it due to the Marotsi to give it a flat contradiction, for the would-be hero arrived at Lialui in a destitute condition, was the recipient of Lewanika's hospitality and protection, and was under obligation to him for men and boats to proceed on his journey. But far too much of this sort of thing has been foisted on the public, giving the general reader a vague and totally erroneous idea of the country and its peoples. There is quite sufficient to tell about Africa that is truly wonderful, and of intense interest to all who desire to acquire a knowledge of the "Dark Continent," without turning it into fiction and fable.

As the day cleared up, I got a few boys, and with my photo apparatus trudged off to the Falls of Gonya. After walking a mile and a half we came to a branch of the river about a hundred yards wide, that cut us off completely from the only point where the cataract can be seen to advantage. There being no canoe near by, and as the water did not appear to be more than waist-deep, our only alternative was to strip and wade it. Our progress was slow, the current being strong and the stones slippery; patience and perseverance, however, triumphed, and we reached the other side in safety with my camera. It proved to be a rocky island, which I crossed, and sat down on a boulder, to gaze on a scene so grand that few men would regret traveling a thousand miles to see. The volume of water constituting the falls, though great, does not represent the entire width of the Zambesi here—perhaps not more than half, as, besides the portion we waded through, a large part is cut off by an island on the west side, that rejoins the main stream about two hundred yards below, in beautiful cascades, a third part coming in still lower down in roaring rapids. The day was unfavorable for photography, as I had to unlimber my apparatus every few minutes and protect it with my waterproof cloak from the torrents of rain, which gave me but few intervals. After four hours on the rocks, alternately scorched by the sun and drenched by the rain, we retraced our steps, gratified beyond measure for the privilege of having been permitted to view the falls, cascades, and rapids of Gonya.

The following day we proceeded with the loads to where the canoes were awaiting us below the falls. Here the river is narrow, compressed on either side by rocky bluffs, giving a rise of fifty feet at the end of the annual wet seasons. It would be a very easy matter to escape the cataract by cutting a canal to this point, the route being almost in a straight line, with very few and slight undulations. The day was far gone before

MISSION STATION, SESHEKE

See page 198

we got on the water again, so that an hour after starting I ordered a halt and formed camp on a sandbank, about a hundred yards below the confluence of the Lumbi. This river is over half a mile wide a little higher up its course, but here comes thundering down a narrow, rocky gorge of not more than fifty yards, as it enters the Zambesi.

January 27th. As the Barotse men are not particularly well acquainted with the rapids below Sioma, I have thought it best to engage a native pilot. I put him in my canoe and let the others follow his lead, as he professes to know every channel among the shallows. A run of three hours brought us to the Kari Rapids, where the waters were so turbulent and forbidding that we had to unload and carry the stuff past the most dangerous places. I have to reserve a portion of each day now for the purpose of hunting, so as to provide meat for our thirty-eight hungry men, the corn they carried with them being finished. But it would be an easy matter to feed five times as many here, as both banks of the river are simply teeming with game.

During the next few days we made but short runs, being frequently delayed in getting our dug-outs safely through the numerous rapids; but the scenery seems more beautiful than ever, the many clusters of wild date palms along the banks adding peculiar charm to the grandeur of the landscape. While camped at the mouth of the river Injoka, I found myself in a forest of mopani. This tree is a favorite in Africa, although it is useless for building purposes. Its leaves when crushed give off an agreeable aromatic odor almost as strong as pimento; no underwood or scrub grows beneath its shade, but a carpet of short clean grass. What a genuine pleasure it is to saunter along under those dark-green trees, without a bush to impede the careless tread, with the exception of an occasional clump of aloes. One can scarcely conceive that there is not a human habitation within fifty miles of a spot so lovely.

I struck fresh antelope spoor, and knew they could not be very far away. A sharp snort drew my attention to a pallah buck standing at short range, and I fired and dropped him; but before the echo had died away, a whole herd came rushing past, skirting the edge of a marsh, and stopping at about a hundred and fifty yards from me. I singled out another and got him, and as they started off, fired again and brought down a third. The shots having been heard by my Kaffirs, a batch of them soon appeared and bore the meat in triumph to camp.

Hunting in Africa is attended with an amount of excitement and interest unknown to the same sport in Europe. The knowledge that the forests through which we noiselessly glide are haunted by so many wild and dangerous animals keeps one constantly on the alert for the slightest sound that might indicate their presence. Every clump of underbrush is scanned lest a lion or a leopard be lurking in its dark recesses, ready to spring on the unwary; while a consciousness of perfect freedom lends buoyancy to one's spirits.

On the 30th, while quietly gliding along in smooth water near the bank, I was aroused by a noise at first like distant thunder, but every second coming nearer and increasing to a terrific roar, like the sound of an approaching express train. I stopped and jumped ashore. It proved to be an immense herd of buffaloes tearing through the thicket, within a dozen yards of where I stood, leaving a track behind them as though a regiment of heavy artillery had just gone by. We got our rifles and gave chase; but they had winded us and swerved round to leeward, and although we followed the tremendous trail for two hours as hard as we could, failed to get within five hundred yards of them, and at last were reluctantly compelled to give up. We got a duiker antelope on the way back. Such abundance of game as swarm in this part of the Zambesi Valley I never even dreamed of. A number of zebras crossed our track, and we observed the spoor of at least six different species of antelope. On reaching the river we found that the men had captured a buffalo calf left behind in the mad rush, and which supplied us with delicious veal steaks for dinner.

We got under way again, but in a few minutes arrived at the Ngambwe Falls. These falls are insignificant in themselves, being only five or six feet high. Both above and below them the river-bed is full of huge boulders, which with the rapidity of the current made the waters so tumultuous that we were obliged to get out of the canoes and drag them by land for a good half-mile, which occupied most of the afternoon. The day was gone, and we camped. I shall ever remember the gorgeous sunset of that evening: the islands so green, and the reflection in the water so pronounced, with a golden-hued shade over all as old Sol retired, making a picture to which no painter's brush could do justice.

Next morning we came upon the finest game scene

it has ever been my lot to witness, or ever expect to see again. In the foreground, close to the water, stood a group of nine zebras, including three young colts. Nothing could have been prettier than the startled mien, the pricked ears, and poise of the heads of these graceful animals, with their beautifully striped coats of cream and rich dark brown glistening in the morning sun. Beyond them a few yards a herd of hartebeest was grazing, and at a short distance a small valley, like a dip in the veldt, was red with hundreds of roy bucks. One of the men jumped ashore and shot a zebra, when we had an opportunity to examine it closely. Surely this is the most beautiful animal in the African forests! But here sentiment must give place to our mundane wants. Zebra meat is rather sweet to the taste, very tender, though not particularly savory; but to this the men make no objection, for to them any meat is toothsome. Later in the day, when we had camped, the hunter went out and brought in two roy bucks; but we are getting surfeited with venison. I would gladly give the finest antelope for a dish of cabbage or a few potatoes; it is now sixteen days since we have tasted vegetables of any kind. At Lialui I prepared a very good substitute for spinach from pumpkin leaves, or a succulent shrub gathered for us by the natives, that served in some measure to appease our craving for green food and aid the digestion, which becomes seriously impaired by an exclusive meat diet.

I have been wearing for the past few weeks a pair of "veldt schoons," native made—uppers of koodoo hide, soles of buffalo, and sewn with strips of antelope skin. They are very comfortable to the feet, and are excellent for hunting in dry weather, but get like a piece of wash-leather when wet. I was obliged to put on a pair of heavy boots this morning, and, having walked a good deal, find my heels badly blistered. I have suffered intensely in the past from the strong boots I brought with me from England, and have come to the conclusion that they are no good for these tracks. With the exception of two or three pairs of tennis-shoes, I have had no comfort in my footgear until I came across "veldt schoons," and I mean to stick to these as long as they will last—then make another pair.

CHAPTER X.

FROM SESHEKE TO BAMANGWATO.

At Sesheke.—Working under difficulties.—Indifference of the natives.—Pay for "working book."—Not quite their equal.—Capabilities of the soil.—Monsieur Goy's letter.—Draining and irrigation.—Canoes capsized.—Kazungula.—The French mission.—Isolation and loneliness.—Premonitions of trouble.—Wholesale desertions.—Lost bearings.—A monopolist.—Tropical scenery.—Victoria Falls.—For hours we stand gazing.—The great fissure.—Baboons.—Batokaland.—Return to Kazungula.—Preparations for crossing the desert.—The tsetse-fly belt.—Pandamatenka.—Rough road.—A broken dessel-boom.—A night among lions.—Program of a day.—No water.—Thirst, thirst, thirst!—Bushmen.

FEBRUARY 1st. Now all is changed; the Elysian scenes in which we have reveled these many days, to us are no more. The country on both sides is again low, flat, and swampy; few trees, and consequently no large game, but aquatic birds abundant, as in the Barotse. We made a long run to-day, from 7 A.M. until 5.30 P.M., when we reached Sesheke, where Dr. Livingstone had his headquarters while exploring in these regions. There is now here a station of the Paris Evangelical Mission, in charge of Monsieur and Madame Goy, who were expecting my arrival, and tendered me a welcome so hearty that I felt very much at home right away. I met Monsieur V——, a young French missionary, who arrived here a few weeks ago; but he has suffered so severely from fever that he is unable to remain, and is now making preparations to return.

KAZUNGULA MISSION STATION

Next morning the chief, Nananwana, and headmen assembled, and much time was occupied in palaver, talking over the prospects of my journey beyond Kazungula, as they have to find more carriers for me by order of Lewanika, for we are still in his territory. We will be delayed here a few days, as the overland caravan has not yet turned up. I sent on the two Jamaicans in charge of the boats and goods to Kazungula, as I find the spot where the camp is pitched very unhealthy, and they are having constant fever. I would have left one or even both these young men at either of the French mission stations; but from the fact of their suffering so much from the fever, I realized that to do so meant the sacrifice of their lives at no distant date.

February 9th. The whole of the past week has been spent at Sesheke, waiting for the loads by land. They arrived yesterday afternoon with all the goods safe; and to-day I have made arrangements to start for Kazungula to-morrow morning. The work on this station, like most new missions in the interior, is discouraging in the extreme. For many months Monsieur Goy, although often prostrated with fever, brought on by exposure and fatigue, has been bravely toiling at the building of a meeting-house, and has at last completed it. He had to go to the forest and with his own hands cut the lumber, load it on his wagon, and drive it home; then to prepare the wood for the frame, put on the rafters, and thatch the roof with grass, almost without aid, for he could not persuade the natives to risk their precious lives by climbing up even half-way to hand him a rafter or bundle of thatch. The few who were employed to cut grass, etc., gave him no end of worry, every pay-day demanding cloth and beads far in excess of the quantity agreed upon, or the nominal amount of work performed.

Last Saturday week, after infinite labor and trouble, the building was ready for holding services, and Monsieur Goy rejoiced at the thought that now, surely, the people would come and hear the gospel in a place so comfortable, yet having cost them nothing. Monsieur Goy proposed to have a formal opening, and went around the villages inviting the people to come. About a hundred and fifty responded to the call, as there was to be a roasted ox distributed. But yesterday, there being nothing promised to eat, the service commenced with an audience consisting of the chief, five lads, and four women. About a dozen more sauntered in before the close of the service, but the manifest total indifference of the natives is even more disheartening than open hostility. There is no difficulty in getting people who come round the station during the week to listen, even with apparent interest, for hours together, to spiritual counsel; but it would be a mistake to conclude that their assents and nods of approval are sincere. One young missionary, in his innocence and zeal, was so delighted with the long conversations he was having daily with three men posing as inquirers, that it formed the subject, meanwhile, of a very interesting letter he was writing to friends at home. But near the end of the week, the trio, lingering round the door to a later hour than usual, were asked why they waited. The answer was prompt, "We are waiting for five days' pay." "Pay for what?" queried the astonished missionary. "Well, now! Did you think we were coming here every day to listen to you for nothing?"

Thus the illusion was rudely dispelled, and, like an honest man, he tore up the interesting letter.

Monsieur Coillard and others have had similar experiences in attempting to get lads to attend school. They expect the same pay for "working book" as for any other form of labor, and the young under instruction at the various schools of the mission are mostly those sent by the chiefs, who are quite willing to have the children taught to read, provided the missionary takes the entire charge of them, supplying them with food and clothing at his own expense. The Christian workers see fresh proofs every day of how little, after all, "the line upon line and precept upon precept" has affected the natives. They steal from him at every opportunity, and very rarely can he obtain any redress from the chiefs; consequently Monsieur Goy and his brother missionaries are obliged to provide themselves with large dogs to protect their property.

But for the sure promise of a day of reaping, if even long delayed, he would often be tempted to abandon the task as hopeless, and retire from the field in despair.

It has been said that slavery has left its stamp on the negroes of the West Indies, so that it is difficult now to eradicate the evil propensities acquired by their forefathers in the days of forced labor. Be this as it may, one thing is certain: great good would accrue to these natives by compelling them to perform some honest work, and keeping them at it, for at least eight hours a day, until they learned the value of manual labor. Their natural conceit, pride, and laziness are traits of character that are almost prohibitive of their accepting the teachings or following the example of the white man, whom the natives, of these parts at least, look upon as—to put it mildly—not quite their equal.

Never, until the present absolute power of the big chiefs over the body and soul of their vassals is broken (which, however, must come at no distant period), will there be any real success in spreading the gospel among them. The missionary is ever conscious that while he is speaking, the people before him, if they think at all, are debating in their own minds, "Were I to become a Christian, what would my chief say?" for well they know that the ethics of Christianity are condemnatory of the life, conduct, and character of their rulers.

Before leaving Sesheke, let me answer the question, "What are the prospects for agriculture in the Zambesi Valley?" by quoting a letter received from Monsieur Goy, who is an authority on the subject, not only by reason of his practical experience of several years in the country, but also because his knowledge as a scientific agriculturist gives special importance to his testimony. Monsieur Goy, I may mention, is a native of Switzerland. He writes:

"I would like to assist incognito at the lectures you will give on your peregrinations through the Dark Continent. Yet I am sure you will not imitate so many travelers, who in their own interest have always overpraised Africa, in estimating too highly its mineral wealth and the fertility of the soil in certain regions. You will render a great service to the general public in describing the country along the Zambesi River, which is supposed to be one of the gardens of Africa, but in reality is most desolate. Being in the tropics, one would expect to meet with all the fruits and products of those regions; but you find nothing else than mealies, Kaffir-corn, and millet, and very inferior fruits indeed. The harvest is generally very small, and, notwithstanding the game and fish, which are abundant, people suffer from scarcity of food every year. We are the only strangers, and yet have to make provision in advance against the time of famine. One would, then, wonder if by active and intelligent work the European cultures could not be introduced here. I can only say that that plan would have little chance of success.

"For five years I have lived in this country, and traveled much, but have not been able to find two square miles of clay soil. I have studied the question more than anything else, as it was my vocation by choice. I had prepared myself for it by a long and special apprenticeship. In coming to the Zambesi I proposed to do agricultural work, but with a purely missionary aim. I left France with much courage and hope for the success of this special mission, which had been intrusted to me by our committee, and began working at Sefula by opening a canal of two miles to drain a marshy ground, and disposing that canal in a way that made easy the watering of my plantations. A great deception was in store for me: the ground, once exposed to the sun, turned out to be pure white sand, and I don't believe that a better result would have been found in any other place. With a great deal of trouble one might succeed in growing a few vegetables for his own use, but nothing to speak of.

My own experience shows that everything imported, animals of every kind as well as seeds, degenerate, and have to be renewed after a couple of years.

"This country, judged with impartiality, is not a country with a bright future, and offers no inducements to civilization. The Europeans who labor here as missionaries do so from a sense of duty, and not from choice."

February 10th. Having bade farewell to the kind friends at Sesheke with whom I have put in a week so happily, we started this morning in a swift canoe, thirty-two feet long, twenty-four inches beam, and twelve inches deep, with five strong paddlers, intending, if possible, to reach Kazungula to-night, a distance of seventy miles. By noon we were in the rapids of Mombova, where I learned that two of my canoes sent on ahead last week got capsized, and the loads, not being properly secured to the canoes, went to the bottom. They were all recovered, however, and, as they consisted chiefly of trade cloth, etc., will be easily dried. We were more fortunate, and reached our destination without any mishaps at 3.30 P.M., making the journey in eight hours' actual traveling. The quicker one makes this run, the better, for it is most uninteresting, being shut in nearly all the way by tall reeds and papyrus on either side, the neighboring swamps exhaling, in the early morning particularly, a vile malarious odor.

On arriving I was warmly greeted by Monsieur and Madame Jalla, of still another French mission station, situated close to the drift, where all who visit Lewanika's country from the south must cross the Zambesi. It was expected that many natives would come and settle here;

but, although several years have passed since the station was established, these hopes have not been realized. There is not a village or a native hut within a mile on this side, and the site is very unhealthy; for when the river is in flood the water rises to within a few yards of the dwelling-house, leaving heaps of débris and mud as it recedes. I found Frater and Jonathan comfortably ensconced in an old wagon, while all the goods were safely stored in a hut. Here I discharge the Barotse boatmen and wait for the carriers to turn up who are to take my loads on the next stage of the journey. They are assembling every day in response to the call of the sub-chiefs sent out by the king to collect them from the various villages; over a hundred are already in camp.

To-day Jack told me that his father (who lives on the other side of the river) objects to his accompanying me farther as interpreter unless I promise bigger money. At present I am paying him twice as much as he could earn any other way, so I quietly told him, much to his chagrin, that I will endeavor to get along without him. A few minutes after, Monsieur Jalla told me that he had often thought of the prospects there might be for mission work in the Batoka country, through which I intended to travel, and expressed his desire to accompany me as far as the Kafukwe River. He knows the Sesutu language well, and several of the men know both it and Setoka, so that the interpreter difficulty is solved.

All being well, we start on Tuesday morning.

Madame Jalla is a brave little woman, and readily consents to being left all alone until her husband's return, probably three or four months hence. The isolation and loneliness of missionary life here can scarcely be realized by workers in more favored spheres. The home life and its pleasures must be held with a light hand, for malarial fever ceases not in its deadly work, sparing no one. No loving care or frequent precaution can do more than lessen the attacks of the invisible foe. The merry voices of the children and the patter of little feet must be heard by the parents as music that is passing. Madame Jalla in a recent letter writes:

"Our little darling Valdo is still very well in health; he is not yet eight months old. You know that the greatest trial of the missionaries on the Zambesi is that up till now they have always lost their children quite young. We have two dear little girls buried here, and that makes us appreciate all the more this third child, who seems so strong and well; but the fever is here, threatening us continually, and our joy in having him is always mixed with fear."

There is as yet no church formed or meeting-house erected on this station. The trials incidental to missionary life are at Kazungula of a similar nature to those experienced at the other stations of this mission. The work to which these heroic men and women have devoted their lives can only be described, at present, as resembling the dead of winter. Now they suffer the chilling blasts of a dreary, lifeless, and frozen apathy on the part of those whose good they seek; but as springtime and the singing of birds must follow winter and the trees put forth the tender leaf, then after a season of shower and sunshine bring forth fruit, until the husbandman is made to rejoice over garnered crops, so to these tried and faithful toilers shall come a day when "both he that soweth and he that reapeth shall rejoice together."

Monday, 16th. We have now a hundred and fifty men in camp, one third being porters, the rest a company of warriors sent by Lewanika to escort us as far as the Kafukwe River. I have been busy all day allotting loads, but somehow with many misgivings. There is a great deal of talk among the headmen concerning the dangers we are to encounter, etc., and, to cap all, a rumor has reached them that an impi of Matebele, the tribe of all others they most dread, has crossed the river into Batokaland and are lying in wait for us. Now these men, who but a short time ago in a war-dance vowed they would annihilate any opposing host, however strong, are paralyzed with fear, and I should not be surprised if, after all, I am prevented from proceeding by the north bank of the Zambesi. Most of these braves have followed us over four hundred and fifty miles, surely not to show the white feather now! Yes, and at the only time when their company is actually required.

All is ready for the march on the morning of the 18th, when a servant reports that my camp is deserted. The cowardly fellows have fled during the night, doubtless to relate to the king a story of the appalling dangers they have escaped. Well, better that they go here than later on, when I might have been in a worse fix; thus I am left alone again with my two Jamaicans. This is a crusher, but, like the African fever, we get used to it. The future is now dark, but in a few days, no doubt, it will brighten. I must look around for some other means for continuing my journey eastward. In the meantime, accompanied by Monsieur Jalla and a few boys to carry some blankets, we set out on a week's tramp through Batoka, so as to see something of the natives and visit Africa's greatest wonder, the Victoria Falls.

We went by canoe as far as the Nampwi Rapids, where we hid the boat and took to a footpath along the river-bank leading to a small village, which we reached at 6 P.M. We turned aside among the long grass and bivouacked under a large tree, thinking it would serve the purpose of a tent; but its shelter, together with the long grass, harbored such hordes of mosquitoes that when supper was ready our hands were so busy keeping off the wretched tormentors that we could scarcely get a chance to carry the food to our mouths. We ate but little, and, being tired, wrapped ourselves in our thick blankets and tried to rest; but it was a weary night. Not ten minutes' sleep could we catch, and our arms ached with the perpetual whacking right and left, which we had to keep up in vain efforts to defend ourselves from the "pesky varmint."

At daylight we had a cup of coffee, and set out on the march. There was scarcely any perceptible path—now through a rocky ravine, then across a broad stretch of grass eight to ten feet high. We had soon more than enough of it while trusting to the proverbial native who knows all about the forest and has a natural instinct for finding his way anywhere in the woods. After following him for two hours, we found by his twisting and turning that he had lost his bearings; so, deposing him from the position of guide, we took our own way, making a bee-line at a right angle to our previous course, and to a point ahead where the hills on either side seemed to converge, and between which we knew the river must pass. We were not mistaken, and with a feeling of relief we found ourselves on the right road.

About noon we sat down in a cool shade for breakfast, rested for a couple of hours, and started again. No large game sighted, but I got a few guinea-fowls and partridges. We halted at 5.30 P.M. under some mopani trees, and in the stillness of the evening could hear the distant boom of the famous cataract.

Daybreak saw us again on the track, which in most places was only imaginary and very rough. But the chief annoyance was from a certain kind of grass that sheds innumerable small, sharp, claw-shaped prickles, which stuck to our clothes, penetrating to the skin like hundreds of needles, scarifying us all over. By noon we reached the village of the chief at the drift, who tries to hold the monopoly of ferrying people over the river about a mile above the falls; but he did not seem inclined to oblige us right away, in spite of the proffered pay and present, only remarking that he would think about it and see us to-morrow. He meant thereby to show how little he cared for white men, and desiring above all that we might eat a little "humble pie" by being under the necessity of coaxing and begging him to favor us. Resenting this idea, Monsieur Jalla went to interview another chief—an old Makalolo named Mosatane, one of the very few remaining of that almost exterminated tribe—who treated us with much more respect, presenting us with a sheep and plenty of meal, and promising to see us over in the morning.

We spent the night in a lovely grove near the river-side. The scenery here is particularly fine. The river, though about a mile wide, is broken up by large islands of from a hundred and fifty to two hundred yards; these islands are clad with the most tropical-looking vegetation we have seen. There are numerous date palms of considerable size, but, like everything else in this disappointing country, the fruit is a delusion, consisting of a large stone covered with a very thin film of edible substance. Looking down the river, we see five columns of spray, white as snow, rising slowly high above the falls, and lingering in clouds that glisten beautifully in the sunlight. Early in the morning Mosataue appeared with the canoes and paddled us over to the west bank, where the falls can be seen to the best advantage. Half an hour's walk brought us close to the renowned cataract, Mosia-na-tunia, or Victoria Falls, as Livingstone named them.

We found a couple of small huts close by, which came in handy as a temporary shelter for us while we stayed. The numerous well-beaten tracks in the bush surrounding the falls suggest the idea that there must be any number of visitors frequenting the spot. Such is not the explanation; they are formed by hippos in their nightly perambulations. These animals abound in hundreds, and there is scarcely a square yard from the verge of the precipice to a radius of a quarter of a mile that does not bear their spoor. According to the natives, once or twice a year is about the frequency with which white people make their appearance here, and the Kaffirs wonder very much what even these come for, for they see nothing extraordinary in this, to us, almost unparalleled wonder. We asked a woman on

VICTORIA FALLS (NEAR THE CENTER)

the east side of the river, and living within two miles of the falls, if she had ever seen them. Her reply was characteristic: "Oh no! What should I go and see them for? Is there any one going to pay me for my trouble?"

In the afternoon we went to view the attraction that had induced us to walk fifty rough and weary miles. The banks are densely wooded with huge trees and thick underbrush. When within a stone's-throw of the water we entered an atmosphere of perpetual drizzle, kept up by the spray that rises unceasingly in great volumes and carried in the direction of the wind, to fall in fine rain. The ground is sopping wet; every now and then we sink to the ankles in mud, and in a few minutes are drenched through. Yet for hours we stand gazing in amazement and awe, contemplating this the greatest natural phenomenon we have ever seen. Now we are on the edge of the chasm; but it is impossible, with either pen or pencil or camera, to give anything like an adequate idea of the majestic splendor of this rival of Niagara.

The river is about a mile broad as it dashes over a precipice four hundred feet in depth, in a straight line across its entire width. The chasm into which the river plunges is a narrow rent not more than a hundred and fifty feet wide, and runs at right angles to its course, getting narrower toward the eastern bank. The opposite side of the fissure is very precipitous, of hard basaltic rock, and almost on a level with the river above; but on account of the dense fog one cannot see more than a couple of hundred yards at a time, and that only when a gust of wind blows it to one side, which, though momentary, bears repeating many times over, and well repays the exercise of patience, for through these rifts we get a magnificent view of the lovely blue water above, flowing calmly and tranquilly onward until it crashes into the seething abyss below. The palm-bearing islands in the distance form a picturesque background to the sublimely beautiful scene. While viewed in sunshine, the double zones of prismatic colors formed in the spray have a brilliancy compared with which an ordinary rainbow is but a faint semblance. Livingstone, Baines, and Mohr have each in turn given their impressions of the Victoria Falls. The latter, a shrewd and keen observer, writes:

"I will now endeavor to give a feeble description of the great cataract itself. The majestic river, a mile wide, comes down from the north-northwest, and flings its waters down four hundred feet into a rocky ravine, varying in width from two hundred and forty to three hundred feet, which runs across its bed. From the river above the falls rise many islands, all adorned with the richest tropical vegetation. The banks are covered with vast but not dense forests, in which occur whole groups of tall-stemmed palms, giving a thoroughly southern character to the scenery. Near the falls the water hurries along with flying speed, and the long ribbons of foam everywhere to be seen make it look as if it were boiling. Near the western bank lies a little island, about a hundred and twenty feet from the brink, and here the bed of the stream seems to dip suddenly, for the water leaps down with a roar and a rush, like a huge sea-wave. At this point, quite at the eastern corner, a ridge of rock juts out, on to which any one not subject to giddiness can step, when he will have, on the left, the fall just described, and in front the long line of the great cataract, which can of course only be partially seen, for the compressed air drawn down with the flood and filled with drops of water escapes continually and rises in eddies, producing the spray-clouds, which gleam like specters far above this great 'altar' of the waters. After looking down for some time into this raging, leaping, foaming, heaving chaos, deafened by the terrible noise of the maddened waters, and shaken by the menacing howl rising up continuously from the depths, which seems to pierce through bone and marrow, one wonders how the rocks, those hard ribs of the earth, can withstand the shock of such a mighty onset.

"After I had gazed at this glorious scene for some time I began to feel stunned, and I went a hundred paces to the south in the direction of our camp. Here I was on rocky ground, within the sphere of the spray veil, and one moment was wrapped in it as in a thick fog, while the next it was suddenly rent asunder by a gust of wind, the most brilliant sunbeams pouring through the gap, succeeded, however, almost immediately by a fresh shower of spray.

"Turning round on this spot with the face to the north, a singular impression is produced, for the abyss and the long line of clouds rising from the earth are visible, but the waterfall is hidden by the intervening trees and bushes.

"Anxious to get a front view of the falls, I now made my way through the forest—which may not inaptly be called the 'rain forest,' its luxuriance being the result of continual showers of spray—and found the ground marked by the countless footprints of elephants and buffaloes, attracted, doubtless, by the cool mud-baths to be had here.

"The upper side of the chasm, running across the bed of the stream, ends in a projecting slab of rock, and before us on the east lies the channel—here two hundred and seventy feet wide—which is the only outlet for the whole volume of water. Stepping on to the slab of rock, and looking to the north-northwest, we have a view of the whole long line of falls. As the river, owing to the late rains, was still very much swollen, I saw them under very favorable circumstances, for the black rock-masses were almost entirely hidden by the indescribably beautiful water draperies, the abrupt naked rock-chasms only yawning here and there through the white veil of spray. When I saw the cataract, the first fall consisted of one long, unbroken, shining, greenish-blue wave, which, as it sped on its farther course, resolved itself into ever finer, whiter, and more delicately rounded cloud-forms.

"This is the point from which the visitor can obtain the grandest view of the incomparable Victoria Falls of the Zambesi. Before us we have the full glory of the falling mass of water, ever moving, ever changing, blustering, foaming, glowing, shining, with small green islands peeping over the very edge of the abyss, and on the left and right, above and below, water, water everywhere, hurrying onward with a continuous roar like thunder. In front of the falls, where the waters from the west and east meet and embrace, hang suspended two double circular rainbows, unbroken by any horizon, the magic hues glowing in the brilliant tropical sunbeams, blue, yellow, and red succeeding each other in the outer, and red, yellow, and blue in the inner ring. . . .

"Livingstone, who made his observations with a pocket chronometer, which showed the mean Greenwich time, gives the longitude as 25° 45′ E. I place my observation forty-four minutes of longitude farther east.

"The height of the veil of spray which hovers above the falls I measured with a sextant and a base-line equal to 550 feet; the angle a was found at 50°, which gives for the opposite angle a the length = 655.5 feet; add to this 400 feet depth of abyss, and we have 1055 feet ascension, a result differing only by 40 feet from that given by Baines. Of course the height varies every day, according to the volume of water in the river, the temperature, and the strength of the wind. . . .

"After the Zambesi has made its way through the pass, two hundred and seventy feet wide, it rolls on in sinuous fashion, describing three or four wide curves. The bed is so narrow that its depth must be enormous to accommodate such a vast volume of water. The banks consist of perpendicular rocks five hundred or six hundred feet high, absolutely inaccessible to men, though many baboons, which have taken up their abode here, climb up and down them with ease."

I have to apologize for the accompanying photographic views of the falls, as they by no means convey the impression of grandeur produced on an eye-witness. They are only "bits," showing the water as it takes the leap clear of the rock into what—the reader must be left to imagine, as the most rugged and imposing portions are so shrouded in spray that the negatives taken appear as if "light struck," or "fogged," while it is not in the power of the camera to "shoot around corners," therefore cannot look over the brink into the four hundred feet of chasm below, where the foaming waters are tossed into billows of snowy whiteness, dashing on to the outlet at the eastern bank. For many miles the course of the Zambesi below the falls zigzags in acute angles every few hundred yards.

On the 24th I walked down as far as the first bend, about a mile and a half distant. This turn is most abrupt, the gorge narrow, and the water very deep, the surface streaked with foam. The left of the "Profile Cliff" photo represents the eastern extremity of the falls, where the waters leave the narrow chasm and continue their course toward the Indian Ocean. While returning to camp I came across a lot of baboons the size of eight-year-old boys, but, being alone, gave them a wide berth.

On the 25th, though loath to leave this enchanting spot, we rolled up our blankets and silently stole away; but not while my pulse beats shall I forget the experience of these three days. Mosatane was on hand to ferry us over, and invited us to his village to see his people. We followed him, and under a big tree in the vicinity of his compound set about preparing breakfast. We were honored by a visit from four of his wives, who brought us meal and Kaffir beer; we particularly appreciated the latter, for we were very thirsty. The day passed rather wearily, being besieged by natives from morning till night. I was mortified to discover

ABRUPT BEND AND "PROFILE CLIFF," ZAMBESI

that the chief object of Mosatane's inviting us to his village was that he might beg from us whatever he set eyes on. He did not get anything, all the same, except what he gave us an equivalent for. One soon gets sick of these people when finding that it is an utter impossibility for them to show a single disinterested act of kindness: be their present great or small, they without exception get angry if they do not receive a deal more than its value in return. Seldom, if ever, have I seen an exception to this.

We observed that the tribal mark of the Matoka is the absence of the two upper central incisors, these being removed in early life. The custom, though a personal disfigurement, is universal. Mosatane reveres the name of Livingstone, with whom he had made many long journeys, and tells numerous stories concerning him, but all in the highest praise of the great explorer. At Sesheke we met two old men, Makumba and Ratau, who also claimed to have been in the service of Livingstone; they vied with each other in extolling his character, and apparently recalled the memory of the years spent in his service with great pleasure.

In the early morning, after a cup of coffee, we were once more afoot; but in an hour or two fever began to assert itself on me, and I struggled along with an aching and throbbing head, while my mouth became so parched and dry that I felt as though the mucous membrane would strip off if I closed my lips. We rested for three hours at noon, and marched again until evening, covering about twenty-five miles. We lay down for the night near a pool of water, but mosquitoes were there in millions, and sleep was impossible. At daybreak, for which we had longed, I struggled to my feet again, still very feverish, but managed to do another twenty miles, which brought us to the place where we had left our canoe. In two and a half hours we were at Kazungula again.

For the past two days I have eaten nothing and done a good bit of tramping, and now feel much inclined to go to bed for a week. The journey to the falls and back has been a trying one, but we were more than repaid for the trouble, and with the aid of Madame Jalla's unremitting kindness I hope to be soon all right again.

February 28th. I feel very much better, only that the twenty-five to thirty-grain doses of quinine make my ears ring unpleasantly, and I can hear nothing else. But what is to be the next move? I cannot delay long here. No other way seems open but to cross the Kalahari Desert, visit Khama's town and see what an African township is like under a Christian native king (for I have seen enough of the other sort); then from Bamangwato to strike north through Mashonaland and reach my goal, the Lakes, in some way, not yet very clear to me. But, believing it to be possible, I will make the attempt.

I crossed the river to the west bank to interview two English hunters who are waiting for an answer from Lewanika to the request for permission to hunt elephants in his country. I found them very short of trade stuff, of which I have a good supply. They having a bullock-cart and oxen with two Colony drivers, whom I had the option of engaging, business was speedily arranged to our mutual satisfaction; and thus, most unexpectedly, ways and means for transport are once more provided. The oxen are kept some ten miles distant from here, beyond the "fly" belt that skirts the west bank of the Zambesi, and they can only come in here at night, when the tsetse is supposed not to bite. They are sent for and will be here by ten o'clock, when I load up and start without delay.

My goods are already across the drift, and in the evening I say good-by to Monsieur and Madame Jalla, who have been the essence of kindness to me. The time spent with them and my experience at Kazungula have been on a par with the fellowship and hospitality I enjoyed at the other stations of the French Zambesi mission, which is saying a good deal. At 11 P.M. the baggage is all aboard the cart, drawn by a span of twelve oxen. It is off at full speed, which is about the rate of a "Trades Procession" or a "Lord-Mayor's Show"; but they will get beyond "the fly" before daylight.

I spent the night in the Englishmen's camp, and next morning, after a sharp walk, reached Leshuma, where the oxen were outspanned awaiting my arrival. At this place Monsieur and Madame Coillard had to camp for over a year, waiting for the decision of Lewanika as to whether they were to be allowed an entrance into the Barotse Valley or not. At length their request was granted; but it must have been a weary time for them, the district is so lonely, wild, and dreary. Nearby is a solitary grave of a Swede named Oswald Bagger, who died here of fever in 1878.

After having lunch we trekked until 9 P.M., when we outspanned for the night. On again to Pandamatenka, where we take on an extra span of oxen. This place is of some interest, especially to Roman Catholics, from the fact that about eight years ago the Jesuits sent up a band of "Fathers" and "Brothers" to organize a mission station here. They had intended settling in the Barotse Valley, but entering the country without first obtaining the king's permission so incensed him against them that he ordered them back forthwith. Pandamatenka being a sort of neutral ground between Khama, Lobengula, and Lewanika, they decided to build under the patronage of G. Westbeach, a trader, whose station it was. Their dwelling-house and church still stand, the latter (see foreground of illustration) now utilized as a stable. The doors and window-frames that remain bear evidence of the skilled workmen they must have had with them; but their mission was a failure, the party being too large and their equipment altogether too elaborate and extensive compared with their very limited knowledge of the country and people. By bitter experience they learned that in such work "the race is not to the swift, nor the battle to the strong." Soon after their advent, and ere they had well begun their mission, one of the Brothers died, a Father was drowned on his way to the valley, the others got disheartened, and the mission was broken up. Even those who escaped from Pandamatenka fell victims to fever elsewhere. Westbeach, too, is dead, and his trading-store stands empty. The present occupants of the place are two half-breed hunters with a few bushmen. Here we found five heaps of stones, marking the last resting-places of Jolly, Cowley, Bairn, Baldwin, and Lowe—Europeans who succumbed to malarial fever.

PANDA-MA-TENKA

We had been told that at this place corn and vegetables were cultivated in abundance, and that we should be able to put in a supply for the journey; but we were contented with a limited purchase, as they charged us at the rate of three pounds per bag for corn and two shillings each for very poor pumpkins.

We trekked early on the 5th of March, the spare oxen driven behind by our Kaffirs. The next three days' journey was through rough country—either rocky belts of woodland, with stones and stumps that almost shook the cart to pieces, or over miles of swamp with black mud and water up to the axle. On Tuesday evening, feeling very "blue," and conscious of an approaching attack of fever, I was sitting in the cart holding my aching head between my hands, when the "desselboom" gave way with a crash, and we were thrown forward on the road, putting a period to our journey for that night, so we camped where we were. But by the time I could get out my blanket and lie down at the foot of a tree the fever had me in full force; the live-long night my head felt as if it would burst—skin hot and parched, temperature 106° F. Several times during the weary hours of darkness slight showers of rain fell, and although I had no shelter I wished it would come heavily and cool me a bit. Near morning perspiration broke out profusely and I was relieved. I took a cup of coffee, and thought I was better and got up, anxious to see to the repairing of the cart. The drivers brought in a small tree they had cut down, and were just commencing to hew it into shape, when I felt a sudden chill, accompanied by faintness, compelling me to lie down again. Such a fit of ague and fever followed as I have seen in others but never until now experienced, vomiting until my eyes were bloodshot, shaking until I had to hold by the root of a bush to steady myself, cold and bloodless, although now the sun was high and the thermometer registered 100° F. in the shade. By evening the new dessel-boom was finished and we trekked again. I was just able to crawl into the cart, but for the next two days could not eat a mouthful, only drink water—and such water! brackish and muddy.

To-day, the 12th, however, I am, thank God, feeling very much better. This is fortunate, for we are never sure that there are no lions lurking in the neighborhood when we lie down for the night. Here, and along our route for the next eight days, they abound. Last night they roared and growled within fifty paces of our camp, trying to stampede the oxen. There was, of course, no rest for either the drivers or myself, as we had to keep guard, rifle in hand, expecting an attack every minute. We met the annual transport wagons, three in number, bound for the Zambesi with supplies for the missionaries. The conductor told me that this morning, the lions, in spite of big fires, dogs, and guns, attacked his oxen, and lacerated one so badly that it had to be killed, while two bore ugly claw wounds. Four dogs went after them, but one, the biggest and bravest, never returned, so we shall have to keep a sharp lookout now.

I am making no attempt at writing a daily journal during this trip. One day is so like another that there is seldom an event worthy of record. The program of an ordinary day is very much thus: At the first reddening of the sky, about an hour before sunrise, the fire is stirred up and the kettle put on; meanwhile mats and blankets are stowed away, the "voige" (water-keg) filled, if we are fortunate enough to be near a "vley" (pool), cooking utensils collected and packed. The oxen are being inspanned, and by this time coffee is ready, which we swallow with a bit of bread baked in the ashes or a hollowed-out ant-hill. The long whips are cracked, the word "trek" is shouted, and the oxen move on; and now for five or six hours we lumber along, through the deep sand, rough rock, or swampy ground, through belts of mopani forest, and on through vast stretches of thorny bush armed with spikes like grappling hooks. By 10 A.M. we probably reach water, where we outspan and rest during the heat of the day, inspanning at three or four in the afternoon and going on till nine, when we bivouac for the night. The oxen are made fast by *reims* to the trek-chain; and after supper we each seek the lee side of a bush or a clump of grass, spread our mat under the starry sky, and wrap up for a few hours' repose.

While this routine may be taken as the rule, it is by no means without many exceptions. At times, for two whole days we will find no water, either for ourselves or the cattle, necessitating long treks. When about half-way across the desert the oxen were inspanned for twelve hours, pushing on to a spot where we expected to find a vley, but which, when we reached it, was almost dry. We had to collect a little from the holes made by the feet of game, but it was so thick and of such a vile odor that we could not swallow it. One of the drivers took a mouthful, and suffered all day in consequence. The poor beasts sucked the mud, refused to graze, loitering around the wagon, and during the night licked the broad iron tires of the wheels to cool their tongues. Played out, we could go no farther without a rest; but about two o'clock in the morning (now the third day of our thirst) we inspanned again, and dragged wearily on, almost at the fainting point for hours, when, just as the first rays of the sun shot across the arid plain, we descried in the distance what appeared to be a small lake, glistening like burnished silver. The oxen seemed to scent water in the air, and, mustering their waning energies, redoubled their speed, and in an hour we reached the lake, cattle and men plunging into it with a mad rush. But our joy was short lived; the poor animals moaned their disappointment, the drivers' faces were pictures of despair. How I looked I don't know, but how I felt may be imagined. It was a salt "pan" (lake), and the water a bitter brine. Slowly and sadly we turned around, utterly disheartened, and went on for two hours more, when we came upon a deep well containing several feet of muddy— but oh, so precious—sweet water. How fondly we sipped it! And with buckets we drew enough for the oxen, having to use the whips vigorously to keep off the herd while each one had its turn.

We rested for twenty-four hours so as to give them a chance to pick up. Two oxen suffering from lung sickness had been left on the road to follow as best they could with the spare span. One must have lingered behind and fallen a prey to lions, as we never saw him again; the other we shot, and used such portions of the flesh as we thought safe. We were not over nice about it, as for two weeks we had been without fresh meat, having seen no game except an occasional guinea-fowl, although we saw a great many fresh spoor of almost every kind of antelope, elephant, zebra, giraffe, hartebeest, etc., but mostly crossing our track, going north and south. I sighted several flocks of ostriches, and succeeded in knocking over two at long range. They were very wild, and without a horse it is difficult to hunt them. In each case they got up and disappeared in the bush, but were found dead next day by the bushmen, who brought me several handsome feathers —the only trophies I possess of ostrich-hunting.

Every few days we meet with small bands of these bushmen (Masarwa) in the most unlikely and unexpected places. They are wild children of the desert, homeless wanderers, and pigmies in stature; during the rainy season of a dirty yellow color, at other times hard to tell. They are spindle-shanked, and possess abdomens entirely disproportioned to their diminutive size. These queer little people speak a language so barbarous, with its perpetual click, click, click, that no white man has been able to acquire it. Many of them are veritable caricatures of the creature man. An armful of reeds or a cave provides all the shelter they ever know; they own no herds, cultivate no fields, but subsist upon the game, edible roots or bulbs, the larvæ of white ants, grasshoppers, and worms that they find in their familiar domains. But this creature, insignificant though he looks, is more than a match for the most formidable wild animal that roams the forest or plain.

In the chase he has no peer in any tribe in Africa, and knows better than any other how to obtain and prepare most virulent and promptly fatal poisons with which to smear the sharp points of his tiny arrows, while his small size and cat-like movements in the grass enable him to approach to within a short distance of his prey, unseen.

I had an opportunity last night of observing the effect of their poisoned shafts, and also their mode of hunting. A little fellow came to our camp to beg salt. While trying to talk with him through one of the drivers, he suddenly held up his hand and motioned us to be silent. He slung the quiver with his arrows over his shoulder, and, grasping his tiny bow, glided swiftly off into the grass in a stooping posture. Looking in the direction on which he seemed bent, we saw at a long distance the heads and necks of two giraffes appearing in the background of an ant-hill. In a very short time the cunning hunter had got within a few yards of them, still unobserved: fitting an arrow to his bow-string, in an instant he had aimed at and hit the larger of the two. The animal gave a frightened jump and leisurely walked away, the bushman returning as stealthily as he went. On expressing our surprise that he had not followed up the game, he in the coolest manner possible asked, "Why should I drive the meat away?" and naïvely remarked, "It will not go far." Nor was his confidence in the weapon misplaced, as we proved by the excellent giraffe steaks we had for breakfast next morning. The little hunter somewhat reluctantly parted with his interesting weap-

KHAMA, CHIEF OF BAMANGWATO

ons, in exchange for a teacupful of salt and three yards of cloth.

These curiosities—the primitive bow of supple wood, and the small bark quiver of cane-arrows, with their detachable ivory, poisoned points—are now in my collection.

CHAPTER XI.

FROM PALACHWE TO FORT VICTORIA.

Palachwe.—A terrible epidemic.—Malaria.—Semi-civilization.—Physically losing ground.—Khama and his country.—Total prohibition.—The Mangwato as a race.—Makalakas.—Darker phases of African life.— McKenzie and Hepburn.—The Matebele.—On the trek again.—My West Indians return.—A monotonous landscape.—Fort Macloutsie.—Hyenas and jackals.—*Multum in parvo*.—Tuli township.—"Show your passport." —A licensed prospector.—Mealies and pumpkins.—Lobengula's impis.— Matipi's kraal.—Whiskey shops.—Syndicates "dead broke."—White men's graves.—"Providential Pass."—A tragic story.—Zimbabwe.—An ancient stronghold.—Fort Victoria.—A hundred miles of sand.

THE journey across the Kalahari Desert puts the strength and endurance of both man and beast to the severest test; but on the 30th of March we reached Palachwe, the principal town of the Mangwato, having been just four weeks on the road. We feel very thankful, too, when we remember the many broken wagons, shattered wheels and dessel-booms we passed on the way, telling of long delays and great trouble to others who had attempted the journey under less favorable circumstances. It is nothing rare for travelers to be delayed for months in the middle of the desert by flooded swamps, oxen dying, or wagons hopelessly broken down, and obliged to send back for assistance. Yet we are here, with a measure of fair health and strength (with the exception of a troublesome cough which annoys me much, and seems come to stay), in a semi-civilized country under the good chief Khama. We outspanned in front of Messrs. Blackbeard Bros.' trading station, where we are invited to stay for a couple of weeks, until arrangements are made for our next move, which must be northward.

March 31st. I was called this morning to see Khama, his wife, and child (the child died the following day), who were all three down with fever. Not only they, but, as the chief tells me, fully half the natives are stricken with a bad type of malarial fever, which has assumed the form of an epidemic, an average of fifteen succumbing to the disease daily; while I am informed that since the year began, close upon three thousand of Khama's subjects have been cut off. He seems greatly distressed about it, imploring me to remain for a few weeks and render what medical aid I can to the sufferers, for this tide of death threatens to decimate the tribe. The night is made hideous by the gruesome cries of the hyenas as they join in the carnage among the many dead bodies but partially interred in the sand of the plain.

A very cursory glance at the situation of the town is sufficient to reveal the cause of its being so unhealthy, although it is the new town of the Mangwato, and only laid out in the latter part of 1889 (Shoshong, their old settlement, sixty or seventy miles south, having become untenable from lack of water). Palachwe occupies a valley at the base and west of the Chupong Hills, and covers an area of some sixteen square miles, with a population of say fifteen thousand people, composed of a number of villages in charge of sub-chiefs. The huts in these "staats" (villages) are built in circles, with a small lekhothla in the center. The soil is coarse, deep sand, wheeled vehicles sinking to a depth of from six inches to a foot on the roads in the town, and for miles around. Gardening is impossible without constant artificial irrigation, which the natives do not seem to understand or care to be bothered with, so that the land in and around the "staats" remains as it has ever been—unbroken *veldt*. Nor does the chief approve of even cutting down the superfluous bush or trees; consequently the fetid, foul air from the excrement and refuse of the cluster of huts hangs around the dwellings, the undergrowth preventing the free access of fresh air. Sanitary regulations there are none, and but few comfortable dwellings that might in some way be made to conform to the observance of laws which we consider conducive to health. No white man can own a foot of land in Khama's country, nor erect a square house, except by his special permission, and even then the chief claims it as his property; so that temporary residents have to content themselves, as a rule, with native huts of the very poorest construction. Rarely can they be truthfully called waterproof, and are not to be compared in any way with those of the Marotsi. The result is, at the close of the rainy season the grass thatch has become soaking wet and rots, when it is little better than a reeking dungheap, under which the night at least must be spent, inhaling the noxious vapors, that go far to produce the annual attacks of fever, which every white man seems to expect as a matter of course. Again, in almost any part of this extensive flat it is unnecessary to dig more than three or four feet below the surface to find water, and in many places it lies in green stagnant pools, giving off an offensive effluvia, particularly at night.

The officials and traders are obliged to send some miles to obtain water for domestic purposes, which is brought to the town in iron tanks mounted on wagons. No one need be surprised that fever makes such ravages in Khama's town of the Mangwato. However, here it is, and, though not feeling over bright, suffering from a sharp attack of bronchitis—the result of the many shelterless nights on the damp ground in the Kalahari—I must do what I can for the many patients, who already begin to come or send for help on hearing that a doctor has arrived among them.

Palachwe derives its name from the *kopjie* in the vicinity. "Mangwato" refers to the tribe, and "Bamangwato" to the country of the tribe, wherever it might locate. In the center of the town (Palachwe) is situated the headquarters of the Bechuana Trading Association, under the management of Mr. Gifford, well and favorably known in La Chapelle in the Canadian Northwest. Within a hundred yards of the Bechuana Trading Association premises stands the hut which does duty for a post-office, and across the road a telegraph station; the line being now open right through to Salisbury places Mashonaland in telegraphic communication with the outer world.

I was called on the 9th to see a young man who had fallen in front of and was run over by his wagon, sustaining a compound fracture of the *femur*. I fear it will be a bad case, as he cannot be persuaded that it will be necessary for him to remain quiet on his back

for several weeks. I will attend him closely, and hope
that union may take place before I leave. Much to my
annoyance, on visiting him the following day I found
the bandages and splints had all been undone by a native doctor, who declared it an utter impossibility that
the fracture should heal without the orthodox fetich
performance being submitted to—burning of certain
herbs, placing the limb in the smoke, etc. I fixed him
up again, and explained, in as strong language as my
interpreter could muster, that if his wizard was permitted to interfere again I should see him no more.

April 26th. It is now nearly a month since I reached
Palachwe; and although the chief and the white residents are anxious for me to stay a little longer, I find
myself physically losing ground and getting weaker
every day. For scarcely twenty-four consecutive hours
during my sojourn here have I not felt the effects of
this trying climate, either in utter prostration from the
malarial poison, or in repeated and long-continued spells
of high temperature. I have decided to get out of this
to-morrow by wagon, and steer northward through
Mashonaland *via* Salisbury. During the month, besides Khama (who has suffered two relapses, but is
now seemingly all right) and hundreds of his people, I
have had seventeen out of the twenty Europeans in the
town under treatment, also several Dutchmen passing
through. Happily, there have been no fatal cases among
them to record; although the fever assumed a very malignant type in five instances, all are now convalescent.
The death-rate among the natives, who have had no
medical aid except from Kaffir doctors, has continued
very high; but now that the winter approaches the

probabilities are that the worst of the epidemic is over for the present.

Among many curios I brought home from Africa, there are none I prize so highly as the magnificent kaross, composed of six hundred and twenty-six tiger-cat tails, which was presented to me by the white men of Palachwe, with the following letter:

PALACHWE, April 23, 1892.

Dr. Johnston, Palachwe:

DEAR SIR: We, the undersigned, on the eve of your departure from Palachwe, beg to hand you this little note, and the accompanying kaross as a slight return for the very great kindness we have all experienced at your hands; and in asking you to accept same we would mention that if it sometimes reminds you of the friends you have made and helped here, it will indeed have answered its purpose.

Wishing you a very pleasant trip and a long life, we are, dear sir,
Yours very sincerely,
CHAS. A. ENSOR, ALBERT E. GILES,
PERCY G. WYLD, P. HOWARD WILLIAMS,
C. H. M. BOON, H. GILES.

Much has already been written concerning Khama, his country, and people, both by missionaries and travelers. The former, as a rule, champion the cause of the native, extolling his virtues and condoning his failings, while the latter are only too often under the necessity of depending on prejudiced parties for their information. What we have to say will be simply comparative, and confined, as much as possible, to personal observation, avoiding sentiment—so indispensable an adjunct to writings on Africa nowadays. We are told the public likes romance; perhaps it does; but there are some who prefer plain facts, and for such we write.

Khama is a noble example of what Christianity and civilization can do for the African. Both friends and foes acknowledge him to be a straightforward, honest, and upright man. Stern and vigorous in administration, he enforces his laws with undeviating firmness and impartiality, particularly in the suppression of the drink traffic. A trader discovered selling drink to a native is forthwith expelled from the country. So extreme are his personal feelings on the subject, that he declined to drink the medicine I prescribed for him during his illness because it was in a bottle, but took it readily when sent in a jug. A native who attempts to make Kaffir beer—so largely consumed in almost every other part of central Africa—is not only exiled with his family, but has all his lands, cattle, and household goods confiscated, excepting cooking-pots and blankets; and with no respect of persons, Khama's own brother-in-law having had to share this fate only a few months ago. In a word, under no pretense whatever are intoxicating liquors supposed to be obtained in Palachwe, not even for medicinal purposes.

Seeing he so jealously guards his people against the baneful effects of strong drink, one would naturally conclude that Khama is equally ambitious for their advancement and elevation socially, by inculcating those principles that should regulate Christian homes and families, and without which no community can be other than debased and immoral. But such is not the case. Any effort to improve their dwellings the better to observe ordinary social laws, as in reference to the separation of the sexes, etc., is speedily vetoed. He lives in one round Kaffir hut himself, and his people must

WATERCART, MANAWATO

aspire no higher; hence we found whole families with grown-up sons and daughters herded together promiscuously in their small round grass and mud hovels. In no instance have we seen the semblance of a partition, not even a bit of calico hung up to divide the sleeping-places, while immorality is more brazen-faced than among the most uncivilized we have met hitherto. The numerous cases of syphilis and venereal complaints that have come under my notice here for the first time since leaving the West Coast prove all too conclusively that something more is wanted besides the exclusion of alcoholic liquors before the majority of Khama's people can be truthfully numbered among the trophies won to Christianity in Africa.

The Mangwato as a tribe are of small stature, and coarse-featured. The tribal mark is formed by making four perpendicular incisions three quarters of an inch long in front of the ears over the zygomatic arch. They make no attempt at dressing the hair; the men cut it short, and the women have their heads shaved with the regularity of a Chinaman. Female decorations consist of an assortment of iron and brass armlets and anklets, and in addition tiers of rings composed of small blue beads reaching almost to the knees. The headmen wear European clothing, and the aspiration of all the Mangwato proper is to dress like white men.

They are averse to manual labor, work of any kind being considered undignified. Their chief occupation is the making of karosses. But this handicraft has seen its best days, as since Khama came under British protectorate the sale of gunpowder, cartridges, or firearms has been so restricted that there is very little hunting of wild animals now. As usual among such people, the bulk of the hard work falls upon the women. They till the ground, stamp the mealies, and act as maids-of-all-work to their husbands and brothers. What we have written concerning slavery in the Barotse applies also to Bamangwato, although perhaps in a milder form. Yet over fifty per cent. of Khama's people are slaves (Makalakas), subject to his orders, his sub-chiefs, or such of the Mangwato as may have permission to appropriate their labor. These Makalakas are the representatives of many tribes conquered and captured in by-gone days, when the Mangwato was a strong and warlike nation. Still, many friends of freedom would be glad to see Khama add to his many virtues and humane laws that of equal rights to all his subjects, and place those victims of "the accidents of war" on a footing with the Mangwato, and not the abject slaves they are at present.

But why, it may be suggested, refer to these darker phases of African life? Well, for one reason, because there are many who desire to know both sides. It would certainly be more agreeable, and perhaps more popular, to write only that which is pleasing; but for the sake of those especially who may be anticipating coming to this country, I am endeavoring in calm deliberation to acquire a knowledge of the regions and people along my route, judging impartially and without prejudice, seeking to record only that which I believe to be indisputably true. Untold harm has actually been done by the publication of one-sided reports, purporting to be faithful descriptions of certain portions of the Dark Continent, but written (when the truth is known) by men who are simply the tools of parties having selfish motives for booming this or that territory where their interests lie, and by writers who cater to that class of readers to whom books of travel are palatable only as they smack of hair-breadth escapes, thrilling adventures, etc.

In many instances young men occupying good situations at home have been induced to resign their positions and come out here with the hope of bettering themselves, only to find that they have been grossly deceived; and if they do not succumb to fever, dysentery, or drink, they embrace the first opportunity presenting itself of returning home, with a very much increased appreciation of the mother country. Even missionary reports often fail to tell the truth concerning the field in which they seek to create an interest, fearing that a full account might discourage contributors. The evil effect of this policy is not far to seek: half of the missionaries we have met during our journey state in so many words that their coming to Africa has been fraught with sore disappointment, both as regards the country and the work.

But to return to the Mangwato. While what we have written in reference to them applies to the tribe as a whole, there are many happy exceptions. The labors of McKenzie and Hepburn during these many years have not been in vain, for besides the chief there are a large number of natives whose consistent and exemplary lives prove that their profession of Christianity is something more than the mere observance of outward formalities; and there can be no question that great and lasting good has resulted from the long and earnest toil of the missionaries.

It was with deep regret that we learned, on arriving at Palachwe, that on account of a dispute between Khama and Mr. Hepburn the latter had retired from the field and returned to England. This unfortunate circumstance has been a great blow to the mission. The splendid brick church in course of erection and near completion is now at a standstill, and I fear will remain so until the London Missionary Society can send out another man.

The contrast between the Mangwato and the Matebele in the adjoining country on the north is very marked, illustrating the power and influence of the chiefs over the people. The Matebele are Zulus who, owing to inter-tribal wars, were obliged to leave the south and trek northward. They are ruled by the savage chief Lobengula, who, while he in no way molests or opposes the four missionaries who live in his country and carry on a work that has existed for over thirty years (being originally established by Dr. Moffatt), like Lewanika, assumes an attitude toward them quite as antagonistic to success as if he were openly hostile. Shaking his clinched fist at his people, he tells them, "You may become Christians if you like, but——" and there he stops, for his people know him well enough to understand what the menace implies. Hence the results, thus far, of these long years of self-sacrificing labor are almost *nil*. This I learned from Rev. Mr. Elliott, one of their oldest and most experienced missionaries, whom I had the pleasure of meeting here with his sick wife, on their way to Cape Town. He also informed me that not half a dozen natives can be found in the whole country who would boldly assert their allegiance to Christianity; one or two dared to do so, and were promptly knocked on the head, by order of the chief.

But our baggage is on board the wagon, our eighteen oxen are ready to be inspanned, and we trek to-night north toward the Zambesi. I have thought it best to send my two Jamaicans, Frater and Jonathan, on to Cape Town, Mr. Elliott kindly promising to take charge of them *en route* homeward. I am sorry to part with them, as I am still a thousand miles from the point in Africa I wish to reach. They have been of great service to me, and the idea of employing Christian natives of the West Indies as assistants to pioneers in Central Africa I have proved by this journey to be quite practicable. But as means of transporting trade goods and luggage seem to get more expensive and difficult to procure the farther east we travel, I do not feel justified in taking them beyond Bechuanaland. But why not leave them with the missionaries, as proposed? At Bamangwato there is no missionary, as I have already stated, and in any case I do not see that the fit time has come yet. Even those left at Bihe I would recommend to return as soon as building operations are completed on the Cisamba station, as it is only in the opening up of new spheres that their services can be profitably utilized. At present little or no effort is being put forth to reach the numerous tribes occupying the vast regions five hundred miles north and five hundred miles south of the road we have traveled from Bihe, save that noble little band composing the French mission on the

Zambesi. They are not constituted to act as organizers of work, and until white men are forthcoming to lead the van, rather than put friends at home to the expense of supporting them, without the prospect of accomplishing anything, we deem it expedient that they remain in their own country, for the present.

Mr. Ellard, a young Englishman in the employ of Messrs. Blackbeard Bros., being threatened with pulmonary trouble, has volunteered to accompany me part of the way at least, in the expectation that the higher plateau may benefit him. So I have laid in a supply of provisions for the road, sufficient, I hope, for two of us, until we reach Salisbury. The prohibitive prices charged here for food-stuffs forbid extravagance; but "necessity knows no law," and past experience has taught me not to depend on what *may* be obtained from the natives on the way. The usual monotony attends traveling through this part of the country. There is but little variety in the scenery; an odd kopjie (hill), scrubby thorn-bush, or small mopani tree, with a great expanse of dry, wiry, sapless, straggling grass, constitutes the landscape. The road, however, is fairly good, and we lumber along, the drivers bawling out the names of the oxen with threats and exhortations, and cracking their long whips. We cover about fifteen miles a night, one trek from sunset until 9 or 10 P.M., and another from 1 A.M. until daylight, when the oxen are set free to graze for the day. This seems a slow mode of traveling, and so it is; but it must be remembered that we have over five hundred miles of a rough road before us, and a heavily laden wagon to be drawn by the same oxen the whole way. On the morning of the 2d

CROSSING THE LUNDI

a driver went out and shot a splendid eland antelope, the flesh of which we found delicious, and made a good addition to our larder, as with care a hindquarter keeps for a week.

We reached Macloutsie on the 3d, where we find a fort, and headquarters camp of the Bechuanaland Border Police. They are here to enforce British authority and protect its interests in Bechuanaland, although what these interests are seems at present problematical. The troops, two hundred and fifty in number, are recruited from Cape Colony and the mother country, and commanded by officers from British regiments. According to Sir Sydney Sheppard, "the expense of the force is about £90,000, and the whole expenditure on the Protectorate is just over £100,000; the revenue at present is very small." (See *The Cape Argus*, weekly edition, July 28, 1892.)

The elevation of the district is much higher than Palachwe, and healthier, there being but three or four patients in the well-appointed hospital at the time of our visit.

Two days beyond Macloutsie the drivers went hunting again, and shot a wart-hog—a horrible-looking animal, with tusks six inches long, and a cartilaginous protuberance two and a half inches in length. A little behind and three inches above each eye the flesh is too rank to eat. Along this part of the road wolves and jackals come howling around the camp at night; but the fires keep them at bay. The track is rough in the extreme, not only from the numerous stones and holes in the way, but, what is even worse, stumps of trees varying in height from a few inches to a foot. The broad wheels persist in mounting them, to come down with a dull, sickening thud that threatens not only concussion of the brain, but of every internal organ of the weary traveler, who tries to snatch a couple of hours' sleep on the top of the cargo, compelling him at last to sit up and improvise a spring seat of his rolled-up blankets, so as to lessen the risk of serious injury from *contre coup*.

On the 8th we outspanned within three miles of Tuli, and walked on in the morning to see this "mushroom" staat that has sprung up since Rhodes & Co. began to boom Mashonaland as England's Eldorado. A small hut at the outskirts surprised us not a little; for the proprietor, besides announcing, on a board of many colors fixed to a pole in front of his establishment, that he was a hairdresser and barber, also intimated that in his twelve-feet-square domicile he was prepared to accommodate, for a consideration, hungry and somnolent wayfarers with refreshment and beds. I entered to have a look at his *multum in parvo* and get a "crop." I found the artist—an ex-policeman—busy with a very refractory subject, a prospector, maudlin drunk. Talk he would, while being shaved, in spite of the barber's expostulations. As a second party in a like condition sat awaiting his turn, we proposed taking a stroll. Intoxicated white men seemed the order of the day; we met them at every turn, although they have to pay twenty-five shillings per bottle for brandy and five shillings per bottle for ale.

Tuli is situated on the south bank of the river Sharshi, and boasts of a small hotel and half a dozen trading-stores, built mostly of wood and corrugated iron. There are, besides, two stores belonging to the British South African Company filled with great quantities of wheat meal, while in the open air are stacked some seven hundred bags of mealies; but evidently the administration of the commissariat department of the company is rather defective, as there is not a single bag of either commodity fit for food. This shameful waste of grain has not been confined to Tuli, however; the same company hoarded a thousand bags of mealies during 1890 at Alibi, until they had to be thrown away on the veldt; and nearly the same quantity was disposed of in a similar manner at Macloutsie. The over-sanguine purchasers probably intended to lay in a supply for the hundreds of horses, which, though brought up from the Colony, refused to live in such a climate.

In the center of the town, on a small kopjie, a fortification has been constructed, and is garrisoned by some five policemen, every white man in the district being under pledge to aid in holding the fort in event of an attack from the Matebele, their most formidable enemy. Having obtained permission of the captain, I proceeded to do some photography from the fort, but was warned not to climb over the breastwork, as the sandbags would not permit of being walked upon!

Whether it was the intense heat or having had nothing to eat from early morning, I know not; but while in the act of pulling the slide a feeling of faintness and giddiness came over me, so oppressive and painful that the operation became anything but a pastime. I got down as soon as I could and sought a friendly shelter, and lay down for a couple of hours, helpless as if paralyzed. But a cup of tea revived me a bit; and the wagons having come up early in the afternoon, so as to get across the five hundred yards of sandy river-bed of the Sharshi during daylight, I walked on after them.

I may remark that not more than ten per cent. of South African rivers can be called permanent. They flow only during the three or four months of the wet season. For another month water will be found in isolated pools, but for the balance of the year they will be perfectly dry. Since leaving the Zambesi we have crossed scores of water-courses, but in not more than two did we find a running stream.

When about to get on the wagon for the purpose of reaching the other side, a policeman rode up demanding to see our passport or license to enter Mashonaland. We made some observations in reference to our possessing a Portuguese passport through their country as a foreigner, but thought it rather extraordinary that a British subject should require a permit to pass through (so-called) British territory. "Can't help that, sir; my orders are to stop every white man from passing through Tuli unless he can show a prospector's license." Vain were our protests that we were not "prospectors"; nor would we know the difference between reef quartz and alluvial gold, if we saw it. A policeman on duty is not open to reason, and, though feeling very ill, we had no alternative but to march back to a small mud hut, where a minion of the law duly registered us as prospectors, and on payment of a small fee handed us strips of paper to that effect. It was now getting late, and we hurried back to join our wagon. To cross the river-bed was no light work, the wheels sinking to the hubs in the wet sand and requiring double spans of oxen to pull it through; but it was accomplished without any mishap, and, having trekked seven miles more, we tied up. Being unable to eat anything, Ellard went out to a Boer camp for the purpose of purchasing some milk. They allowed him to have a quart, and let him down easy by charging only two shillings and sixpence.

We are now out of Khama's country, Sharshi being the northern boundary. From the time we entered it at Leshuma, ten miles south of the Zambesi, we have traversed in a sort of semicircle over six hundred miles of his territory, and have come to the conclusion that it may suit Kaffirs well enough, whose daily wants are limited to a few mealies or pumpkins (I have seen no other products of the soil in any quantity during the ten weeks of my wanderings in British Bechuanaland), but it can never be of any use to Europeans for purposes of colonization. There are prairie farms in the United States and Canada any single one of which yields annually more agricultural produce than does the whole of Khama's kingdom. "Irrigate, irrigate," says the farmer. With what, pray? For eight months in the year there is scarcely a running stream in the country; during that time the only water to be found is in the pits and stagnant pools called "vleys," scattered few and far between over the veldt, becoming reduced in number as the season advances.

We crossed the Umpagi on the 10th, and are now in the Banyai country. The roads are still very rough, being cut up every few yards by *spruits* and *sluits* from a few feet to several yards in depth, requiring the frequent application of the brakes to prevent the wagon from crushing the oxen as it plunges into the ravine.

The Banyai natives are refugees from various tribes, and have their kraals among the fastnesses of the hills, where they have been driven through fear of the Matebele. Like the Mashonas, they are very poor, having been similarly plundered of almost everything they possessed by the raiding warriors of Lobengula, who not only seize their cattle, but take captive and enslave their women and children, assegaing their men. The dress of the women consists chiefly of large coils of beads round the waist and ankles. They shave their heads with the exception of a round spot on the crown about three inches in diameter, and over all, of course, grease. The men, as usual, are more simple in their attire, contented with the regulation small tab of wild-cat skin fore and aft.

Four days more saw us outspanned by the Booby River, surrounded by numerous grand kopjies rising abruptly from the plain, some of them to the height of eight hundred to a thousand feet, bare and bald, seemingly one solid block of granite, closely resembling those we first saw in the Cisange country west of Bihe. While out hunting, the drivers encountered a lion, but there is no exciting story to tell of the adventure, for with commendable discretion they sought refuge in the camp. Two days ago four lions attacked the oxen of a transport rider, killing several; but thus far we have escaped them.

Next day we halted at Matipi's kraal, and bartered for some vegetables with salt, gun-caps, and matches. I climbed an adjoining kopjie for the purpose of taking photos, and found quite a village near the top, composed of poor little huts built in the nooks and crevices

ZIMBABWE RUINS

of the rocks; having no soil in which to fix the upright sticks, the foundations were strengthened by layers of mud.

The following day we crossed the Gondogne. There is a small whiskey shop here, run by white men, nominally for the convenience of travelers, and one of many that have been opened between Tuli, Salisbury, and Umtali since the British took possession, and generally situated as near as possible to the regular outspanning places. The Salisbury correspondent of *The Cape Argus Weekly*, April 6, 1892, writes:

"The following list will be interesting to many, and also useful to those intending to trek Mashonalandward. Wayside places on main road, Tuli—Salisbury. From Tuli:

M. Pagre's, 15 miles. Campbell and Drummond.
Umzingwan, 35 miles. Hinds and Ferman.
M. Gobu's, 80 miles. Withers.
M. Tibi's, 92 miles. Drummond.
————, 106 miles. Dillon and Perkins.
Nuenetsi River, 122 miles. Sanderson.
Lundi River, 155 miles. Grant.
Toqwi River, 182 miles. Saunders and Prinslotz.
Fern Spruit, 194 miles. Bowden.
Fort Victoria, 204 miles. Various hotels and stores.
M. Kari's, 234 miles.
Imytsitsi. Werrit and Young.
Fort Charter. Dunn.
Umfuli.
Hanyani.
Six-mile Spruit. Mashonaland Auctioneering Co.
Salisbury.

"The places left blank have been filled, but so far I have not received the names. From Salisbury to Umtali the following is the list:

    16 miles from Salisbury. Duncan and Kerr.
    32 miles from Salisbury. Graham and White.
    Marandella's, Bottomley. Head and Moore.
    M. Chiki's, 78 miles. Lewis.
    Laurencedale.
    Kesapi Drift, 108 miles. Reid Bros.
    ————, 130 miles. Bates and Watson.
    Odsi, 150 miles. Holberg."

Albeit they are of but little benefit to a hungry man, as we have inquired in vain for bread at every one we passed. This, with the fact that out of a hundred wagons now on the road to Salisbury seventy carry an average of two thousand bottles of intoxicating liquor each, is not much to the credit of Europeans, nor to the company under whose patronage it is admitted. It is the unanimous opinion of those we have met that whiskey dealers will get their fingers burned this time, for there is neither money to buy nor people to drink a tithe of the stuff that is pouring into Salisbury. This rush is owing to the scarcity of liquor and provisions last year. The rivers being full, wagons were detained on the road until whiskey brought £30 per case; champagne, £5 per bottle; Boer meal, £12 10s. per bag; and one-pound tins of provisions, 10s. each. The times have changed materially since then. Many of the mining claims have not turned out to be such bonanzas as was expected; four syndicates have smashed up, dismissed their men, and abandoned in disgust the fields that refuse to yield sufficient of the precious metal to pay working expenses; while almost every day we meet bands of disappointed prospectors returning down country, poorer men than when they passed up, full of hope, a year or so ago. One graphically described things in general by remarking, "It ain't no country for the white man anyhow, even if gold is there, where to live he has to be a-eatin' of quinine all day long."

We could not but sympathize with one young fellow, whose health seemed completely shattered, and who but eighteen months before had gone up in company with two brothers, but now returns alone, both the brothers having died of fever after sinking their all, some fifteen hundred pounds, in fruitless search for "the wealth of Mashonaland."

We crossed the Lundi River on the morning of the 19th—a tough bit of work, taking two spans of thirty-six oxen, pulling their hardest, to get the wagon through. The river, though low, had a good stream running. During the rainy season the Lundi rises very high, and, owing to the rapidity of the current, becomes impassable for transport wagons, many being delayed on the bank for months at a time. Then fever, aided by the canteen close by, gets in its deadly work. There were no fewer than fifty-seven white men's graves, mostly on the south side, made during the last wet season.

We are now in Mashonaland. The landscape grows more hilly and rugged as we move northward, while the same smooth-faced, rocky kopjies predominate here as we noticed farther south. The vegetation on the plains is richer, the trees larger, and the scenery in general much more interesting; but there are no signs of cultivation anywhere, and the few natives who come out to trade seem to set great store by their meager stock of garden products. One brings half a pound of mealies in a basket little larger than a coffee-cup, while another swings in his hand one small sweet potato suspended by a string, and for which they each ask a shilling or a yard of limbo, but go away satisfied, toward evening, with a tablespoonful of salt.

We have now traveled twenty-three days without seeing a native village, with the exception of the kraal at Matipi's. Through the Naqua Pass the high, rocky bluffs on each side present quite an Alpine appearance. Emerging into the open country, we outspanned, and were entertained the whole day by a concert of unearthly whoops and yells issuing from a glen where a Mashona kraal lay hid. A big beer-drink was evidently on hand. We continued our journey the same night through "Providential Pass," where the Pioneer Column was so agreeably disappointed in not being attacked by Lobengula's warriors; hence the name.

On the 22d we reached the Toquani, another hard "river to cross." Last year at this place three prospectors on their way to Salisbury had a melancholy experience. The eldest of the party having been gored by an ox, one of his companions boldly ventured to cross the swollen river on horseback to call medical aid from Victoria. He had reached the center of the stream, when a crocodile seized him by the leg, mangling it fearfully, and dragged him down to some reeds, where he lay in a helpless condition all night, doing his best to keep the monster at bay with his revolver. At daybreak his moans brought friends to his assistance, who carried him to Victoria. But it was too late; gangrene had already set in. He succumbed next day, and was laid to rest by the side of a young Englishman whom fever and hunger had cut off a few days previously (kind-hearted countrymen had planted a few flowers on the graves, and erected a palisade of sticks to protect them from the hyenas), while the comrade for whose sake he had attempted to ford the river died by the wayside.

We reached Victoria on the morning of the 24th and outspanned at the new township. I walked back to the fort, about four miles, for the purpose of picking up Kaffirs to carry my photo apparatus, blankets, and some provisions, and started about noon to visit the Zimbabwe ruins, fifteen miles southeast by east. By sundown we were busy cooking our supper in an open space near these marvelous memorials of a great but long defunct people. The night was bitterly cold for a bed on the bare earth, and we had only enough firewood to last a couple of hours; so we hailed with relief the first streak of day, and got astir stiff and cramped. With dry grass we made up sufficient fire to prepare a cup of hot tea, which had a wonderful effect in reviving our spirits. I then set about seeking points of vantage for the tripod, but found it impossible, even with a wide-angle lens, to get the curious tower within the rotunda. Its position is much confined by high trees and broken walls, while the long grass and weeds would require half a dozen men clearing up for days before the camera could be brought to bear successfully on much that is most interesting among these grand relics of a people whose identity so far is a matter of speculation.

After taking a view of the rotunda from the northeast, we gathered our traps and climbed to the top of the kopjie, where the remains of the ancient fort are to be found. Here again we were foiled in the attempt to get pictures; everywhere the summit of the southeast portion has been built upon, and so closely that one can only walk in and out among the narrow passages and small rooms, but nowhere could we find sufficient distance to focus upon more than a few feet of wall at a time. Why these Phœnicians, Arabians, or whoever they may have been, should have crowded themselves and their stronghold into such a limited space is explained when in walking around to the north side we find the only entrance is through a crevice between two huge rocks, so small as to admit of but one person at a time; while the boulders present a perpendicular front about forty feet high, uniting with others of the same character to form a wall across the kopjie almost as impregnable to the weapons of modern as it must have been to those of ancient warfare. Access from any other direction is impossible on account of the high, smooth-faced, rocky cliff of ninety feet on the opposite side, which in several places has been supplemented by the addition of walls from fifteen to twenty feet in height, and built so as to form a continuation of the precipice.

To those archæologically inclined we would recommend the book entitled "The Ruined Cities of Mashonaland," by J. T. Bent, Esq., an expert and scientist who

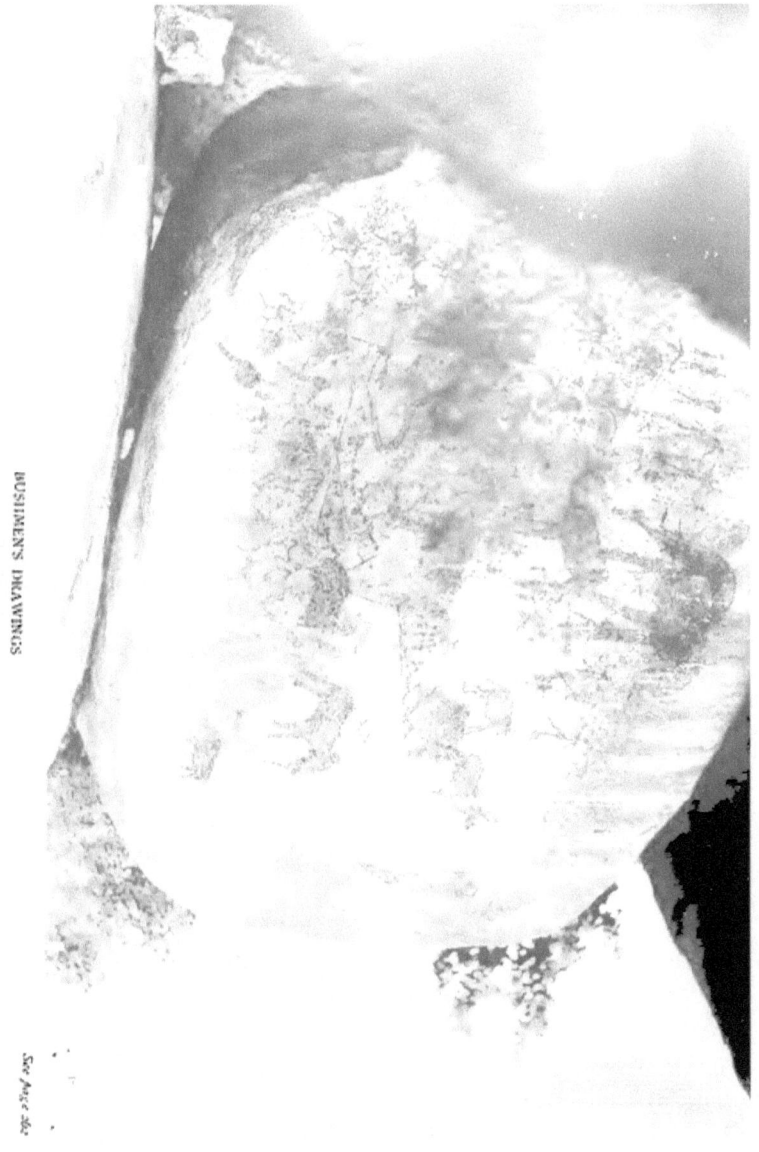

BUSHMEN'S DRAWINGS

See page 80.

visited these ruins a short time ago, and from whose description we take the following extracts:

"The prominent features of the Great Zimbabwe ruins, which cover a large area of ground, are, firstly, the large circular ruin with its round tower on the edge of a gentle slope on the plain below; secondly, the mass of ruins in the valley immediately beneath this; and thirdly, the intricate fortress on the granite hill above, acting as the acropolis of the ancient city. These we will now discuss in their order.

"When we reached the Great Zimbabwe the circular ruin was on the inside a dense mass of tropical vegetation; creepers and monkey ropes hung in matted confusion to the tall trees, forming a jungle which it was almost impossible to penetrate, and added to the mazy labyrinth of walls a peculiar and almost awe-inspiring mystery.

"It was the work of some days to clear this off with the aid of native workmen, while at the same time we proceeded with our excavations in the neighborhood of the tower and other prominent portions of the building.

"As for the walls themselves, they were nearly free from vegetation, for, owing to the absence of mortar, no lichen, moss, or creeper could thrive on them, and those few things which had penetrated into crevices were of a succulent character, which formed their branches to the shape of the interstices. To this fact is due the wonderful state of preservation in which these ruins are found.

"What appeared at first sight to be a true circle eventually proved elliptical—a form of temple found at Marib, the ancient Saba and capital of the Sabæan kingdom in Arabia, and at the Castle of Nakab al Hajar, also in that country.* Its greatest length is two hundred and eighty feet; the wall at its highest point is thirty-five feet above the ground, and fifteen feet at the lowest; its greatest base thickness is sixteen feet two inches, and its thinnest point is about five feet. . . .

"The labyrinthine character of the interior will be best grasped by a glance at the plan. Entering from the northern portal, we at once plunge into its intricacies. The great and astounding feature is the long narrow passage leading direct from the main entrance to the sacred inclosure, so narrow in parts that two people cannot walk abreast; while on either side of you rise the stupendous walls, thirty feet in height, and built with such evenness of courses and symmetry that as a specimen of the dry builder's art it is without a parallel. The large blocks of cut stone used in Egyptian, Greek, and Roman masonry must have been comparatively easy to deal with as compared with these small stones of rough granite built in even courses in a circular wall of immense thickness and height. The idea at once suggests itself that the people who erected these walls had at one time been accustomed to build in bricks, and that in the absence of this material they had perfected a system of stone-building to represent as nearly as possible the appearance of brick. Also another reason for the use of small stones may have been to enable them to construct the tower and curves with greater accuracy. The facings of the stones are all uniform, but most of them run back into the wall irregularly, acting in the same way as *throughs* in our dry-built

* Encyclopædia Britannica.

walls at home in preserving the building from falling. In this narrow passage, at point 8 is the remarkable hole, executed with perfect neatness through the thickest part of the wall, about the actual use of which I am able to give no definite theory. It could not have been used for drainage or defense; and in the fortress above there are two similar tunnels equally inexplicable. . . .

"I will now proceed to describe the hill fortress approaching it from the valley below. . . . The kopjie itself is of great natural strength, being protected on one side by gigantic granite boulders, and on the south by a precipice from seventy to ninety feet in height, and on the only accessible side the ancient inhabitants constructed a wall of massive thickness, like those of the ruins below. This wall is thirteen feet thick on the summit, with a batter of one foot in six; it is thirty feet high in parts, and the flat causeway on the top was decorated on the outside edge by a succession of small round towers alternating with tall monoliths. Seven round towers in all we made out, about three feet in diameter, and several others had been destroyed by the fall of a portion of the wall. This system of round towers and monoliths produces one of the most peculiar and unique forms of decoration I have ever seen. . . . In one place is a narrow sloping gully four feet across, ascending between two boulders, and protected, for no conceivable reason, by six alternate buttresses and a wall at the upper end, forming a zigzag passage narrowed in one place to ten inches. Walls of huge size shut off separate chambers. In all directions everything is tortuous; every inch of ground is protected with buttresses and traverses. Here, too, as in the large circular building below, all the entrances are rounded off, and I imagine that here we have quite the oldest portion of the ruins, built at a time when defense was the main object. When they were able to do so with safety, they next constructed the circular temple below, and as time went on they erected the more carelessly put together buildings around, which I have described."

A number of Mashonas have taken refuge on the hill-top, forming quite a large kraal, and so far escaping the raiding and plundering impis of Lobengula; for no sooner are the Matebele known to be on the war-path than the natives betake themselves with their small cattle through the crevice, where, once inside, three or four armed men are more than a match for a regiment.

By 11 A.M. I had finished my work, and, delighted with our visit to Zimbabwe, we set out for the wagons; but on coming to a brook we remembered that we had omitted breakfast. We stopped and boiled water in our "billy," threw in some tea, and this served to wash down the bit of bread we had saved for this repast. This done, we were off once more.

The extremes of temperature are so great at this season of the year that it is hard to tell whether we suffer most from the cold during the night or the sweltering heat of the day. We have no time to delay thinking of it, however, as we do not wish to keep the wagons waiting; we generally like to trek about sundown.

By four o'clock we had covered the fifteen miles to Victoria, of which place there is little to say, except that there are several temporarily built stores, and a few police of the British South African Company. But why so few are there, no one knows. A foolhardy confidence is placed by the company in the professed friendship and pacific attitude of Lobengula toward the English; but those who best know the crafty old chief of the Matebele declare that an attack on the Europeans is inevitable, and that at no distant date. For, even now, although Lo-ben is receiving a pension of one hundred pounds a month in gold, his younger braves are fretting like sleuth-hounds in the leash for liberty to—as they say—wipe out the white invaders of their country. A fort has been constructed with a broken-backed provision-shed in the center, and a trench and breastwork that would be no formidable barrier to the advance of a company of schoolboys, not to speak of a charge of Zulus. Mr. Bent, the archæologist already referred to, comments on this place as follows:

"In point of fact, the scenery of Mashonaland is nothing if not quaint. . . . Fort Victoria has no redeeming point of beauty about it whatsoever, being placed on a bare, flat plateau, surrounded in the rainy season by swamps. Nearly everybody was down with fever when we got there; provisions were at famine prices—for example, seven shillings for a pound of bacon and the same price for a tin of jam; and the melancholy aspect of affairs was enhanced by the hundred and fifty saddles placed in rows within the fort, which had once belonged to the hundred and fifty horses brought up by the pioneers, all of which had died of horse-sickness.

"The diseases to which quadrupeds are subject in this country are appalling. One man of our acquaintance brought up eighty-seven horses, of which eighty-six died before he got to Fort Victoria."

Four miles more, and we reach the wagons, rather footsore, and a bit hungry. The oxen are being driven up as we get into camp. An hour more, and we are on the trek again, traveling slowly, on account of the deep sand, grass fires sweeping through the scraggy bush for miles on either side. Two days of this and we find ourselves on a great desert plain, where we look in every direction for some sign of life on this vast stretch of sunburnt earth—in vain. We cannot even obtain wood enough to cook our food, having to collect dry ox-dung for this purpose, little thinking that this was to continue, with the exception of one or two narrow belts of thorn-bush and "wait-a-bit," for nearly a hundred miles.

CHAPTER XII.

FROM FORT VICTORIA TO INYAMACAMBE.

Fort Charter.—A deserted village.—Chartered companies.—Salisbury at last!—The wealth of Mashonaland.—A vegetable market.—The argument of the upper ten.—British influence.—Missions in Mashonaland.—A lion-hunt.—The parson scores heavily.—By Tete or Sena, which?—Fantastic kopjies.—Termite mounds.—A narrow escape.—Policemen.—"Tie him up till morning."—Umtali.—Massikassi.—Among the Portuguese.—A friend in need.—War in the Humbi country.—Bartering with the natives for food.—Abandoned wagons.—A primitive dug-out.—Courteous natives.—Wading the Kuhamadzi.—Gorongoza Mountain.—Digging for water.—Spontaneous combustion.—Baobabs.—Lovely sweet oranges.

WE passed Fort Charter on the night of June 5th. This is the place where the company's Pioneer Column endured the greatest hardships, through the mismanagement of the commissariat department, the men suffering with hunger, with only an occasional pannikin of mealies to appease it; while seventy per cent. were without boots and clothed in rags, at the same time working their hardest, building the fort, and getting the numerous wagons, machines, and guns through the mud. And all for what?

The fort is situated on a slight rise on the dreary plain, the only outlook being a vast expanse of white sand. I found two solitary white men in charge. One was running a "gin-mill" in the magazine, but intending to close up in a week or two, as travelers are too few to make it pay, the main road being lately diverted through another district. The other is the telegraph operator, who is in danger of forgetting the Morse alphabet for want of practice.

On the morning of the 10th we outspanned at "Six-Mile Spruit." The large native kraal in the vicinity turned out to be completely deserted, the natives having fled in terror from the outrages committed upon them by white policemen. The cooking-pots, calabashes, and baskets of the Mashonas scattered around the huts were suggestive of hasty flight. I walked through among the silent dwellings, and found in one the decomposed corpse of a woman, apparently about twenty-five years of age. The whole scene was sad and sickening in the extreme. Further information from reliable sources only augmented our horror at the depravity of the brutes, who had thus added another blot on England's fair escutcheon. And yet we have heard the hope expressed by philanthropic and Christian people at home that with the opening up of Central Africa by British protectorates and chartered companies an entrance would be secured to the heart of this hitherto unevangelized field for the gospel of Christ. But it is much to be feared that not in this generation will the deep-seated dread and bitter hate of the Mashonas toward the white man be eradicated, whether he represents the church, government, or commerce.

Dr. Guthrie, of honored name, hit the mark when he said in reference to British colonization: "Not more fatal to the Canaanites the irruption of the Hebrews than our arrival in almost every colony to its native population. We have seized their lands, and, in a way

FOOTMILL FOR BRICK-MAKING, BLANTYRE

less honorable and even merciful than the sword of Israel, have given them in return nothing but a grave. They have perished before our vices and diseases; our presence has been their extermination. Nor is it possible for a man with a heart to read many pages of our colonial history without feelings of deepest pity and burning indignation. They remind us of the sad but true words of Fowell Buxton. 'The darkest day,' said that Christian philanthropist, 'for many a heathen tribe was that which first saw the white man step upon its shores.'"

By 8.30 P.M. we are on the outskirts of Salisbury. I walked on ahead of the wagons so as to choose a suitable place where we might pitch our tent. The night was bitterly cold, and the bleak open veldt anything but inviting. Fearing that we might inadvertently squat on private property, we interrogated two gentlemen on the question who were passing at the time. One of them, a German, happened to be the owner of the land, and most cordially suggested our taking possession of an unoccupied hut close by, kindly placing it at our service so long as we remained in the district. This was a most unexpected but acceptable windfall, as a hut is warmer in the night and cooler in the day than a tent—no small consideration when we remember that the thermometer registers up to 90° F. midday, and frequently 32° F. at night. The wagons coming up, our baggage was unloaded and safely stowed in our new abode.

Salisbury at last—headquarters of the British South African Company, and the most northerly point reached by the Pioneer Column in 1892. The business shanties are built along the base of an isolated kopjie, forming one long street, while on the opposite side of the valley, and about a mile distant, are situated the official huts belonging to various departments of the government, the military camp, and the public hospital. At present there seems to be stagnation in every line of business in Salisbury. Miners are discouraged over the fifty per cent. of their "finds" being claimed by the company, and are leaving for pastures new, while there are but few coming in to take their places. Large consignments of liquor and provisions are being piled up at the doors of the traders, until they have now more than sufficient to supply the needs of the small community for several years to come. Bankruptcy is the order of the day. Sales by auction are held twice a week, where goods are sacrificed at less than their original cost in the colony, so as to realize sufficient to meet present demands. All this has caused a deplorable reaction, and those who have extolled "the inconceivable wealth of Mashonaland" as "impossible to exaggerate" are in worse than bad odor with the unfortunate inhabitants. Every other night indignation meetings are held. At one of them the following cablegram was formulated and dispatched to the directors in England: "In consequence of the stagnation in this country through the company's fifty-per-cent. charge, a full representative meeting was held on the 11th inst., strongly protesting against the claim, which is to the detriment of the country's progress and of the welfare of all inhabitants, and respectfully but firmly requesting an immediate reduction to ten per cent."

The cruelest deception of all seems to be the encouraging of farmers with their families to trek from the south to these highlands, with the promise of thousands of acres of fine farming country free. No one looking out on the dreary wastes we have traversed during the last forty-five days could hope to earn even a bare living from the arid soil. Good crops of wheat or grain it certainly will not yield, except in the few low-lying spots on the banks of the spruits, and these only Kaffir-corn or mealies. We have talked with several white men who have put the matter to the test during the past two years with results almost *nil*. Potatoes have been planted, but they no sooner begin to form than the white ants eat them off; and this termite occupies only the best land.

We were invited by one of the authorities (who, having, as he said, large stakes in the country, tries to look hopefully on its future) to visit the vegetable market. We did so. A jackass could have carried away all the garden produce displayed without being overloaded. I leave the reader to draw his own conclusions as to the productiveness of the soil from the fact that a small basket of potatoes not much bigger than walnuts was offered and found purchasers at two shillings per pound.

To obtain anything like farming lands we must leave the high veldt and try such districts as lie east and northeast of Victoria or the Mazoe Valley. Far from Mashonaland being even a fair average country for farming, none but those who have "an ax to grind" in booming it will speak of it other than as a failure for such purposes. That there is gold in the country there can be no question, and for those who are willing to risk their lives in an insalubrious clime to find it there is no doubt a future of some promise; but as for aught else, it is but another "South Sea bubble."

Imported domestic animals are short-lived, and those indigenous to the country are correctly described by Mr. Bent thus: "The characteristic of all domestic animals in Mashonaland is their small size. The cows are less than our Guernsey breed, and give very little milk; the sheep and goats are diminutive and unhealthy looking; the hens are ridiculous little things, and their eggs not much bigger than pigeons' eggs at home; as for the dogs, they are the most contemptible specimens of the canine race I have ever seen in any of my wanderings. This does not look well for the prospects of the agriculturists."

The great argument "that the country is new, that much will yet be accomplished, but we must await developments," and laying special emphasis on the beneficial results accruing to every country that has the good fortune to be under British influence, serves but to remind me of a circumstance that is reported to have occurred here a short time ago. Two miners on coming into Salisbury had treated themselves to a few bottles of "Glenlivet," retiring to their hut to consume them; and when no longer able to maintain their equilibrium, one asked the other, "How do you feel?" "Feel!" was the reply—"I feel—that I am under the sphere—of British influence."

On the 14th, accompanied by Dr. Rand (to meet with whom so unexpectedly here was a mutual joy, having known each other years ago in Jamaica), I returned to Six-Mile Spruit, for the purpose of taking some photos of the village, to find nothing but a mass of blackened ruins. We draw our own conclusions from this, and regret having prematurely spoken of discovering the body of a woman in one of the huts, as interested parties had doubtless got wind of this; hence the evident incendiary. Special care had been taken to see that the burning of the hut with the body was done thoroughly. That it was not the result of a bush fire was manifest from the fact that the grass for several yards round the hut was unscathed. On removing the débris and exposing the remains of the woman, however, Dr. Rand found the bones in sufficient form to enable him to corroborate my statements.

While rambling in the bush a short distance from this place, Dr. Rand drew my attention to an overhanging rock under which was a large stone, its flat surface literally covered with bushmen's drawings, very ancient and interesting. The artists, as a people, have long since disappeared from Mashonaland, although specimens of their work are to be found in many districts, particularly in the Mazoe Valley. They represent, generally, wild animals and all sorts of game, battle scenes, etc., and are done in colored pigments, red, black, and yellow predominating. On close inspection the pigments appear to have eaten into the rock; hence their preservation.

The week spent at Salisbury passed very rapidly and pleasantly. Making the acquaintance of the leading people of the district was a material help to my gathering information on points of importance to intending emigrants.

I met "Major" and Mrs. P—— of the Salvation Army, who came up about a year ago with the intention of establishing a recruiting center, but so far without success; the class of men found in mining camps resent being sought after by the Army. The "Major" seems to be an intelligent man, but has only a faint hope that some day in the distant future they may be able to do something, should the projects in hand for the country succeed; otherwise the field will have to be abandoned. The Church of England has also a representative here, though there is no church or meeting-house yet; but a few people on Sunday mornings attend a service held in a small hut.

The most successful and enterprising mission is the Wesleyan Methodist, under the superintendence of the Rev. Isaac Shimmin, an earnest and energetic missionary, who, although in Salisbury less than two years, has succeeded in building a very neat little chapel, seating about two hundred, and opened a fortnight ago, free of debt, most of the money having been subscribed in the district. It would be hard to find a more suitable man for such a sphere. His manly, frank, and honest bearing has won the confidence of the whole community; but it draws the line at going to church; very, very few turn out to the services on Sunday.

On Wednesday evening, by request, I lectured in the chapel to a full house on the subject of my journey from the West Coast; and probably never again shall I have the opportunity of addressing an audience so entirely composed of those who could best appreciate an account of the trials, privations, and dangers incident to African travel, every individual man being in a position to sympathize more or less from actual experience. A liberal collection was made at the close toward the seating of the new building.

The missions in Mashonaland, however, so far, are for the evangelization of the Europeans; no effort is being put forth to reach the natives.

A few weeks ago Mr. Shimmin scored heavily against four or five leading sportsmen in the town, who, in response to the request of some natives of a distant village that the white men might come and kill a lion which was taking off their meager flocks of goats, arranged for a hunt. Mr. Shimmin formed one of the party, in spite of an ill-disguised protest on the part of the hunters to a "parson" going on such an errand, anticipating, of course, that a man of the "cloth" would be in their way. The bush where the lion was said to be lurking being reached, a very short time elapsed before a low growl revealed his whereabouts. Immediately several shots were fired at random, which served only to enrage the brute, and with a bound he charged his assailants, who took to their heels, with the exception of the "parson," who stood his ground with his rifle at the "ready." The monster sprang on the hindmost of the fleeing sportsmen, bringing him to the ground with fearful force, and inflicting a ghastly wound in his leg. For an instant the lion, with his forepaws on the prostrate man, raised his head to look around, when Mr. Shimmin, taking steady aim, planted a bullet in a vital spot, rolling the beast over—dead. The man was saved. But where were his comrades? They came back on hearing the shot, shouting with great agitation, "Where is it? Where is it?" The "parson" pointed for answer to the inanimate carcass.

It has been a treat to meet so many friends in this far-distant land, but we must be on the move homeward. Two ways are open to us, viz., by Tete to Blantyre and Nyasa, or *via* Umtali to Sena and up the Shiré River. We have tried our best, backed by the influence of Mr. Doyle, the interpreter, and others, to get carriers for the first route; but no money will tempt them to go. A few Shanghans came and booked, giving me a little hope of getting through by what would have been the shortest way; but at the last moment they backed out. The fact is, the company have been sending down policemen in that direction of late, to punish recreant chiefs for infringement of its laws by burning their villages, and to which Mr. Bent refers:

"A fine of cattle had been imposed on the chief, accompanied by a threat that if the fine was not paid by a certain day the kraal would be burned down. The fine was not paid, and Major ——, with a band of men, rode out to execute the orders, borrowing two of our horses for the occasion. As we passed through the village the ashes of huts and granaries were still smoldering, broken pots and household goods lay around in wild confusion, and all the inhabitants had taken refuge at one of the neighboring villages. As we passed by this, it is needless to say we did not meet with an altogether cordial reception. We dismounted and went among them, asking in vain for beer, eggs, and fowls. The Morunko (white men) had taken them all, they said, and they received our overtures of friendship with silent and, as we thought, ominous contempt."

As a result of this, carriers from this side unprotected naturally fear retaliation.

ANGONI SLAVE WARRIORS

Failing the Tete road, I take the next best, *via* Umtali, which has one advantage: transport for the first hundred and ninety miles can be done by bullock-wagon.

On June 19th we left Salisbury. I am not altogether disappointed at being obliged to take this direction, as I shall have an opportunity of seeing Umtali and learning something of Manicaland. The road gets more diversified the nearer we approach Manica. Some of the gorges and canons are very fine, and the rocky kopjies present most fantastic and peculiar features. At a distance the rugged peaks appear like ruins of ancient castles or monasteries so familiar to tourists in Italy; otherwise they have the same characteristics as those observed south of Salisbury, consisting of masses of solid granite, and almost void of vegetation.

It is remarkable that with the granite kopjies appear also the huge ant-hills such as we last saw beyond the Kwanza. There have been many doubts and a great deal of speculation expressed by travelers as to whether these mounds, so numerous, and varying in size up to eighteen feet in height, and even a greater diameter at the base, are the work of ants at all. This is excusable, in a measure, on the West Coast, where the activity of the termites has ceased constructing such memorials of their existence, probably for centuries; but here there can be no doubt on the subject, as during the dry season we observe a number of chimney-like structures, from a few inches to two or three feet in height, and averaging eight inches in diameter, on the mounds. On closer inspection we see the ants, all alive, working their hardest, bringing from below the particles of earth of which the building is composed. They go on uninterruptedly until the wet season, when the rains break down their edifices of untempered mortar, and so *ad infinitum* increase, year by year, the proportions of the great ant-hills, that in some districts appear at a distance like the conical roofs of so many native huts.

The journey to Umtali occupied only eleven days, and there were but few incidents worthy of note, except, perhaps, that I had rather a narrow escape from what in many instances has terminated fatally to either man or beast, sometimes to both. As game is only found some distance from the road, the transport rider in charge of the wagon having with him two good horses, one or other of us was accustomed to go out every day for a hunt while outspanned. On the 28th, near the Odzi River, in company with a young gentleman holding the official position of the company's forester (like us, he was bound for Umtali), I started as usual for the bush. After riding some miles we raised an antelope and gave chase, clearing the narrow sluits and spruits at a good gallop; but, unfortunately, in attempting to head off the animal I took a course that led along by the side of a brook to leeward of a steep bank and near to some reeds, among which the buck disappeared, when my horse plunged headfirst into a game-pit. These wretched traps in this part of Africa are exactly like an ordinary grave, about seven feet long and five feet deep, and a little over two feet wide, but narrowing down to a few inches at the bottom, which generally bristles with sharp spikes, although, luckily, not so this time. It was so well hidden with long grass that I could not see whether we had got in broadside or lengthways of the hole. I was not kept long in doubt, for the horse made a second plunge to free himself, and down we went together, jamming my legs against the sides of the pit. Happily for both of us, the ground was soft and loose, and I managed to extricate myself in a short time by knocking in the bank at the end with the butt of my rifle. The plucky animal with a struggle succeeded in getting clear of the hole, but was too frightened for more galloping over the veldt that evening, so we had to return to the wagons.

When about three treks from Salisbury, a circumstance came under my notice that confirmed in a great measure reports I had heard of the doings of some of the British South African Company's police. A certain captain with three men, who had been sent to arbitrate some matters with the natives in the Mutassi district, were returning to headquarters, when they overtook on the road four Mashonas driving two small oxen. On seeing policemen approach, of whom they had heard enough to make them dread a closer acquaintance, they, of course, ran off into the bush; whereupon, according to the captain, who was my informant, the police put spurs to their horses, rode down one man, whom they tied up on the spot, and began firing on the others with their Martinis. Walking some distance in advance of the wagon, I found at a wayside hut this noble band of Englishmen, who seemed to think they were doing valiant service for their Queen and country by attacking four harmless and defenseless Kaffirs on the public road. The night was very cold, but there, outside, sat the Mashona, secured by an ox reim tied round his waist; while inside was the captain, swearing roundly at his men for their bad shooting, who in turn excused themselves on the ground that it was dark.

I could not make out why he wanted to murder the natives, and asked for an explanation. "Why," he replied, "they were about no good, or they would not have run away when they saw us coming. Bring in the fellow, interpreter, and ask him what the —— made him run."

"Great chief, I was frightened."

"Where were you going?"

"Going to my kraal."

"Where did you get the two oxen?"

"I don't know where they came from. I only overtook the boys who were driving them a short time before we saw you coming. But I believe the cattle had strayed and were being brought back to their owner, the chief of —— staat."

"Take the fellow outside, and tie him up till morning, when we'll see about it; meantime, let me have a glass of whiskey."

Such scenes are of too frequent occurrence, and could English people but know the treatment received by natives at the hands of some of their filibustering representatives in Africa, a more humane system of extending British rule would speedily be inaugurated, while some who aspire to be classed among the heroes of the Dark Continent would be tried at the Old Bailey for their lives. The Magoma case has yet to be brought to light, but "murder will out."

We reached Umtali on the morning of June 30th, and

learned that a few weeks ago a wagon road had been cleared as far as Massikassi. I decided to defer the carrier question until we get there, and proceed thither with my stuff by wagon. We stayed only one night in this village, which differs but little from such places as Macloutsie or Fort Victoria. It is situated at the base of a large kopjie, and consists of some two dozen wattle-and-daub huts, every third one devoted to the sale of drink.

When within some six miles of Umtali, and after crossing the Odzi, we noticed a very marked change in the nature of the soil: no more sandy wastes, but rich red earth or black loam. The solitary kopjies gave place to long ranges of mountains forming the great Manica gold-belt, and, judging from the general configuration of the country, it bids fair for farming, although the uncertainty of the seasons must always remain a great drawback to large investments in that direction.

The evening of July 1st saw us trekking toward Massikassi. For the first two treks the road was fairly good, as we were mostly on the grassy plains; but the balance of the way was simply execrable, the trees having been very carelessly cut down, leaving stumps two feet high. Every five hundred yards there are ravines from thirty to fifty feet deep, with sides so abrupt that though the brakes were screwed home until the wheels stood still, the wagon would plunge forward with a rush, shrouded in a cloud of dust, at a speed that threatened to crush the oxen and end in a general smash-up, and giving rise to the fear that we should soon have nothing but the pieces to collect of both oxen and wagon.

The next four miles was over rough veldt, among great rocks and sluits, where no attempt had been made to prepare the way for wagons. We succeeded in reaching Massikassi safely on the morning of the 4th. This place commands a view approaching the nearest to Scottish Highland scenery we have struck in Africa. To the west, long ranges of hills well clad with vegetation, while eastward widens out before us the beautiful valley of the Rovue, bounded on the north and south by mountains rising to the height of six thousand feet. We find here, besides the Portuguese village, where Captain Andrada and Commandant Battencourt with several sub-officers are quartered, the camp of the English Boundary Commission, consisting of eight officers belonging to engineer regiments. Most of them are absent surveying, and not likely to return before Saturday. This handicaps me, as they, with the Portuguese Commission, have taken all the available carriers that can be depended upon for long journeys, such as Inhambanes and Sofalas; natives of Manica are cowardly, and would be almost certain to desert on the road.

I passed the interim in submitting to a couple of sharp attacks of fever, and when well enough accepted an invitation to dine with the commandant, whom I found very genial and hospitable. I spent one evening at the old Portuguese fort, about a mile down the valley, now in charge of the Companha Mozambique, who retain an Englishman, a Frenchman, and a Portuguese as their representatives. It is some seventy years since the Portuguese built this fort, and their right or claim to this part of Manicaland was never disputed until a few months ago, when the British South African Company took it into their heads to bring down a lot of police with a Maxim gun and a seven-pounder. They posted themselves on a neighboring kopjie and menaced the fort. The result was a most unjustifiable fight, in which the Portuguese were defeated with heavy loss, their fort captured by the company's men, and by them looted. This high-handed proceeding, however, was severely censured by the English home government, and the company withdrew. The fort was repaired, and is now the very picture of peace and tranquillity. A fine garden occupies the open space in the interior, and bananas are flourishing all around the stores and dwellings.

On Saturday the commission returned, and the Portuguese captain most readily expressed his willingness to assist me with men, and by Tuesday morning had collected seventeen carriers, lending me at the same time several of his own servants to act as guides. This is a small caravan, but quite sufficient for my few belongings now. The difficulty of obtaining carriers seemed so serious at Salisbury, that I, having become inured to exposure and hardship, decided to minimize my outfit. Finding that porters can now be paid in gold or rupees, I disposed of a quantity of my cloth and bulky trade goods, also my tent, so that I have again to sleep in the open, as on the journey from Zambesi to Palachwe, where the halts at night were too brief to allow of pitching the tent.

As eight of the porters are natives of Gorongoza, a country through which we have to pass, it was thought advisable to pay their capitaô (headman), but to retain him at Massikassi as a hostage to insure their abiding by their contract; otherwise they would probably leave me in the lurch when near their homes. The others were natives of Inhambane and Delagoa Bay. There is one very satisfactory item to be noted here, namely, that none of these men are slaves in the ordinary acceptation of the term, except in so far as they are the vassals of their respective chiefs. They come of their own free will from the coast and distant parts of the north country to seek employment of the Portuguese, and are well paid for their labor. For the three weeks' journey to Sena they each get thirty shillings in gold, and I find them in food besides.

On the 13th of July we set out from Massikassi, taking a course due east, although our most direct route would have been through the Humbi country to the west of the Gorongoza Mountain. But we were under the necessity of giving that country a wide berth, on account of its disturbed condition, arising from the recent war between Goveia and Makombe, in which the former was killed, with a great number of his followers. The natives being so elated over their victory, we were advised not to attempt going through, but to cross the Pungwe River at Makaka, a hundred and eight miles eastward.

The path was narrow and led through tall grass for most of the day. We made but sixteen miles and camped for the night. Our order of march here differs somewhat from that on the West Coast. The Bihean makes an early start and travels until about noon, when he halts for the day and proceeds to prepare his hut, with as much care as if he intended to take up his abode there for a year instead of a night. Here it is

GROUP OF YAOS, SHIRE-HIGHLANDS

seven o'clock before they get on the track, and they go on for ten miles and stop for breakfast; two hours' rest, and another ten miles' march before sundown. There is no hut-building, nor even a skerm, but good fires are kept up all night. This is essential to our safety, for all this region abounds in lions. No sooner do we compose ourselves for the night, wrapped in our blankets, three or four of us stretched out around each fire, than from every point of the compass we hear the hungry roar of these surly brutes as they seem to invite each other to combine in an attack upon us, every minute coming nearer, until within two or three hundred yards, when they lie down and wait their chance should our fires burn low, kindly reminding us of their proximity by a continued repetition of low grunts. But in spite of this we are too tired to keep awake all night watching; a certain number of men are therefore told off for sentry duty and to keep up the fires, each man taking a spell of two hours during the night.

On the second day we made a long march of twenty-five miles, as water was scarce, but were rewarded for this extra exertion when we happened at last upon a clear running brook.

By noon on the 16th we arrived at Chimoia, where we had to lose a couple of hours buying meal and rice for the men. In the west rations are served by an allowance of calico for a certain number of days; but here we have all the bother of trading with the natives, as cloth is not in so much demand, and they want a variety of goods for their food-stuffs—red white-eye beads chiefly, salt, handkerchiefs, etc. A good deal of rice is grown in these districts, but very little else except Kaffir-corn. It is not that the soil is poor, as in most parts of Africa where we have been, but the native seems to have no ambition in the victualing line beyond mush, and a bit of game, when he can get it. Manicaland is a rich country, not only in gold, but in the capabilities of the soil; any tropical products would thrive well if given a chance.

There is no very distinctive tribal mark among the Manicas and coast natives, except that the men have the lobe of both ears slit and in the hole carry their snuff-box—generally the empty shell of a Martini cartridge. The women have the upper lip pierced, and insert a lead or silver plug with a flat round top on the outside, like a reversed collar-stud.

We are now in the tsetse-fly belt. We passed seventeen wagons to-day that have been left to their fate on the veldt for several months—the result of a rash venture on the part of a company to transport goods from Beira up into the interior. The "fly" killed off the oxen, numbering some four hundred and valued at seven pounds each, and so the wagons, of an average value of one hundred and thirty pounds, had to be abandoned. Most of them are now so dilapidated and scorched by bush fires that it would not pay to remove them.

Mr. Bent, in describing his journey to the coast east of the point where we turned northward, writes:

"Ample evidence of the ravages of this venomous insect (the tsetse) are visible on the roadside. Dozens of wagons lie rotting in the veldt, bearing melancholy testimony to the failure of Messrs. Heaney and Johnson's pioneer scheme. Everywhere lie the bleaching bones of the oxen which dragged them; and at Mandigo is an abandoned hut filled to overflowing with the skins of these animals, awaiting the further development of the Pungwe traffic to be converted into ropes, or *reims*, as they are usually termed in South Africa. Fully two thousand pounds' worth of wagons, we calculated, as we passed by on one day's march, lies in the veldt, ghost-like, as after a battle.

"Then there are Scotch carts of more or less value, and a handsome Cape cart, which Mr. Rhodes had to abandon on his way up to Mashonaland, containing in the box-seat a bottle labeled 'Anti-fly Mixture'—a parody on the situation.

"But the greatest parody of all is at Sarmento itself, a Portuguese settlement on the banks of the Pungwe. Here two handsome coaches, made expressly in New Hampshire, in America, for the occasion, lie deserted near the Portuguese huts. They are richly painted with arabesques and pictures on the panels. 'Pungwe Route to Mashonaland' is written thereon in letters of gold. The comfortable cushions inside are being moth-eaten, and the approaching rains will complete the ruin of these handsome but ill-fated vehicles. Meanwhile the Portuguese stand by and laugh at the discomfiture of their British rivals in the thirst for gold. Even the signboard, with 'To Mashonaland,' is in its place. And all this elaborate preparation for the pioneer route has been rendered abortive by that venomous little insect, the tsetse-fly. In his zeal to carry out his contract, Major Johnson committed a great error and entailed an enormous amount of misery when he telegraphed that the Pungwe route was open, and circulated advertisements to that effect, giving dates and hours which were never carried out.

"Heaps of people, for the most part poor and impecunious, flocked to this entrance to their Eldorado, and, after waiting without anything, and in abject misery at Chimoia, had to return to Mapanda, where the condition of affairs was desperate—people dying of fever, the doctor himself ill, and no food, for the Portuguese governor of Neves Ferreira, Colonel Madera, boycotted the English and forbade the natives to bring them provisions. Assistance was brought to them by Dr. Todd, of the *Magicienne;* but many died, and the rest, disappointed and penniless, had to return to Cape Town."

We reached Makaka early on the 18th, having averaged twenty miles a day from Massikassi. We give the boys a rest, and cross the Pungwe to-morrow. While waiting at this village, the fact is demonstrated to us that "woman" is by no means to be considered the "weaker vessel" here. On expressing surprise at the absence of the usual lounging men around the kraal, while a whole crowd of women were busy stamping corn and singing their liveliest songs, the reason was given that this being the harvest time, the women had their hands full of work; and that as the men persisted in idling all the morning, and constantly getting in the way of their wives, the latter seized sticks and quickly made a clearance of the male sex, who had sense enough to offer no resistance, seeing they were very much in the minority, but were impressed with the parting order, that they were not to return without permission.

The river Pungwe here is about a hundred yards broad, and presents a beautiful view from this point looking down the stream, its many windings being seen to a great distance shimmering in the sunshine, and the overhanging trees reflected on the bosom of its clear, cool waters. We crossed early in the morning in a very primitive dug-out with the outlines of a boomerang, the original shape of the tree, and proceeded on our journey toward Sena, taking a course a little east of north.

We stopped at Mabute for breakfast, and I had a long palaver with the natives, who were exceedingly polite and respectful, the headman bringing me a present of meal and a fowl—a plain proof that white men are rare in these parts. Our faces and arms get pretty well scratched by the grass, which becomes still more rank and tall, in some places reaching a height of fourteen feet. The luxuriousness of vegetation here is remarkable. The immense fields of corn now being reaped speak volumes, not only for the land, but for the diligence and industry of the women, who are, with few exceptions, of good physique, and possess by no means unpleasant features but for the disfigurement of the upper lip. They contrast as widely with the poor Mashonas as do their respective countries.

A sort of light bamboo grows in great abundance all along our route, valued highly by wagon-drivers in the Colony as whip-sticks. I was surprised to see, while passing through a kraal, a small boy spinning a rough top, whipping it up with great vim by means of a barkwhip. I wondered if the idea was original with him. I find the natives we meet on the path or in the villages very civil. The women make an awkward attempt at a curtsey as we pass, while the men salute by performing a kind of double-shuffle with their feet, readily answering any question, and frequently accompanying us long distances to guide us through the intricacies of the numerous tracks.

They prepare a very superior bark-cloth by cutting from a sort of fig tree large felt-like masses of the bark. After soaking it in water for a short time it is hammered with wooden mallets on a smooth log. When it is beaten out quite thin and all the holes neatly mended, by the aid of a very primitive native needle and fine fiber, it is again beaten with a mallet on which lines are cut, giving the finished cloth a ribbed appearance. If the portion of the tree from which this layer of bark has been taken is bound up tightly with plantain-fiber, a new bark forms in process of time.

Since crossing the Pungwe three days ago we have been gradually ascending; but now, following the base of the Gorongoza Mountain, our highest altitude has been reached, and we now begin to descend, keeping to the ridge of the tableland. Water is plentiful, and we come across villages every few miles. On the plains to the east, buffalo, eland, and zebra are to be found in great numbers; but they keep clear of the hills.

On the evening of the 21st we crossed the Kulumadzi, flowing southeast. The stream was low enough to permit of our wading it, its width being about forty yards. But the scenery every way we looked was bewitching—the water coming noisily down from the hills, rushing and dashing among the numerous big boulders that occupy the river-bed. We linger to rest for a while on the bank, so refreshing and cool it seems after the long day's exhausting march. We have just emerged from the gloomy somberness of the primeval forest, through which we have been tramping for over five hours, and where the rays of the sun could scarcely pierce through the dense and tangled herbage—the gigantic cable-like creepers festooned among the branches, parasites of enormous growth clinging to the ancient timbers, where stillness reigned unbroken by even the twitter of a bird or the sough of the wind.

Next day our path lay through a more open country, and the soil is no longer black loam, but changed to rough marl, the small pebbles causing the carriers to complain much of sore feet. The grass and undergrowth are shorter, and the general aspect of the country is not so pleasing as it has been for the past few days. Gorongoza Mountain is now behind us, and we have on our left the hills of Masara.

We crossed the river Nymandura about 9 A.M., and halted for breakfast by the beautiful Munedeze. Four hours more brought us to Goveia, a Portuguese village much the worse for wear. The resident representatives of Portugal are three men of middle age, the tallest not exceeding five feet four inches in height, and all of a very despairing appearance, with a sort of calm and resigned expression on their faces, the result, I suppose, of eight or nine years doing nothing. They kindly proffered us the use of one of the five large mud houses, once official residences, but for years unoccupied, and crumbling back to mother earth. As some of our carriers belong to this district we gave all a day off, continuing our journey on the 24th.

We have had no water for ten miles, and then only a small stagnant pool; nine miles more, and we obtained a little by digging in a dry river-bed. We saw at a long distance large herds of antelopes. Everywhere there is evidence of plenty of game, including elephant; but as the season for grass fires has begun, the larger animals have been driven east. Another month the young grass will be springing, and they will return; so that here we have one of the finest hunting-grounds in Africa, within ten days of the sea.

We passed several small villages during the day, but all deserted, owing, probably, to the scarcity of water, or perhaps the late war. Soon after starting on the morning of the 25th, we crossed several small streams, after which we found no water for twelve miles, and then only by digging. On camping the same operation had to be repeated before we could get enough of the precious fluid to prepare supper. At this place I observed some women dyeing white calico black, by means of a jet-black juice exuded from the pods of a tree; and, judging from the cloth worn by the people, that had been submitted to the process, the dye seems to be permanent.

July 26th. Having slept last night in a hollow, we found ourselves surrounded by a thick fog this morning, and by noon fever came on. I stopped at a village to buy meal for the carriers. Again a headman brought out a fine large basketful of meal as a present to the white man. I gave him a jackknife in return. The afternoon march was very hard; what with the hot fever and not a drop of water for fourteen miles, it was no play. The men were crying out for meat, but exhaustion compelling me to lie down by the wayside every mile or two, I was quite unable to go into the

LIVINGSTONIA

See page 310

bush after game. Fortunately, however, I sighted a fine buck grazing about a hundred and fifty yards from the path. On raising my rifle my hand shook so much that I had to lean against a tree to steady myself. I fired one shot and dropped him, but had to leave the carcass in charge of my gun-carrier until the men should come up, for my mouth and throat felt as though it would be a case of spontaneous combustion if I did not reach water soon. At last we arrived at a village where a native took me to a hole, five feet deep, dug in the sand, with about half a gallon of water in it—not very nice, but never more appreciated.

The 27th was another thirsty day, thirteen dry miles, but the scenery magnificent. With the exception of the first twenty-five miles after leaving Goveia—of rough, stony, rather sterile country—the rest of the way has been a perfect panorama of beauty, with numerous fine palms and gigantic baobabs. The latter peculiar tree, to which nature has been so liberal in the matter of trunk and so stingy in allowance of branches or foliage, yields large pods containing a substance tasting like cream of tartar, and is often called the tartar tree. But the tree that appeared most striking was a kind of large acacia, called by the natives "njerenjere." Its bark is very smooth, bright sea-green in color, looking for all the world as if it had been treated to a coat of "Aspinall's enamel" from the roots to the tips of the smallest branches. It is used by the river men for making paddles, and by all natives for producing fire. Almost every man carries a piece of this wood about with him, and when he wants a blaze he bores a hole in the chunk, in which he places a little tinder or specially prepared bark, and then, inserting a straight stick, which he holds against his head, by an ingenious arrangement of string he twirls the stick and in a short time smoke is seen to rise.

About sundown we reached the village of Inyamacambe, a daughter of the late Goveia. The chief brought us some lemons and a basket of lovely sweet oranges, the first we have seen in our journey. I noticed with great pleasure a clump of lordly mango trees, all in full bloom, making me think of Jamaica, as these were the first I had seen since leaving home.

CHAPTER XIII.

FROM SENA TO BLANTYRE.

River craft.—On the Shiré.—The Wissmann expedition.—Landed at Chiromo.—Trouble with Her Majesty's customs.—" What is to-day?"—The chief of Mbewe.—A defenseless position.—Blantyre.—Might is right.—Misguided men.—Boycotted.—Wild hallucinations.—Courting a martyr's death.—Dr. Ellinwood speaks.—Abortive asceticism.—Faith cure.—Cheap missionaries.—Poor economy.—A foreign tramp.

TO my intense satisfaction we reached Sena by four o'clock on the afternoon of July 28th. Five months ago I left the Zambesi at Kazungula, and now see its broad waters again, but a good deal nearer home, thank God! It has taken fifteen days' actual marching to come from Massikassi, a distance of fully three hundred miles, giving us an average of twenty miles a day. I am not much the worse, except that my feet and legs are badly swollen; but my next stage, I trust, will be accomplished by boat, and they will get a rest.

Sena has evidently been a very important Portuguese settlement in days gone by. It has a large, strongly built stone fort, impregnable to hostile natives; the fine old arched gateway, the stones of which are time-worn, is an interesting specimen of ancient masonry. The town itself is very scattered, and consists of the substantial dwellings of some sixty Portuguese inhabitants, and several trading stores conducted by Banyans, a Dutchman, and some half-breed Portuguese, while at some distance back the black population have their huts.

The governor very hospitably invited me to stay at his house until arrangements should be made for the river journey, which invitation I gladly accepted, and must own that he could not possibly have shown me more kindness. Although unable to speak much English, and I less Portuguese, we got along well, and I found him one of the genial, good-natured sort. He has a number of slaves in his household, and, so far as I could see, treated them with much more consideration than some people do their servants.

We have seen natives both here and at Massikassi in stocks and goree-sticks, although not chained together in gangs, as described by Sir John Willoughby; nor were they ordinary slaves or laborers, but convicts undergoing sentence for gross crimes—poisoning, assassination, incendiarism, etc.

I met the commandant, Capitaô Môr, and other officials of the government at a dinner-party, and the following evening went out to a very pretty place called Inhascereira, situated about five miles to the northwest of Sena, and right on the bank of the Zambesi. A judge and a doctor reside here during a few months of the year. They are both very bright little men.

Now for Nyasa! I chartered for ten days a river craft, thirty feet long, six feet beam, and two and a half feet deep, with a comfortable little cabin in the afterpart. My crew consisted of twelve *marineros* (paddlers), a *patraô* (steersman), and a *kadamo* (pilot) at the bow. Sunday being so near, I dismissed them with instructions to be at the boat on Monday morning. Most of them put in an appearance at the stated time, but my *patraô* had got drunk on his advanced pay, and a soldier was sent by the governor to wake him up by an application of the palmatory (a flat disk of wood with eighteen inches of handle). By 9 A.M. he was sobered a bit, and we were afloat on the Zambesi again.

Two hours' rowing and we turned into the Ziwiziwi, progressing slowly on account of the many sandbanks. I shot two crocodiles with explosive bullets, hitting them right behind the shoulder as they lay on the sand. One measured fifteen feet six inches, the other fourteen feet. By 10 A.M. on Tuesday morning we came out on the Shiré River, and headed upstream. There is apparently little difference in size between the Shiré and the Zambesi; the current of the former, however, is the stronger. There is nothing to be seen of much interest, except the crocodiles, some of them monsters; a hippo now and again shows himself, but they are fewer here now than in former years, the steamers having driven them higher up. For two days the land on either side has been low and swampy, with reedy banks and very malarious.

August 3d. Reaching Port Herald, I was invited to breakfast by the administration agent, from whom I learned that small-pox had broken out among the men of the German expedition, under Major Wissmann. They are now camped a short distance down the river, where they will probably be delayed for some time, the river at present being very low, and their barges, etc., drawing too much water. I understand that the purpose of this party is the placing of a steamer on Lake

Tanganyika, for the suppression of the slave-trade. Whatever may be the protective influences expected from the presence of a steamer on the lake, it would seem that the measures to be adopted in getting it there are not likely to be pacific toward the natives. Yesterday a gentleman expressed to an officer of the expedition a hope that the natives *en route* might be found friendly. "Friendly!" was the sneering rejoinder. "I much prefer them hostile, for then we fight them and take what we want; whereas when they are friendly we have to pay for everything. I sincerely hope we shall have some fighting soon, as I want to get my men in training."

Soon after leaving Port Herald we passed the river cargo-steamer "James Stephenson," fast on a sandbank. The steamers, I understand, find great difficulty this year in getting up and down, on account of the shallows and snags, making navigation almost impossible. In another twenty-four hours we arrived at Chiromo, at the mouth of the Ruo, on the confines of Nyasaland, having accomplished the journey from Sena—a hundred miles—in four and a half days. I have had no trouble with the men; and this has been my experience with all the porters or boatmen employed from the Portuguese. They are well trained, hard-working, and obedient.

And now we are in British territory, I believe; but the knowledge of this fact is fraught with no thrill of joy to me after what I have seen of so-called British rule and influence in Africa. I had no sooner stepped ashore than I was accosted by an official of Her Majesty's customs with "Any firearms, sir?" "Yes," I re-

GRAVES, LIVINGSTONIA

plied: "an 'Express' rifle, a fowling-piece, and a revolver." "Must leave them all here until you obtain a permit from the administrator, H. H. Johnston." "And where might that gentleman be found?" "In the Shiré Highlands, five or six days from here."

To wait twelve days for this permit was out of the question; yet I was not very keen about venturing on the next stage of my journey unarmed, through a country abounding in leopards and lions—even within half a mile of where we were standing. A law to prohibit the sale of guns or gunpowder to natives I can quite understand; but to take from a lone traveler his only means of defense in Africa, without the option of obtaining a license, is a proceeding that even the Portuguese would be ashamed of. I protested, but the official was immovable, and there was nothing for it but to submit.

Chiromo is an important government station, having a custom-house, post-office, etc. The English occupy the north and the Portuguese the south bank of the Ruo. The two British gunboats are here, H. M. SS. "Herald" and "Mosquito." I spent a pleasant evening on board the "Herald" by invitation of Commander Robertson, meeting the officers and doctors of both vessels.

I sought out Mr. Simpson, a Scotch trader, who has a large store and has done an extensive business here among the natives for many years. He gave me a hearty welcome, and pressed me to stay with him a couple of days, promising to get me carriers for the overland journey to Blantyre. Mr. Simpson complains bitterly—and I fear not without reason—of the administration of British Central Africa (now incorporated with the British South African Company) by Her Majesty's commissioner, who exercises his authority in such a peremptory and bullying manner, through his Zanzibari and Sikhs, that a great deal of discontent is rapidly springing up among the chiefs, who declare that they have never given over their country to the English. A tax of six shillings per annum is levied by the British upon every male native over fourteen years of age, while the Portuguese demand only one rupee, resulting in some of the natives going over to the latter, while others are threatening resistance to the unreasonable and unjust demands made upon them, from which they derive no return or benefit whatever.

It struck me as being rather peculiar that I should have been required to take out a license in order to pass through Mashonaland; and now on coming again into British possessions, so called, to be deprived of my rifle, in a country where it is absolutely indispensable, not only in procuring meat, but as a means of defense against wild animals, strikes me as being more peculiar still. Only yesterday Mr. Simpson came across a lion and lioness with two cubs, within a mile of camp.

Saturday, August 6th. There has been a great deal of disputing on the station as to the day of the week, some maintaining that it is Friday, others Saturday. I settled the matter in this way: having purchased at Sena a small basket of eggs for use on the journey, and knowing how many I had at starting and the number used each day, the arithmetical problem resulted in favor of Saturday.

On Tuesday I got carriers together and started at

11 A.M. overland for Katunga. Much of the journey was very rough, on account of the long grass and thornbush. We passed Mona about 2 P.M., and arrived at Masanjeras a little before five in the evening, making eighteen miles. I found a white man in a good-sized house, which he had built for the purpose of occasional trading. He kindly offered me a shelter for the night. Next morning we continued our journey through the fearful grass. The rugged footpath was very narrow, winding along the base of the Tyolo Mountain all the way. We sighted large herds of buffalo and waterbuck. Palm trees are abundant on the plain, and some are very handsome. This valley is thickly populated. We passed many villages during the day, the largest, Mbewe, close to the Shiré. The chief, Maquire, quite a young man, came out to greet us, with some two hundred natives at his heels; he bade me good-evening very cheerfully in English. I afterward learned that he had been for some time at the Blantyre mission, and bears a good reputation among the white people of the country.

The sun was setting, and we pressed on to seek a camping-place for the night; we pitched on a spot clear of grass, right on the river-bank. Mosquitoes attacked us in hordes, which, with the frequent barking of leopards, the low growl of a lion in our near vicinity, the constant snorting of hippos, and the eerie consciousness of our defenseless position, permitted no sleep (for which I have to thank the unfair exactions of officialdom). At break of day we continued to follow the river-bank, passing a village about every twenty minutes, and reached Katunga about 9 A.M. I turned into the premises of the African Lakes Company, where Mr. Baird is manager, who sent out to get carriers for Blantyre; and, as by the time they were all collected it was late in the afternoon, I decided to stay until next morning. We started early, crossing the plain toward the hills, commencing the ascent about eight o'clock. We had stiff climbing for a couple of hours, then the road, dug out of the mountain-side, was tolerably level and in good order. We got some fine glimpses of the Shiré Valley from our high altitude. By 3 P.M. we passed the fortress-like store of the African Lakes Company at Mandala, and in fifteen minutes more were in Blantyre.

I met Dr. Scott, who took me to the Manse, where I was introduced to the missionary in charge (*pro tem.*), Rev. A. Heatherwick. The magnificent church, the substantial and home-like residence, the crowds of boys and girls being trained by the mission, have all been so well and frequently described that a detailed sketch of them by me is unnecessary. I learned that the company's steamer, "Domira," would not be down to the south end of Nyasa for some ten days. This is disappointing, but cannot be helped, as I must go and see the stations on the famous lake before returning home; besides, doubtless letters are awaiting me at Bandawe, which I must get somehow. Were it not that I longed with an intense yearning to get back home, I could put in a few weeks at Blantyre very happily; and I much require the rest this beautiful spot and pleasant surroundings afford.

I visited Mandala, headquarters of the African Lakes Company, where a large trade is carried on with the natives, and through whom supplies are forwarded to branch stations, and to the various missionaries on the lake. Bad accounts of the disturbed condition of the country on the east and north of Nyasa arrived; news of a fresh outbreak was daily expected, the hostility of the Arabs being very bitter, and they are all too successful in winning over the numerous chiefs to their side. To this may be added, as a reason for discontent, the maladministration of Her Majesty's commissioner, who seems to possess no principle and no policy in directing the affairs of the country, except the very questionable one of "might is right."

On Sunday I attended the various services in the church, the congregation consisting chiefly of the two hundred native boys and girls under instruction and boarded on the mission premises. The form of service, though nominally that of the Established Church of Scotland, contrasted strangely with the simplicity to which I had been accustomed in my boyhood in the Highlands of Scotland. It closely resembled the more ceremonious ritual of the Church of England—the surpliced clergyman, the processional white-robed choir, intoned prayers, turning to the east during the repetition of the Creed, tapers on the altar, reading-desk on one side of the chancel and pulpit on the other, etc. But perhaps this is the form countenanced by the Church of Scotland in modern times. Dr. Scott conducted service in the morning, Mr. Heatherwick in the evening; both of them are evidently zealous and devoted men. The former is indefatigable in his attendance on the sick of the district, including all classes, whether belonging to the mission or not. No journey is too long, no hour unreasonable for him, provided the call comes from a sufferer.

The grounds around the mission are very fine; much has been done in planting trees of eucalyptus, cypress, fir, etc., by a Scotch gardener who has been here for many years. I visited the little cemetery near by, the last resting-place of some twenty-three white people who have died here, in almost every instance from fever. One grave, that of a man named Henchman, suggested a terrible lesson to those fanatics, now so numerous, who have either come or intend coming to Africa as missionaries on the "faith alone" plan. This man came up the river last year with his wife and two children. Although warned again and again not to attempt traveling in Africa without some tangible means of providing for his family, his only answer was the stock phrase, "The Lord will provide." Arriving at Blantyre, he left his family in charge of the missionaries and proceeded to Angoniland, where he proposed to establish a station. After a short time he returned to Blantyre, and, taking his wife and children with him, set off again, provided with but a meager supply of provisions and a very small quantity of barter goods. A few weeks sufficed to open his eyes to the blunder he had committed. The natives, discovering that he was unable to pay his way, coolly boycotted him, refusing even to supply them with food, until they were brought to the last extremes of distress. He persisted in his sufferings; but his wife, having common sense as well as faith, dispatched a letter to the African Lakes Company begging for men to bring them back. This was promptly done, the Blantyre mission taking them in and providing for them again. The bubble of Henchman's dream regarding a mission supported by "faith alone" having burst, it was now either work or want. He sought and obtained employment at road-making, under the administration. But a few months of tent life and exposure to the sun were too much for him; repeated attacks of fever so disabled him that he had to seek Blantyre once more, this time too late. In three days he died, leaving his wife and children alone in Central Africa, among strangers.

One might imagine that such an example would deter others from hazarding their lives in foolhardy attempts to prove that the present system of missions in Africa —receiving their support from home—is all a mistake. But no! Such men are too obstinate to be led by any counsel other than their own conceit. Only this morning, August 20th, I have been to see a delicate little shadow of a girl, ten years of age, apparently dying of fever, in a hut near Mandala. She was brought here by her father, a Mr. Booth, who, with a companion named Maugin, arrived a week ago, with the intention, as they say, of commencing a plan of operations in mission work, which, with the aid of hundreds of the same mind as themselves, who are to follow soon, is to result in the evangelization of all Africa during the present century. They are provisioned for only a few months, and almost penniless. I have advised Booth, for the sake of his poor little motherless child, if for nothing else, to abandon his mad theory and go home; but he laughed at the bare idea, and pitied my lack of faith, assuring me of his confidence that he has a great work here to perform. To all appearance he is quite prepared to sacrifice his only child to the hallucination that possesses him.

August 26th. I have just returned from the mission cemetery, where we have laid the body of the young man Mangin, already referred to, by the side of poor Henchman. The door to his peculiar mission did not open up before him as readily as he had anticipated, and necessity compelled him to accept employment in a brick-field. But three days' fever, and his career is closed. By this sad event Booth's faith has received a rude shock; but will it bring him to his senses? Oh no! Like the Zulu savage, who courts death in the battlefield, or the Hindoo fanatic, who throws himself beneath the wheels of the Juggernaut car, he believes that such a sacrifice will merit a great reward in the world to come.

In missionary speeches we have heard such expressions as, "The survivors will pass over the slain in the trenches and take the African fortress for the Lord." * This sounds very brave, but it is questionable if the cause of missions might not be better served by the adoption of a course less tragic; and if, instead of courting a martyr's death by following the impulses of ill-balanced minds, these enthusiasts would but submit to be guided by the counsel and practical experience of godly men, who for years have adopted measures suggested by the knowledge they have acquired of the country and its people, for the effective promulgation of the gospel of Christ. The time has arrived when this subject demands of all who are seriously interested in Africa's missions a full, free, and dispassionate discussion.

* Krapt.

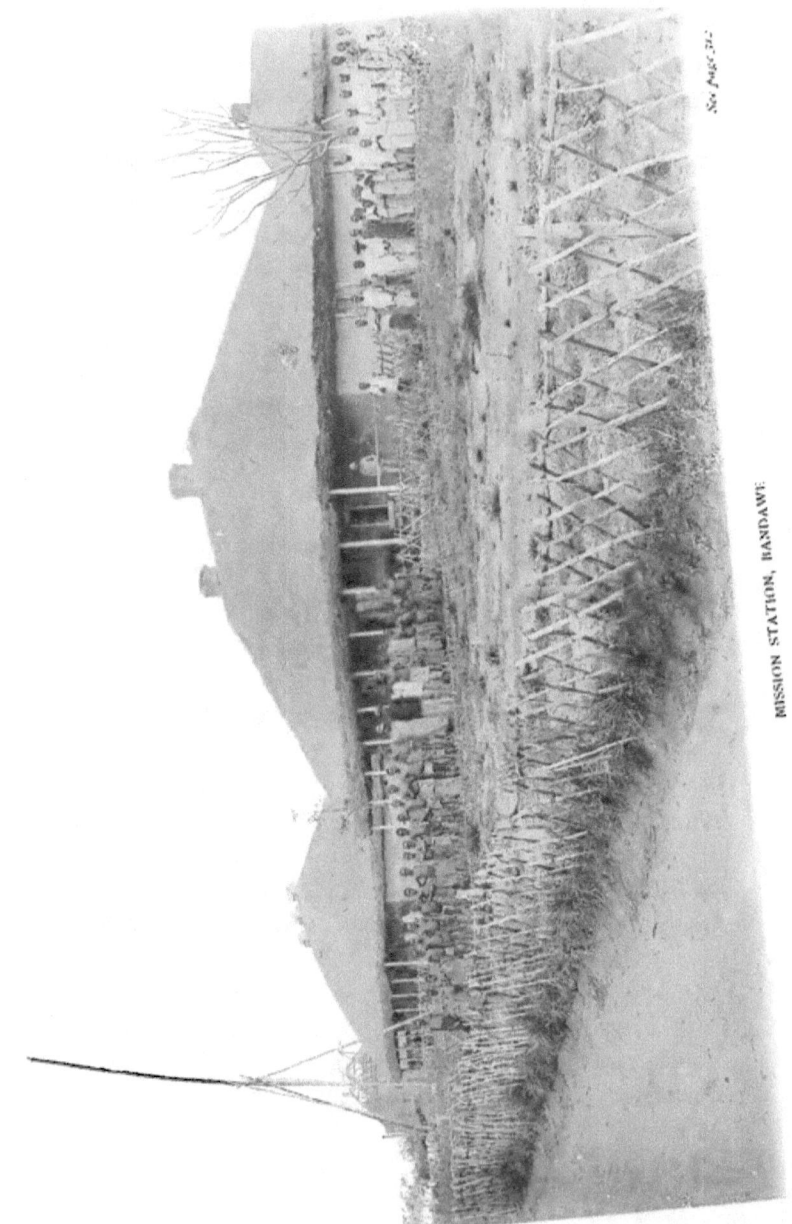

MISSION STATION, BANDAWE.

The Rev. Dr. Ellinwood, in *The Missionary Review of the World* for December, 1890, speaks out so faithfully and to the point that we cannot refrain from giving here a portion, at least, of his able article:

"It seems desirable that the foreign missionary enterprise shall be so administered as to quicken the faith and arouse the zeal of the whole church, rather than to encourage the idea that it is to be carried on by the conspicuous self-denial and self-immolation of a few.

"There is needed a faith which, instead of dispensing with the use of means, shall lead to a great increase of means; which shall, on all hands, call forth more praying and more generous giving; which shall inspire self-denial not merely in some sickly swamp in Africa, but in the wealthy and comfortable Christian homes of America.

"The world cannot be converted by a few startling object-lessons in toil and suffering. We are not encamped before Philistines, whom it is God's purpose to conquer by the faith and valor of a few Davids while the hosts of Israel simply stand still and see the salvation of the Lord. Instead of a benefit there may be positive injury in such examples. They involve a false theory of Christian duty; they excuse the avaricious and ease-loving; they seem to remove the burden of responsibility from the church as a whole. Not only do the missionaries need fixed and reliable salaries, to free them from anxiety and keep them in health and secure their success, but the church *needs to pay these salaries.* Its own spiritual life demands at least that small share of the common burden, and any theory which maintains that a fixed support is not necessary for foreign missionaries, and which so far removes responsibility from those who stay at home, is a downright injury to the whole spiritual life of Christian lands, and in the end will retard the conversion of the world instead of hastening it.

"Such theories do harm upon the mission fields as well as at home. I am aware that the plea has been made that Orientals are accustomed to associate habits of self-mortification with religion, and that they will be more readily influenced by men who are in a sense ascetics; but there is another side to this matter. Asceticism has for ages proved useless and abortive, and what is now needed is the plain, unostentatious, and vigorous devotion of an alert and healthy Christian life. The gospel of common sense is inwoven with the gospel of redemption, and where this is wanting positive harm is done.

"What are the recent facts in this connection, and what has been their influence? Nine missionaries sent out in connection with what is known as the 'Kansas Movement' were landed, some months since, at Sierra Leone. None can doubt the sincerity of their devotion.

"They had doubtless been pained by the criticisms of a worldly church upon the 'luxuries of foreign missionaries,' and they resolved to cast themselves on the Lord, and without salary, and without even medical care, devote themselves to the establishment of a mission in western Soudan.

"For the sequel we refer the reader to the statements recently published by the authorities at Sierra Leone. The British minister at Washington has lately transmitted to the Department of State a letter from the governor of Sierra Leone, including a report from the colonial surgeon at Freetown relative to the case of the nine American missionaries at that place. The report states that upon their arrival they began to live in native fashion, eating native food, cooking and washing for themselves, and even collecting their own fuel in the rainy season, hoping thus to gain the confidence of the natives. On the 9th of July two of the party died, both of whom had been such stanch believers in faith cure that they had taken no medicine. Two days after, a third died of exhaustion, from neglected fever, having been ill for nine days. As the fourth patient in the list refused the services of the physician, the latter reported to the governor that the missionaries, by the course pursued, had originated a malignant type of fever, which endangered the whole community. He therefore quarantined the house, and advised that the survivors of the party be sent back to America. Upon this the patient consented to be treated.

"Nothing could possibly produce a more unfavorable impression upon a community of foreign residents, in regard to the whole work of missions, than an event of this kind.

"And public sentiment throughout Christendom will condemn not so much the misguided young missionaries as that self-excusing sentiment in the church which seems to call for such sacrifices. So long as a missionary cannot receive a modest salary without being exposed to criticism by those who ought to be his cheerful supporters; so long as there are thousands of money-getting Christians who are ready to say of the faith missionary, 'There is the man that I believe in; he is not after the loaves and fishes; he is not going to live in luxury, etc.'—so long will sensitive young men be found who would rather brave danger, and even death itself, than to depend on such grudging supporters. At Sierra Leone starvation led to fever and death, and by all accounts came near to breeding a pestilence; yet people will soon forget it, and the plea of 'cheap missionaries' will be renewed.

"Is it quite sound, either as theology or as fact, to assume that God intends a different measure of faith and a less regard to means on the foreign fields than in the work at home? Is there any more reason to suppose that a fortuitous support can be relied upon for missionaries than for our own pastors? The whole theory of 'faith missions' proves too much; for, unless it be assumed that God has two different economies for the work of the church, then every department and every interest ought to be conducted upon trust, and all salaries, all pledges, all contracts, should be dispensed with.

"The intervention of broad oceans does not change the general laws of Christian service nor invalidate anywhere the divinely authorized principle that 'the laborer is worthy of his hire.'

"Nay, a guaranteed support is even more indispensable on the foreign field than at home. If one is to carry economy to the verge of starvation anywhere in Christ's service, a savage community in a malarious country is the very last place for the experiment. If the ministry cannot be self-supported in this country, where they are surrounded by friends and abundant resources of every kind and a great variety of occupations which open before them, how much less in an African community, where labor of every kind can be secured for a pittance, where few comforts of life can be found at the best, where no business enterprise presents itself as a possibility, and where any missionary, undertaking to live as the natives live, must be almost certain of sickness and death.

"The worst of all in these rash experiments is the sending out of married men, with the increased hazards that must come to a family. If single men were disposed to take such risks alone, as an explorer would venture into an unknown region, the case would be somewhat less serious; though no explorer ever proceeds without a thorough outfit of supplies and the means of preserving health.

"It may be safe to assume that no man has a right to expose a young wife to the perils of such a situation, subject as she must be to the incidents of married life, and with all the additional burdens and trials which a woman must encounter. . . .

"About a year ago a letter was received from a young missionary who felt that he must yield to popular criticism and live on a much smaller salary than that which was assigned to him, which was about seven hundred dollars. He proposed to dissolve his connection with the board and throw himself for support upon the students of one of our colleges. I urged him to consider carefully the subject, since, irrespective of the question of amount in salary, it would tend to dissever the students' movement from the regular organized boards of the different denominations, which would be a calamity. Many months passed before a reply came, at the end of which time he informed me that he had tried the experiment thoroughly of living on half salary, native food and in native houses, and had given it up.

"He had tried honestly and earnestly to commend himself to the people, who, as he supposed, would be influenced by one who came nearer to their ideas of what a religious man should be. But he found he was only despised, and that he really made no impression for good. He lived too well to pass for a fakir, and not well enough to claim respect as a missionary. He was neither one thing nor the other. By the Hindoo community he was looked upon as a foreign tramp. He had made a conscientious and heroic effort, and his experience should inspire the young men of our country with zeal, coupled with just views of the missionary work."

NATIVE WOMEN, BANDAWE.

CHAPTER XIV.

FROM NYASA TO CHINDE.

Bush fires.—A strong current and head wind.—Myriads of red ants.—Tampans.—On the back of a hippo.—Lake Nyasa.—Livingstonia.—A storm on the lake.—Anchored at Bandawe.—The Free Church Mission.—"Black ivory."—"Longed to enslave them."—Not soliciting commiseration.—Ungrateful.—Lip "improvers."—"Muavi" ordeal.—Fertile hills of Angoniland.—Liberty of conscience.—Baobab Island.—A choral service.—Return to Blantyre.—Bound for Chinde.—The Indian Ocean.

ON the 28th news arrived that the steamship "Domira" is unable, on account of shallows, to come farther down the river than Mponda, the southern extremity of the lake, where she is now at anchor. This necessitates a tedious journey of several days' pulling hard against the stream; but in company with the captain, in whose boat I will make the trip, we started early this morning for Matope, a distance of thirty-five miles. There is nothing very interesting on the road; once away from the vicinity of such places as Blantyre, Zomba, or the Melangi Hills, it requires a party of a very sanguine temperament to see the beauties of the Shiré Highlands. The ordinary traveler sees only the drooping and sapless foliage of the sun-stricken and stunted trees, surrounded by tall wiry grass; while at this season the atmosphere is thick with smoke from the bush fires that annually sweep over the whole country, leaving it for a time a blackened waste.

Every few miles we come upon these bush fires blazing furiously on both sides of the path; but we make a run for it, and get through with only a sniff of the flames. The native system of cultivation is responsible, in a great measure, for the wintry aspect much of the landscape presents, particularly where there is a large population. They shift to a fresh spot of land every second or third year, denuding the larger trees of their branches and felling the smaller ones three feet from the ground, leaving the brush to dry and wither, when it is gathered into heaps before the rainy season and burned. The next process is simply making a hole by a stroke or two of the hoe, dropping in a few grains of maize, covering them up with another stroke, and so on, until the field is sown out. They see no good in planting bananas, coffee, cotton or fruit trees, as they are seldom long enough in one place to reap crops that require years to mature.

The present almost prohibitive freights charged by river steamers from the coast to Katunga, and *vice versâ*, must seriously militate against the rapid agricultural development of the Shiré Highlands, as the high rates must leave but a small margin to the growers who wish to export cotton, coffee, etc. In the case of some products, such as sugar, it would cost more to transport to Chinde than it would realize in the London market. The construction of a railway, as far as Ruo at least, is the only remedy; for, even if the charges were less by water, navigation on the Shiré gets more difficult every year. The river has never been known as low as it is now, while the sandbanks are constantly changing, and pilots find the channels of one week the shallows of the next.

Next morning we had our boat loaded, and started up the Shiré against a strong current and a head wind. Having two sets of boatmen, we continued to move along slowly but surely until late, when we stopped for the night. I spread my bed under the eaves of a native hut, preferring the outside to the inside, as being less likely to encounter the disagreeable kind of company found in these domiciles generally. I was just becoming oblivious to earthly things, when I started up with a sensation of being tickled in the face by a number of red-hot needles. Striking a light, I found myself besieged by myriads of ferocious red ants. The only reliable weapon of defense against such an attack is fire, and this I wielded so effectively for half an hour, that I had, at last, the satisfaction of seeing the enemy routed with great slaughter, and was able to rest for the balance of the night in peace.

One species of vermin that infests the native huts, in addition to the trio usually accompanying squalor and dirt, is the horrible tampan, resembling a tick in size and shape, but of a dingy black color. Its bite is very painful, and produces a swelling that remains for some time after the burning sensation from the poison has passed away, often inducing fever. In some huts they can be gathered up in dozens from the earthen floors, and on account of this the traveler can seldom accept the shelter of a native dwelling. A bivouac even in the rain is preferable to the torture of being bitten by tampans.

Next morning we shoved off again, keeping a sharp lookout for the hippos, which keep bobbing up unpleasantly near our heavily laden boat. They seem more ready to go for intruders on their domain at this season, as many of them are accompanied by their young, some not larger than an ordinary pig, and often seen standing on the back of their dam.

We reached Milouries village after midnight. I avoided the huts this time by placing my mat in the open yard, to the lee of a reed fence; but a strong wind with frequent showers of rain made it anything but comfortable. Early in the morning we moved out into the stream once more, determined, if possible, to reach Mponda without further stoppages. The boys, being promised a fathom of cloth extra pay, consented to row all night. This proved rather risky, as toward the small hours of the morning, when the captain and myself were enjoying "forty winks," yells from the boatmen and the sudden upheaval of the boat brought us to our feet. We felt sure that the next minute would find us struggling in the river; but, happily, our two tons of cargo were not so easily tipped over, and we escaped a ducking. It was only a drowsy hippo trying to balance us on its back, in rather shallow water.

About nine o'clock on Friday morning we entered Lake Pomalombe, the oars stirring up the yellow mud at every stroke. We crossed the lake in six hours, and before dark got alongside the "Domira" as she lay at anchor in the stream opposite Mponda. I am sorry to learn that she will not sail for some three days yet; for although she has been lying here for ten days already, there is not a single package of her cargo on board. I find I have four fellow-passengers, who came up the river a few days ago; three of them are young missionaries—two, Germans, for the north end of the lake, and one, an Englishman, for the Universities Mission at Lokomo; the fourth is one of the company's agents. As the passenger accommodation is limited to two small bunks, some of us have to shift on deck as best we can.

On the west bank of the Shiré the native city of Mponda stretches out for a great distance—the largest collection of native huts we have seen in Africa. The population consists mostly of Yaos and Nyanges. The only attempt at mission work among them was made some years ago by four Jesuit priests; but they found the place too unhealthy to remain more than a few months, when they retired from the field and went to work at Tanganyika.

There is but little confidence placed in the professed friendship of the chief, and he is quiet only from fear of the big guns that look over on him from the opposite bank at Fort Johnson. This fort has been constructed as the headquarters of the British administration, and is garrisoned by about twenty Indian Sikhs and a few Zanzibari. There is nothing very imposing about the fort proper, it being little better than a low bank of sand thrown up in the form of a square, and surrounded by a ditch.

We got up steam at 10.30 A.M. on Tuesday, making "Monkey Bay" by sunset, where we dropped anchor for the night. This is a snug and pretty little harbor, with plenty of water, and hemmed in by hills on all sides, except the narrow entrance. A vessel would be safe here from almost any storm. Next morning we were delayed for several hours taking on a supply of firewood. This completed, we started again, and reached Cape McLear by noon. I went ashore to see the Livingstonia mission station, where a native teacher is in charge, and, I am informed, doing a good work among the children of the district. He is a quiet, sensible, unassuming young man, and speaks a little English; but for him, this would be truly a deserted and dreary spot.

There are several large buildings composing the mission premises. These are the results of the early labors of white missionaries, who were one after another cut off by fever, four or five during as many years, including the lamented Dr. William Black, the position of whose grave is indicated in the photograph by the bronze medallion and tablet riveted to the rock, at the head—a loving tribute to his memory from friends in Scotland. This was sufficient warning not to persist in occupying the station by Europeans; for though planted in a lovely spot environed by granite mountains clad to the summit with small trees, it is but a few feet above the level of the lake, hence a very hotbed of malarial exhalations. The survivors decided to move northward and transfer the mission center to Bandawe.

We left Cape McLear the same evening and crossed the lake to Maganga, where we left some letters and packages for the Mvera missionaries. The moon rose bright and clear on the placid waters as the ship's prow turned out to the deep. Far into the night we sat up enjoying the delights of a moonlight trip on Nyasa;

NATIVE WOMEN, LIKOMA

but as the morning broke there was every evidence that we were soon to get a taste of the opposite extreme. The sky became of a dull leaden color, overcast by dark, lowering clouds, sharp gusts of wind increasing in frequency and force, until Nyasa could scarcely be recognized as the same lake that only a few hours' ago lay around us a very picture of tranquillity. Now lashed into a fury, its great waves swept the decks and threatened to swamp our sturdy little craft as she bravely headed to the wind, shipping tons of water at each dip of her prow. We were compelled to pass Kotakota without calling, lest we might be driven ashore. Most of the day the storm continued, but toward evening the wind abated, subsiding as suddenly as it had arisen.

In the afternoon a number of Atonga laborers were being paid off previous to landing them at one of the ports on the lake shore. One of them was busy tying up his bundle of cloth, and while spreading out and admiring half a yard of Turkey-red, the wind whipped it out of his fingers and blew it overboard. In an instant the owner dropped his loin-cloth, and over the rails he went with a jump, feet first into the water. As he rose to the surface he spied his precious twopenceworth on the crest of a wave, and struck out boldly until he reached it. Fortunately for him, there were some repairs going on in the engine-room, and we were at only half speed; even then, by the time he turned round to come back he was half a mile astern. The captain good-naturedly put about the ship and picked him up.

By 9 P.M. Thursday we were anchored off Bandawe,

and, late as the hour was, went ashore in the ship's boat to get my letters; having been fourteen months without a single word from home, I could not wait until morning, now that I was so near. On landing, we made for the mission house, but on reaching it I was almost breathless. The cough, which during the last few days' rest on the water had eased off a little, became aggravated by the short walk through the deep, stiff black sand, and a severe paroxysm came on, so that it was some time before I could speak. All the inmates had retired except Dr. Elmslie, who handed me the longed-for package. But the latest from Jamaica is dated December 13, 1891, so that there is still a blank of nine months; surely some of my letters must have gone astray. I trudged back to my shakedown on the ship's deck. A high breeze was blowing, but the night was not cold.

Next morning I returned to Bandawe Station, so as to visit it by daylight. Dr. Elmslie gave me a cordial invitation to stay there until the return of the steamer from Karonga, when I purposed proceeding to Lokomo. Bandawe is situated on a sandy promontory, bounded on the west by the Angoni Mountains, about a hundred and seventy miles north of Mponda. The mission premises, which are built of brick, with grass roofs, form a straight line, running north and south, consisting of dwellings, school or meeting-house, carpenter's shop, and printing-room. Like all other stations on the flat lake shore, it is far from healthy. The heat is intense, and although the soil is deep sand, within a few inches of the surface it is quite moist, giving off an unwholesome vapor from the accumulation of organic matter swept down from the adjoining hills every year. Here, as we have noted elsewhere, the missionaries have tried to grow almost every kind of English vegetables, but without success. They are obliged to depend mainly on imported food-stuffs, with occasional supplies of sweet potatoes from the hills.

The chief feature of the Bandawe mission is its large day-school. A number of the boys are boarders, but a good many come from the neighboring villages as day-scholars. The natives are now beginning to appreciate education, but it has been a long, hard struggle to attain even this; for here, as on the Zambesi, many abandon the pursuit of knowledge after the first week or two, when wages for "working book" is denied them. But one and all fully realize the benefits accruing from the presence of the missionaries among them, not only for the medical aid they receive, but also protection, as attacks from hostile tribes or the slave-traders are now rare.

In reference to the latter, it must be said that, while there can be no question that a very extensive traffic in "black ivory" still exists around Nyasa, and while it will ever be the earnest purpose of every true friend of the African to do all that can be done to stamp out this fearful scourge, we must take care that mere sentiment is not permitted to control the pen that reports the doings of the Arabs and their native allies. That this is no imaginary danger is conclusive from facts gathered during our sojourn in these regions. For example: a leaflet addressed to the children of the Free Church of Scotland, in the form of a letter from a missionary at the north end of the lake, headed

"———'s Three Hundred Slave Children," reads as follows:

"All my little scholars at the school are from the Wankondê villages—the very children that the Arabs fought for and longed to enslave. They are, every one of them, naked and helpless. God has rescued them from the slaver's cruel hand, and they look to us. Could not the children of the Sabbath-schools at home do a little for the three hundred naked, helpless Wankondê children whom we have graciously saved from the cruel goree-stick and slavery?"

What these statements are worth may be gathered from the following facts. In the first place, the children referred to never *were* slaves, and therefore not objects for rescue (even to use his own words, the Arabs only "*longed to enslave them*"), but attend a school organized some years ago by Mr. Fotheringham. Moreover, they are provided with both food and lodgings by their parents, who in almost every case live in the villages of the neighborhood. Nor are they or their parents in any way soliciting commiseration, seeing that their lot is cast in one of the richest and most productive parts of Nyasaland, and that they are exposed perhaps less than most tribes to Arab raids, protected, as they are, by the guns on the fort of the African Lakes Company.

What has been the result of this pathetic account of slave rescue? Why, the people of Scotland could not be deaf to such an appeal, and in a brief space twelve hundred pounds were contributed. What has been done with it? Nothing! because the object for which it was given existed only on paper.

NYASA FLEET, LIKOMA

See page 321

Such policy on the part of any man is suicidal to the cause he seeks to advance. There are plenty of genuine and just claims on the sympathies of the benevolent, without conjuring up such yarns as this. Philanthropists do not like being *sold* any more than slaves, and the next call, though probably deserving, will suffer in consequence.

Dr. Elmslie had his ardor somewhat damped on the question of liberating slaves last week. Hearing that a slave caravan was passing through a village a couple of miles from the station, three teachers with a few lads took their guns and started off to interview the half-breeds in charge. On the appearance of the mission boys in the camp, the supposed slavers, suspecting that white men were not far off and fearing trouble, took to their heels. Many of the caravan followed suit, leaving fifteen of their number, mostly women, behind. These the teachers brought on to Bandawe, where comfortable huts were assigned them and plenty of food, although, on the whole, they did not appear to have suffered much on the march. The doctor sat down forthwith to report the circumstance to the home committee; but what was his surprise next morning, on visiting their huts, for the purpose of obtaining fuller information concerning them, to find that, with the exception of one woman and her child, the whole gang of captured slaves had run away during the night, and returned to the very people from whom they had been rescued the day before. Rather an unromantic termination to the affair. But it teaches the important lesson that we must discriminate between slave-trading and domestic slavery.

The whole life of Central Africa is permeated with a system of slavery, which the natives themselves have no desire to see abolished, although it must come in time. But high-handed measures will accomplish little in this direction; rather let force be concentrated to arrest the cruel and bloody work of the Arabs, who raid and capture slaves for gain only.

I succeeded in taking several photos of groups of native women who were employed on the premises as laborers in the construction of a dwelling-house. I here give one of these groups. Those in the foreground are mostly old women, showing the deformity of the features produced by wearing the *pelele* in the upper lip. This repulsive custom is not confined to the old;·but no sooner was the camera placed in position and my head hidden beneath the focusing-cloth, than up went the hands of the younger women to their mouths, and the rings, etc., were whipped out quick as a wink. The old women, however, are less sensitive, and in them this lip "improver" reaches the maximum of size, in some cases to nearly the diameter of a napkin ring; and when such attempt a smile, the contraction of the risorial muscles throws the lip up with a jerk, and forms a circle round the tip of their flat pug-noses that peep through the opening, while a row of V-shaped, cat-like teeth is displayed, giving the wearer a most ludicrous appearance.

The girls have their lips pierced when very young. A straw or thread is inserted to keep the hole open; then a small piece of bamboo or bone, gradually increasing in size, until the orthodox ring can be worn. But the *pelele* assumes many forms—a bit of ivory, or wood shaped like a cotton reel, or, what is greatly admired, a piece of white quartz from an inch to two inches in length, looking very much as if they had stuck in the end of a wax candle.

The practice of tattooing the body is usual, but without any apparent tribal pattern or design, as we noticed among the Ganguellians, in which district it is quite universal, both sexes being elaborately tattooed. The Ganguella tribal mark among the men seems to be an arrangement of four large diamonds, though other forms are used to adorn the main pattern. The women tattoo freely, but prefer lines across the body to more complicated figures. There are different methods employed to produce these decorations. In one the knife-point is inserted under the cuticle to admit the charcoal, pigment, or even, in some instances, gunpowder; in others the skin is merely scratched with the knife; while in a third the usual plan of tattooing is followed, when some sharp-pointed instrument is used to prick in the desired—disfigurement.

Along the shores of Nyasa, as among all the tribes north of the Zambesi, trial by ordeal, or the "muavi" test, is practiced extensively, and is resorted to, not only for the purpose of "smelling out" witchcraft, or to convict persons suspected of crime, but in the most trivial quarrels is often the arbitrator for settlement of the dispute. Only to-day a man came rushing into the mission yard appealing to Dr. Elmslie for help, as he had taken a long and a strong pull from the poison-gourd. One of his wives and himself having had a disagreement, it was mutually decided that they both take the test, which they did. The wife infused the poisonous decoction of bark and took the first drink, and immediately commenced to vomit—a sure indication that she was in the right. But the husband was not so fortunate, for, having finished the potion, it did not react as he had hoped, and, fearing death, repented of what he had done, and made for the mission house, when a prompt emetic put him out of danger.

As a rule, natives who are conscious of their innocence take the test readily, as they have the fullest confidence that the "muavi" will convict only the guilty.

When a chief suspects a revolutionary spirit, or any lack of fidelity on the part of his subjects, the witch-doctor is dispatched to assemble the recreant villagers and organize a big muavi-drinking, so as to sift out the traitors. All classes and both sexes are put on their trial, without respect of persons.

Three months ago a case of this kind occurred a short distance from here, by order of the chief, Chikusi. One of the Livingstonia mission staff refers to it in the *Free Church of Scotland Monthly:*

"The chief sent his singánga (witch-doctor) and the royal 'muavi' as a trial of their subjection. That in part accounted for its importance. It seems that everybody in the villages, men, women, and children above nine or ten years old—many of our school-children among them—had drunk it, and that a few from a distance only remained for Saturday's drinking. Seven in all were found dead—cast out to the vultures—including an old white-haired man and wife, and the headman of the villages, but no children. Dr. Henry insisted on the burial of the corpses. Some seemed only too willing to do so, now that the singánga dare not interfere. The possessions of those who died were taken off to Tshipolopolo (the sub-chief who brought the charge against the victims and appealed to Chikusi for the trial).

"Another mauvi-drinking took place last Friday, at which two of our schoolgirls—little things of ten or eleven years old—and a woman died. The excuse was the death of a man in their village."

Although this custom exists in the Barotse Valley, the Marotsi prefer to pour the poisonous decoction down the throat of a dog or a fowl, and judge of the innocence or guilt of the indicted party by the effect the poison produces on the animal—vomiting being supposed to be proof positive of innocence, while purging indicates guilt.

The favorite ordeal of this class in the Barotse is that of the "boiling-pot." The last that took place at Lialui was brought about by a slave carrying a piece of raw meat through Lewanika's reception-room, a few drops of blood falling on his mat. The consternation and alarm of the great man at this, to him, an omen portending every ill, may be imagined, and not a moment was lost in summoning all the sorcerers and wise men of the capital, when it was decided to try the effect of the "boiling-pot" in shedding light on the subject.

The natives are assembled as for the "muavi" trial. Those suspected of having evil designs against the king are singled out at the instigation of the witch-doctor, the names of whom he professes to read in his basket of tricks. Of such there may be many—twenty, thirty, forty, or more—who are each in turn required to dip their hand three times into the boiling water.

If innocent, it is supposed that this should have no effect on their skin, which, strange to say, is very often the case, especially on the thick and shriveled skin of the old; but with the majority large blisters are produced, and they are pronounced guilty, and sentenced either to be knob-kerried, speared, or thrown to the crocodiles.

Returning to the subject of mission stations, I think it has been demonstrated beyond the shadow of a doubt that only high altitudes—as far as possible from the low-lying swamps, or valleys hemmed in by hills—should be selected as sites. If stations must be planted on the flats, let them be occupied only occasionally by white men, and then only during seasons of the year when the exhalation of malaria is least active. The Angoni Hills, for instance, have proved comparatively healthy; the land is fertile, cattle thrive, and much in the way of vegetables, so essential to the health of Europeans, can be grown in abundance.

The Livingstonia Mission has two stations in Angoniland since 1882: Njuyu, where a church has been formed with nine members, and Ekwendeni. There are not the same hindrances in East Central Africa to Christian work as exist farther south and west; the intense darkness and gross ignorance are all over alike, but the power of the chiefs is not so great. They exert little or no influence over the home-life of the people; nor is attendance on religious instruction, efforts to improve their condition or rise in the scale of civilization, vetoed by autocratic rulers, as in the Barotse or Matebeleland. In a word, there is liberty of conscience. This is a point of great importance, and a very encouraging augury for the future of missions in the vast regions bounding the beautiful Nyasa.

On Thursday, September 14th, the "Domira" returned from the north end, when I learned, to my dismay, that she would have to put up at Lokoma for repairs and go back to Karonga for passengers. This is a sore disappointment to me, as I shall miss the October steamer from Quilimane, and shall probably have to wait a whole month at the coast for the November mail. But I am helpless in the matter, for a land journey is not to be thought of, owing to the disturbed condition of the natives on both sides of the lake. I got on board, and crossed over to Lokoma early on Friday morning.

This is an island ten miles from the mainland. It is about five miles long and three wide, with a population of over two thousand natives, speaking the Chinanji language. There is but little vegetation on the island except baobabs; these are numerous, and some of them very large. The soil is poor, as may be said of most of the lake shore; the only products are sand and stones, and a stunted species of manioc. Half a mile from the beach we find the headquarters of the Universities Mission, surrounded by several small hills, that look as if they were formed of débris thrown up from some big excavation.

The mission premises consist of a number of detached reed huts, the domiciles of the several members of the staff; the church, also of reeds; and a schoolroom, store, and boys' dormitory, built of stone and mud. Archdeacon Maples, well known for his untiring energy and devotion to mission work, and, withal, genial, hospitable, and kind, is in charge of the station. He is assisted by some seven or eight white workers, men and women, and also by several native teachers from Zanzibar. The mission has two small steamers, the "Charles Jansen" and the "Beta." The former is used chiefly for visiting the numerous villages along the coast, and is under the command of the Rev. W. Johnson.

The *modus operandi* of the service on Sunday morning should satisfy the most exacting ritualist. The church is floored with mats, on which the natives squat, prostrating themselves one by one as they come in. A few benches are placed near the altar for the white portion of the audience and for the native choir, who are surpliced in white and cassocked in purple. These enter at the commencement of the service in procession, headed by a large brass cross; the priests bring up the rear, crossing and bowing themselves in front of the altar before taking their places. The service is principally choral, and the archdeacon, being a splendid musician, adds great effect to the chanted liturgy by his brilliant execution on the organ. The choir-boys give evidence of careful vocal training, their intoning and chanting being performed with automatic precision.

The congregation embraces a large membership, the majority being women, who wear the distinguishing badge—a small cross round their necks; in many instances, however, their fetich charms are not displaced by this latter addition to their adornments.

I believe this mission is considered a great success by the ritualistic party. And if advanced High-Church lines indicate success, surely we have it here. To say nothing of the full choral service, with its priestly

KATUNGA AND HIS WIVES (LIVINGSTONE'S OLD SERVANT)

robes, prostrations, and genuflections, its confessional and highly decorated altar, its crosses, crucifixes, etc., we have, as indicating advanced High-Churchism, the Sunday afternoon football and cricket matches, in which the clergy take active part.

Thursday, 21st. Another weary week of waiting for the return of the "Domira"; but she is here at last, and by sunset we are heading for Cape McLear, and in thirty-six hours more anchored again at Mponda. Here I left the steamer, and in an open boat proceeded down the Shiré. Going with the current, we made good progress, and early on the morning of Tuesday, the 26th, landed at Matope. Carriers being in readiness, after a hurried breakfast we started for Blantyre. The hills were stiff to climb, and the day excessively hot, so that it was far into the night before we reached the mission station. Next day I engaged carriers to take my luggage to Katunda, purchased some provisions for the road, and started on Thursday morning, with many *adieux* to my Scotch friends at Blantyre, whose open-hearted and unpretentious kindness has done so much to restore, strengthen, and cheer me, arriving among them, as I did, worn out, weary, and sick from my long journey, with its varied and trying experiences of privation and difficulties.

Leaving Blantyre, we set out for the river. Coming upon some water at noon, I stopped and made a cup of cocoa; but as there was no shade from the relentless heat of the scorching sun, we delayed but a short time, and reached Katunga at 7 P.M. I put up at the African Lake Company's station again for the night, and next morning found the boat and paddlers I had previously engaged all ready; and by nine o'clock we were afloat, bound for Chinde. The run of eleven days down this river was uneventful, though we called at the "customs" Chiromo, when I got back my firearms, and had some good shooting on the flats. Rain fell heavily for several days in succession, from which I had no protection but a slight awning of grass at the stern of the boat, so that everything got badly drenched, giving me wet blankets to sleep under for four nights, and inducing a sharp turn of fever. But we reached Chinde safely on the 10th of October, where, with what joy no tongue can tell, I view at last the Indian Ocean, toward which I have been traveling these many months.

Having missed the German mail for this month, I have secured, through the courtesy of Commander Finnis, R. N. of H. M. S. "Swallow," a passage on board a transport steamer, now in the river discharging cargo for the lakes, and leaving in a few days for Port Said *via* Zanzibar.

CHAPTER XV.

A RETROSPECT.

A summary.—Jamaicans.—Missionaries wanted.—French mission stands alone.—Testimony in favor of West Indian assistants.—Unoccupied fields.—Sparse population.—Interpreters.—Medical missions.—Extravagant waste of ability.—Native doctors.—Conclusion.

IN looking back over the past eighteen months since landing at Benguela, and over the thousands of miles I have traversed, the question arises, How far has the purpose of my journey been realized?

So far as my desire to see and learn the condition and need of these regions is concerned, I have been gratified beyond my most sanguine anticipations; for at most I had only expected to be able to make straight for Nyasa through the Katanga country—after all, a road no longer unknown, since the remarkable journey of Mr. Sharp and the ill-fated expedition of Captain Stairs, both of whom started almost simultaneously with myself, although from opposite directions. But I have been permitted to travel through the interesting and but little known Ganguella country and the famous Zambesi Valley; to see one of the world's greatest wonders, the Victoria Falls; to taste the bitters of the Kalahari Desert; to visit Bechuanaland and render medical aid to the good chief Khama and his people during the fever epidemic; to trek over the desolate and dreary wastes of Mashonaland; to watch the miners pegging out their claims in Manicaland; and to roam through the beautiful and fertile—but to the geographer almost blank—country of Gorongoza; besides being privileged to wander among those places for which the sympathies of the Christian world were first enlisted by the beloved Livingstone—Lake Nyasa and the Blantyre Highlands.

Apart from this, I had anticipated testing the question how far the services of the Christian natives of the West Indies might be requisitioned as aids in mission work in this vast continent. My hopes in this direction were founded partly on reports from those in the field, made public through missionary papers and published letters, and partly from the fact that every few months there seemed to be fresh detachments going out to Central Africa, some under the auspices of societies, and some not; until, in common with many others, I felt that if ever the Jamaican is to be brought back to benefit his fatherland, it should be now.

It is unnecessary here to repeat what has already been explained in the first chapter in reference to the six young men who accompanied me for this purpose. As to how they journeyed with me to Cisamba, where four of them remained, the other two going as far as Mangwato, the reader already knows. But when I state that, from the time Bihe on the west was left behind and we arrived at Blantyre on the east, with the exception of the French mission on the Zambesi I did not come across a single missionary laboring among natives, it will be better understood why I failed to find places for the appointment of colored men, as all the way I was looking for pioneers engaged in the work of founding new stations, with whom there might be possible openings for colored assistants, but found them not.

This, of course, has been a sore disappointment to me, but has in no way weakened my former conviction that, provided white men with sympathy for, and tact in dealing with, the colored race are forthcoming to enter the unbroken and fallow fields of the interior, the services of the Jamaicans in manual labor as builders, planters, etc., would be found invaluable. In a short time their aptitude for acquiring the language would fit them for itinerant evangelists, while their color would give emphasis to their words beyond even those of the white teacher, for whom, as the number of concession-hunters and speculators increase, a marked prejudice in the native African mind grows stronger year by year.

But why not include the mission in Mangwato and those of Mashonaland with the French mission? Because, although there is a church nearly completed in Khama's town, there was no white missionary at the time we passed through, and the stations at Salisbury and Umtali are so far intended only to meet the requirements of the influx of gold-seeking and mining Europeans; but I have neither seen nor heard of any effort being made to reach the natives in Mashonaland; therefore, missions to white men are not included in the question under consideration. The fact remains that the French mission stands alone as being actually engaged in the evangelization of the heathen in the great belt of territory referred to.

It is not from mere personal partiality toward colored

men that I am led to think highly of the prospects for their future usefulness in the mission fields of Central Africa, but now from actual experience, and the testimony of those to whom they have rendered service, as expressed verbally and by letter. The first of the latter was from the Rev. W. T. Currie of Cisamba, referring to those left with him, and which I received while in the Ganguella country:

CANADIAN STATION, CISAMBA, WEST AFRICA,
September 15, 1891.

DEAR DR. JOHNSTON: Let me briefly wish you farewell, with a sincere "God be with you till we meet again." Your visit to this station has been for us most pleasant. After a long season of loneliness and heavy work, which had greatly tried my strength, you came with a strong arm and a warm heart to cheer and help in time of need. If, in return, I have been able to assist you in any way, rest assured that I have done so with the utmost pleasure.

The men you have left with me at this station supply a long-felt need of our work here.

The bearing of the men has thus far increased our respect for and confidence in them. They have already won the affection of my boys, even though they can speak to them but few words. They have begun the study of the language, and can sing most of our hymns; have several times helped my boys when holding evangelistic services in the native villages. Their special value to us at present is perhaps in the line of building, and I am sure, from what they have already done, that they will be able and willing so to relieve us from much work that we may devote much more time than we otherwise could to the instruction of the young, and to the preaching of the gospel to the people at large in this country. . . .

Yours sincerely,
W. T. CURRIE.

Mr. Currie is one of the very few having the tact and firmness, coupled with uniform kindness, so necessary in a missionary who has the management of colored workers; so that when he left the station on account of ill-health for a prolonged furlough, the men I left with him lost heart, got discouraged, and concluded to follow, overtaking Mr. Currie at the coast, eventually returning with him to England, and afterward finding their way back to Jamaica.

In one particular, the return of these men to the coast proved a most fortunate incident, as they found Mr. Currie down with a severe attack of fever, and rendered very opportune service, as the following extract from a subsequent letter from Mr. Currie states:

"Please remember me very kindly to the native brethren. Often do I seem to hear their voices singing so sweetly, as they did at our prayer-meetings. God bless them! They kindly cared for me when I had no power to raise my head, and surely I cannot soon forget them."

The Rev. W. Elliott, with whom I intrusted Frater and Jonathan (who had traveled with me as far as Bechuanaland) and who left with him for the Cape, writing to the headquarters of the Jamaica Mission, notifying their departure for home, says:

"We shall be very sorry to lose them indeed. Their bright hearts and faces have cheered our depressed spirits, and their hearty willingness to help in *all* the work of the journey has made them favorites with us all. I earnestly hope to get the help of one or more of them, or their friends, in our Matebele mission in a year or two, or perhaps earlier.

"Jonathan carries away a sad heart from Africa because he has been able to do so little for the Saviour.

He and Frater have both done much for us, and you know what value Christ puts on a 'cup of cold water' given to His children.

"I hope to have a talk with them both about getting help for our Matebele, and I shall write to Dr. Johnston too on the same subject when I know more of our own movements than I do at present.

"We part from them as from friends long tried. May God give them *bon voyage* and a happy return to their homes."

As to the prospect for future mission work, several places along my route impressed me as being very hopeful as well as needy "fields," such as, commencing at the west, Ciyuka in Bihe, Ongandu by the Kukema River, Kongovia by the Kwanza—both the last-named in the Ganguella country; while farther east Kangamba, and, passing over the Barotse Valley and Bechuanaland, we come to the little-known but thickly inhabited region of Gorongoza. In none of these places has mission work been attempted in any form whatever; and why I would especially emphasize the importance of these places as inviting spheres is: first, so far as the climate is concerned they were the healthiest districts we came across; second, they were among the very few places where we were able to obtain vegetables, proving that the soil was sufficiently fertile to yield something more than the ordinary Kaffir-corn; third, owing to the natives being governed by petty chiefs there is more freedom and liberty of conscience allowed, and the work, therefore, not open to the objections that present themselves under a big autocratic chief; while the interviews we held on the subject with the various headmen of these countries confirmed our opinion that missionaries would be well received and kindly treated.

At Ongandu, Kongovia, and Kangamba in particular the populations are large and very accessible, their villages being grouped in each case within a short distance of their respective ombalas. We cannot indorse the reports so often made of the densely populated condition of Central Africa, but quite the contrary. Once in three or four hundred miles one strikes a moderate-sized town; about every hundred miles a group of villages; a small village, perhaps, every other day's march. This certainly was my experience after crossing the Kwanza until we reached Manicaland, and this fact gives all the more prominence to the places we have mentioned.

I earnestly hope to see the day when a mission on a sound practical basis shall be established at each of them.

Gorongoza is but a short journey from the East Coast; landing at Beira by either German steamers from the north or by the Union Line around the Cape, proceeding up the Pungwe River to Saramento, and then, after three or four days' marching, Gorongoza Mountain would be reached.

Those places west of the Zambesi must be approached from the West Coast, either from Loanda, Novo Redondo, or Benguela. At present the latter must be preferred, as carriers are difficult to obtain at the first two. The cost of conveying a load of sixty pounds would be about thirty shillings.

But on no account would it be advisable in the beginning to take out ladies or children. The work should be commenced by young men, several at each station; and as the language or anything like a vocabulary has not yet been reduced to writing, it would be essential that the young missionaries should have the ability and educational qualifications necessary to undertake the drudgery of this task. Interpreters might be obtained from among the half-caste Portuguese, hence a previous knowledge of the Portuguese language would be found almost indispensable.

Much of the first year would be occupied in clearing a place for the settlement, preparing and getting into the soil seeds and plants for the kitchen-garden, making furniture, and providing, as far as possible, for their future comfort. On account of the expense in hiring labor for this work—for we suppose, of course, that the white men will not attempt outdoor toil themselves (*which means the shortest road to a premature grave*)—a plentiful supply of trade cloth, beads, knives, gunpowder, lead, etc., should be provided, sufficient to meet the probable emergency that six or eight months might elapse before their next caravan arrives from the coast.

After two years, and when everything is in order and the home made comparatively snug, it will be time enough to talk about bringing out wives. But even then, should there be children, it were kinder to leave them at home, as this is no country for them. Some are of the opinion that the example of a missionary family home-life as an object-lesson to the natives must stir their aimless minds to emulation. Some time, perhaps, this may come; but for years the contrast will be too great for them to see anything to imitate. In reality, the domestic life, habits, and customs of the white man excite in the African only a curiosity similar to that of a country bumpkin's first introduction to a menagerie. And to say the least, even were some good accomplished thereby, the exposing of children to the base and degrading scenes that must surround them every day among a barbarous and savage people cannot be justified under any pretense whatever.

One qualified medical man could easily look after the health of the Europeans on each of the first three stations, as there is at most but a couple of days' journey between them; but Kangamba, being more isolated and farther interior, would require a larger staff of workers and its own physician.

Too much stress cannot be laid on the importance of medical missions in the foreign field as well as at home. Rarely a day passed during my whole journey that I did not prove the value of being able to prescribe for the sick; and I might say that, under God, I owe my life in more than one instance to the pacific effects of medical aid rendered to suspicious and hostile natives. Right at Catambella, our first stage on the West Coast, I opened my "Burroughs & Welcome" medicine-chest to physic fever-stricken carriers, many of whom were to take my own loads. Quinine, antipyrin, and rousers soon established a reputation for me as a fever-doctor; while on the march those suffering from gastrointestinal catarrh, galled shoulders, and ulcers were mustered daily and treated promptly and successfully. All along the route I had numerous opportunities of alleviating the sufferings of not only many hundreds of natives, but several missionaries, hunters, and traders, and, in Mashonaland and Manica, miners and Portuguese officials.

It is with the greatest satisfaction that I look back over my personal experiences throughout the long journey, to the benefits accruing to sufferers from my profession as a medical man. Not the least of these was my timely arrival at Mangwato and sojourn there during the month of April, 1892, when the devastating fever epidemic was at its height. The many expressions of gratitude from both blacks and whites in Khama's country and elsewhere convince me that in this, if for nothing else, my journey was not in vain. The monetary expense of the expedition, the hardships and trials endured, pale to insignificance when compared with what we were permitted to see accomplished among those who were otherwise hundreds of miles from medical assistance. And the fact that through the whole of our traveling not a single death occurred among my men must be attributed to the well-stocked and at all times available medicine-chest.

The question has been put to me repeatedly by medical students, Would you recommend Central Africa as a field for men holding University degrees in medicine who wish to devote themselves to mission work? Is there a sphere for such there? I can only say that the answer depends very much upon circumstances. If there is a party of white missionaries going out, a fully qualified physician should certainly accompany them. Nothing can justify the appointing of white men and their families to posts in the far interior without placing a doctor within easy access of their station, *and in this particular lies the chief necessity for the qualified medical man.*

He will of course find abundant opportunity for practice among the natives; but from all I have seen of the general class of diseases prevalent in Africa and brought under the notice of the medical missionary, it certainly seems an extravagant waste of ability, as he will find that a very small percentage of the knowledge and skill acquired during years of study is ever required or brought into exercise. It is a recognized fact that the Central African will rarely submit to have even a tooth extracted, far less consent to a surgical operation, even if death could be averted thereby, as amputation conflicts with the anticipation of his disembodied spirit returning in a form superior to his present existence. In the matter of accouchement it is contrary to native law that a man, physician or otherwise, should be permitted to be present, far less to aid women in childbirth. A doctor who has been for the last seven years resident in the country informed me that only once in his whole experience had he been present in such a case, so that his knowledge of midwifery, so far as the native is concerned, is quite dispensable. And there is no room for orthopedic or plastic surgery, for all deformed infants are destroyed at birth, as being under the ban and displeasure of the gods.

Again and again I have watched the daily routine at the dispensary of medical mission stations, and the work of the physician consisted chiefly in dressing ulcers, preparing lotions for ophthalmia, administering emetics as an antidote to the effects of "muavi," strapping up a spear wound, prescribing for indigestion incidental to their coarse fare, or a simple cough mixture for the bronchitis to which they are liable during the cold season; but seldom did we see a case so complicated that a missionary with a very ordinary knowledge of the properties of drugs in common use could not have treated successfully.

Although we are inclined to sneer at the native doctors, it must be owned that, with all their cabalistic practices and the superstitions and orgies that pervade their exorcising of disease, some of them effect cures by means of herbs to us unknown, and the secret of which we might well covet. Dr. E—— of Bandawe tells me that more than once for weeks he has continued to treat ulcers with every means and appliance known to our profession, without avail; owning himself baffled, the patient resorted to a native doctor, and returned in a short time, to Dr. E——'s astonishment, with the wound completely healed.

A case in point may be cited that occurred, April, 1892, in Bechuanaland, in the presence of a number of Europeans. A Boer while trekking northward with his family was delayed for some weeks in camp from the greater number of his cattle having died of lung sickness. His wife was in a low state of health, suffering from numerous boils and festering sores. While dressing them one day, she failed to keep off the hordes of flies that had gathered round the putrid meat in the vicinity; blood-poisoning and pyemia quickly supervened, and death seemed imminent. An English surgeon who chanced to be on the road was summoned, but after careful examination he pronounced the case hopeless, when one of the Boer's native drivers begged permission to call a bushman doctor. Consent was given, and in a short time the bushman appeared. He sat silently watching the patient for a little time, and then went off at a trot over the veldt for some distance, gathered a variety of herbs, and on returning put a large pot with water on the fire, into which he threw his collection of medicines. When the infusion was ready he urged the patient to drink, which she did, bowl after bowl; while with the same decoction he bathed the sores, and within twenty-four hours all danger was over, and the woman ultimately made a good recovery.

It is with no thought of vaunting the qualities of the native doctor that we give such an example, but that it may be understood that the native African is not totally without medical aid of a kind, even in the absence of white men.

In the face of these facts we are forced to the conclusion that the appointment of qualified medical men to mission centers chiefly for the benefit of the native population is superfluous, and that the work assigned to them might be quite satisfactorily accomplished by mere tyros in the art of healing.

Mr. Currie of Cisamba has not been able to take a full course in medicine, but, having a great interest in the study of native diseases and their treatment, had, during the time of my visit there, a larger number of patients coming daily to his dispensary than I have seen at any station in Africa—even where the missionary was an M.D.

Much the same may be said of Monsieur Coillard, and I am fairly convinced that the expenses of medical missions in Central Africa may be very much lessened, without their value being materially diminished, were a short course in the practice of medicine included in the curriculum of our missionary colleges—the studies to be directed by an ex-African medical missionary thoroughly conversant with the prevalent ailments endemic to the regions for which the various students are destined. Yet this suggestion retracts in no way from my first statement, that wherever Europeans are stationed the presence of the best and most skillful physician obtainable is absolutely essential; for where the lives of valued workers are at stake the thought of expense should not be considered.

My weary journey across Africa is ended. I long with intense yearning to get back to that snug little island, the gem of the Caribbean Sea—Jamaica, wherein I am proud to have a home; for in all my travels I have seen no spot so lovely, or that can half compare with the "Isle of Springs." Yet I thank God that I have been permitted to travel through the great continent, notwithstanding the many trials, hardships, and dangers I have had to face, without losing a single native follower by death, and without firing an angry shot.

And now that it is over, I humbly and gratefully acknowledge the protecting care of Him whom I trust, and who has never failed me even in the darkest hour. And if the knowledge acquired of countries through which I have passed, or of people and tribes I have met, can be of service to those who are seeking to spread the light and truth of the gospel, or advance the cause of civilization in this dark and benighted land, I shall rejoice in all I have endured for its sake.

APPENDIX.

Equipment.—Tents *versus* huts.—Clothing.—Firearms.—Barter goods.—Commissariat.—Medicine.—Tabloids.—Fever.—Insomnia.—Water.—Coolers.—Light.—Photography.

THE intending traveler must be guided in the selection of his outfit and equipment by a knowledge of the nature and character of the regions through which he proposes to journey, as it makes a material difference whether his route lies through districts where occasional supplies may be obtained, or penetrates the interior beyond the boundary of supply stores.

Again, the facilities for conveyance of goods must be considered, as, if wagons can be used, provision for the journey may only be limited by the traveler's means; while if carriers must be procured, the less he can do with, the better. To the latter class I would offer a few suggestions from my own experience, having special reference to Central Africa.

EQUIPMENT.—Personal outfit should include: tent, made of Willesden canvas, about seven feet by eight, with double roof, and tarpaulin ground-sheet for the floor; small folding-table and chair; iron frame folding-cot weighing twenty pounds; a thin cork mattress; two or three blankets, large and of *good* quality, with a rug or plaid, and a small horse-hair pillow. Don't forget a piece of good mosquito-netting, and *never* pass the night, whether in a tent or in the open, without its protection, for it is undoubtedly a great preservation to health, the meshes shutting out the miasma, which is always worst at night. There are many ways of rigging up the netting, but the simplest of all is to take a piece of strong calico, say blue " pentado," seven feet long and three feet wide; around the edges of this sew a length of netting five feet wide; to each corner stitch a piece of strong tape, and the arrangement is complete. After the ground-sheet, mattress, and blankets are spread for the night, get four of your carriers' spears, and stick one into the ground at each corner, from which, by means of the tapes, suspend the net at a convenient height. After getting into bed, tuck the edge of the netting in under the mattress all around. But whatever shape you may adopt for your mosquito netting, remember that it is positively indispensable.

A rubber ground-sheet is essential in case you require to sleep in the open; but this is the only article of rubber goods one need take, as air-pillows and suchlike give way in a few months.

TENTS.—Tents are very useful in wet weather, but they get intolerably hot during the day, unless they can be opened at both ends to permit a free current of air to pass through; and this has the drawback that the contents are exposed too much to the prying eyes of the natives, and so exciting their cupidity. West of the Zambesi they may without serious inconvenience be dispensed with altogether, as the carriers prepare quite commodious round huts in an hour or two of sticks and grass, cool on the hottest day and warm at night, while if the thermometer goes down very low, a fire can be built in the center. This cannot with comfort be done in a tent, as there is no outlet for the smoke, and in any case would destroy the canvas.

KITCHEN UTENSILS.—A block-tin canteen, such as is supplied by Langdon of London, contains all the necessary utensils for the camp kitchen, and may be had in various sizes, to suit one or half a dozen persons. I would advise that the kit be examined before purchasing, to see that lids, handles, etc., are thoroughly riveted, as, from the carelessness of natives and the open camp-fire, solder holds but a very short time. See also that the lid of the pot be made of sheet-iron and not of tin, so that it will serve the purpose of a Dutch oven.

CLOTHING.—Two or three suits of good tweed might come in handy when approaching or visiting civilized centers; but for the veldt, good light-colored "elephant cord" will be found much more durable and satisfactory. It is most suitable for marching in the form of knickerbockers, and one jacket of this material will last a year, as it is only worn in the cool of the morning and after getting into camp; and it must be very rough usage that would require more than two or three pairs of breeches. With these, thick, heavy worsted stockings must be worn; but when traveling through long grass they need to be protected by leggings, say of canvas, as, if the grass is dry, it sheds small seeds and sometimes sharp needle-like burrs, that are retained by the rough, woolly surface, penetrating to the skin and causing great irritation. The worsted stockings are at the same time a sure defense against ants of every description, as, no matter how fierce, their mandibles get entangled in the meshes of the knitting, and thus are rendered harmless.

Footwear should be of two kinds. Light tennis-shoes of canvas, but not rubber-soled, are best suited for marching over sandy plains, but soon weary the feet if the path becomes rough or stony; here we must have thick-soled leather boots, a size larger than usual. I do not mean by this "top-boots," such as are sometimes worn by sporting-men at home; they are found much too hot and heavy; but the shoe *par excellence* in dry weather is the native-made "*veldt schoon.*" For more than half my journey I used them in preference to every other, finding them noiseless in hunting and very easy to the feet. They are generally made with soles of buffalo hide and tops of "koodoo" or other antelope.

Underclothing should be chiefly of wool, so as to avert the evil effects arising from chill; and loose-fitting, to allow for shrinkage, as new travelers are not generally experts in the art of washing. The shirts should be made of a light, soft tweed, with a breast-pocket on each side; if some of them are only half-sleeved it would be no harm, as one generally prefers during the day to have the arms bare from the elbow at least.

Headgear is purely a matter of choice. Some vote for the helmet of pith, cork, straw, or felt; others, like myself, prefer an ordinary broad-brimmed light-colored Terai or wide-awake. The helmet I find a nuisance. It gets knocked off in the jungle by the overhanging branches of the trees; it is always in the way; if you wish to rest at noon you must either sit up so as not to crush it, or lie down without its protection, while the soft felt is obviously more accommodating.

FIREARMS.—In reference to weapons, if firearms are carried for the sole purpose of procuring meat, a twelve-bore shot-gun choked in one barrel and a .577 "Express" rifle D. B. will be found sufficient for ordinary game. But if danger from hostile natives is anticipated, in addition to these a few Winchester repeaters, 45.90 caliber, will be found invaluable. If a revolver is carried at all, it should be a big one, for the sake of the moral effect its appearance produces on the natives —a regulation Webley, and well plated, as this saves a lot of trouble in looking after rust-spots. As to cartridges, it will be seen, after my experience related on page 91, that it is of first importance that the intending traveler should get his goods from a trustworthy agent, or direct from the manufacturer, and then to personally inspect his ammunition, to make sure he is not taking old stock.

BARTER GOODS.—No specific advice can be given in reference to trade goods, as every separate district has its own peculiar fashion in beads, color or quality of cloth, size of brass, copper, or iron wire; and information on this head can best be obtained from mercantile houses who supply the traders nearest to the point of entrance. But let it be understood that the goods above named are standard currency in some form or other in every part of the country; but this cannot be said of other articles often included among barter goods, such as clothes, hats, old military uniforms, fancy things, etc.; these will be received, but only as presents. Sometimes by hard experience one finds out how necessary it is to be sure what the market demands before purchasing, so as not to be laden with unsalable stuffs. A quantity of beads (fifty pounds' weight) was sold to me by one in the country as the very thing required for barter in the distant districts of the interior; but after carrying them for three months, I had to deliberately throw most of them away in utter disgust, and feeling very sore at being swindled, for no native would accept them; and but for having procured a fair supply of the right kind from an *honest* man who had no wish to palm off his bad stock on an unsuspecting stranger, I should have been in a bad fix.

Trade cloth is generally done up by the wholesale houses in water-tight bales of from fifty to sixty pounds each, suitable in size, shape, and weight for a man's load. For personal baggage and sundries, tin cases are most suitable; wooden boxes, leather portmanteaus, etc., are quickly destroyed by the white ants. The most convenient size for tin cases is $26 \times 15 \times 9$ inches; and I certainly would not be inclined again to spend forty to fifty shillings each on what are called watertight tin boxes. Six of mine were of this description, made by one of the best manufacturers in London. I never doubted their ability to keep their contents dry under all circumstances until two of them were thrown into the Zambesi by the capsizing of a canoe. On being recovered they felt very much heavier than before, and yet there was no water dripping from them; the fact was, they were water-tight on the wrong side. The water got in easy enough, soaking the leather buffing round the rim, which swelled and effectually imprisoned it. They were full of water, and many of my most valuable articles, put there for special safety, were completely destroyed.

PROVISIONS.—Lay in a good stock of flour, rolled wheat, oatmeal, rice, barley, and plain biscuits; coffee, tea, cocoa; dried fruit; desiccated potatoes, compressed vegetables; salt; canned goods—corned beef, sardines, etc. Sugar is bulky and heavy, but will never be missed if to the above stock is added a few packages of saccharine tablets. Condiments, etc., will of course be included according to discretion. These foods named are the substantial stand-byes.

But a few medical comforts and luxuries must not be forgotten, in case of sickness, such as extract of beef, arrow-root, condensed milk, preserves; and a bottle or two of Cognac must not be omitted, as there are times of extreme prostration in attacks of dysentery, or as the result of fever, when a tablespoonful of this stimulant may turn the tide in the patient's favor. But alcohol in any form, except for medicinal purposes, particularly if taken during the day, is the shortest way to fevers, and renders the traveler less able to resist them when they come.

MEDICINES.—These are next in importance to food, and should be carefully selected, and not all put up in one medicine-chest. Several small boxes, each containing a few special drugs, should be packed away in different cases, so that in the event of one or two loads getting lost, stolen, or strayed there will be less danger of being left without a remedy when attacked by illness, as has been the unhappy experience of some.

TABLOIDS.—I would strongly recommend that the

drugs be in the form of tabloids, as prepared by Burroughs & Welcome. As I have stated elsewhere, the Edinburgh Medical Missionary Society presented me, on leaving Scotland, with a Stanley medicine-chest, containing a bountiful supply; and although it was under water twice and traveled thousand of miles in all kinds of weather, temperature, and atmosphere, for eighteen months, alternately carried by natives, conveyed in canoes, or bumped in bullock-wagons, at the end of the journey the drugs that remained were in as good condition as when I started out.

The following will be found among the most valuable for Central Africa: Livingstone's rousers; comp. cathartic; quinine; arsenic ($\frac{1}{30}$ of a grain each); antipyrin; phenacetin; calomel and podophyllin; lead and opium; aloin, strychnine, and belladonnæ; sulphonal.

Messrs. Burroughs & Welcome supply a small book with each medicine-chest, containing plain and concise directions as to the properties, uses, and doses of the various medicines.

FEVER.—The principal disease, and from which none who penetrate the interior escape, is fever in some form or other, generally bilious intermittent, yet all too frequently, particularly near the coast, the malignant and dangerous remittent hematuric, or black-water fever.

Opinions differ as to the treatment of the various fevers, but most are agreed that quinine is our "sheet anchor"; but I have much more faith in its effects as a prophylactic than in its antipyretic property, not only from personal experience, but also from the evidence of many I have met and on whose testimony I can rely. Five-grain doses of quinine daily while approaching or passing through districts known to be malarious mitigated the severity of an attack, and often warded it off altogether, while others in the same caravan who neglected this precaution were completely prostrated every week or two; but they also, on adopting the habit of a dose every morning, experienced almost complete immunity for months together.

Apart from the ever-exhaling malaria in swampy regions, long delays in camp, with their attendant worries, etc., sitting in damp clothes, whether from perspiration or rain, and omitting to change them on getting into camp, until one is chilled, are the most prolific causes of fever.

A practical and handy little brochure on "Health Hints for Central Africa," by Horace Waller (than whom there are few men better qualified to give counsel on this subject), is published by John Murray, London. It is convenient for the pocket, and contains valuable advice and information that should be in the possession of every one who would travel in malarious countries.

The premonitory symptoms of an approaching attack are, first, languor, depression, irritability of temper, and, in some, excitement and talkativeness; the renal secretion becomes frequent and almost colorless, indicating the necessity for something like "Livingstone's rousers" to stir up the liver, a timely dose of two or three sometimes averting an attack.

But when once the nausea and vomiting sets in, further resistance is useless; one must simply lie down to it, when all the blankets and rugs within reach will be requisitioned to give some warmth to the cold and shivering frame, while the acute frontal headache, pain in the back, and general feeling of "haven't-got-a-friend-in-the-world" completes the misery of one's condition at this stage. A few hours of this, and the chilliness gives place to heat, the skin becoming dry and burning, and the tongue parched; then happy and fortunate is the patient who can get his hands on a bottle of soda-water.

If this stage is prolonged, it may sometimes be cut short by a drink of hot gruel or tea with a drachm of spts. æth. nit., when the attack enters on the third part of the program of its course, by profuse perspiration, giving almost instant relief. The temperature runs down rapidly. Now for a big dose of quinine.

It is of little use taking quinine during a paroxysm, as ten to one it will be rejected by the stomach; and small doses in repeated exacerbations of high temperature is equally futile. Thirty grains have often to be administered, taking advantage of a remission when the temperature is at its lowest, before beneficial results are obtained.

To relieve the persistent headaches, antipyrin in five-grain doses will be found very helpful; but better still, and safer, I would mention phenacetin. One (or at most two) five-grain tabloid acts like a charm, soothing and quieting the nerves, and producing a feeling of restfulness that is delightful. In the sleepless nights accompanying fever I have found sulphonal give great relief, but would caution against its reckless use. Messrs. Burroughs & Welcome give the maximum dose at forty grains, but this I found too high. I would limit to half the quantity, or even less, as giving equal benefit without the unpleasant effects of forty grains, which produces a nervous condition, with vertigo and a swaying, staggering gait when attempting to walk.

For fever recurring every day and continuing for weeks, quinine has but little antidotal power; but it will generally yield to one tabloid of arsenic ($\frac{1}{30}$ of a grain) every four hours. Strychnine may be advantageously added to this, and can be obtained in the combined form.

WATER, generally so impure, is responsible for much of the fever and dysentery incidental to traveling in Africa. It should be the ambition of every one to train himself to accomplish the day's march without drinking, for it becomes very much of a habit, dipping from every pool or stream that one comes across, and only increases the craving for more. By a little exercise of self-denial, one will in a few weeks find he can cross stream after stream without any desire to drink, and on getting into camp a cup of tea or cocoa will refresh him, and thus avoid the risk of drinking unboiled water.

COOLERS.—If there should be no certainty of water being obtainable at the noonday rest, a supply had better be carried. But in what? is the question. All sorts of water-bottles and canteens have been invented. Many give the preference to the enameled-ware flask covered with felt, the latter to be kept moist so as to keep the contents cool; but if there is water to be found wherewith to keep continually wetting the felt (for it dries in a very few minutes), why carry any? While, if there is no water for the felt, a drink from the flask is far from refreshing.

To those who can appreciate a draught of real cold water, even when the sun is hottest, I would say: Construct from a piece of sail canvas a bag, say eight inches square, sewed all around, excepting an inch and a half at the upper corner, into which the neck of a bottle may be tied, and you have a water-vessel that as yet is unsurpassed. This is the home-made form, but it may be added to in not only being made more elegantly, but a flat piece of vulcanite may be fastened to the under side, to protect the clothes when it is to be slung over one's own shoulder. But similar bags may be made of a larger size and handed to carriers who have light loads. If they are kept clean and filled with boiled and filtered water every morning, there will be no lack of cold and non-injurious water at every halt.

LIGHT.—A word or two on the subject of lights. Oil-lamps are unadvisable, as it is inconvenient to carry bulky cans of oil; the same may be said of candles. But a good ball of wick and two or three molds will "fill the bill," and provide the means of preparing light *en route* as required; for anywhere and everywhere in Africa bee's-wax may be had, and from which enough candles may be made in a couple of hours to supply the traveler for a month. These candles, too, are not open to the same objections as the sperm and composite, as they do not get soft and melt with the intense heat.

I would recommend a small bull's-eye lantern with a quart or two of paraffine to supply it, as there are occasions when traveling at night is necessary, and when compass readings are to be taken, etc.; then such a protected light will be a great convenience.

PHOTOGRAPHY.—It may not be amiss to give a brief sketch of my experience with photographic appliances, for the benefit of those who may wish to provide apparatus, material, plates, etc., for a similar campaign.

My outfit in this line consisted of a plain Waterbury 8×10 camera, with single back, rising front, folding tailboard, and hinged ground glass; one Ross 8×10 rapid symmetrical lens, and one 8×10 wide-angle portable symmetrical. I had half a dozen holders for plates and half a dozen ditto for films, with vulcanite slides specially made for me by the Scovill & Adams Co. of New York, who supplied all my apparatus.

Five gross Carbutt 8×10 special plates, sensitometer 25, and three gross Carbutt films of same size and rapidity. These were packed in hermetically sealed zinc packages containing two dozen each, and after developing were repacked face to face, nothing between, in their original form—a method which I can certainly recommend, as, though put to the severest test possible, all my negatives arrived in Jamaica without a single breakage or damage.

Developing material I carried dry: soda sulphite, soda carbonate, potash carbonate, acid pyrogallic, acid sulphuric; and for fixing, soda hyposulphite and alum.

One ordinary folding-tripod with seven-inch top, three rubber trays, a folding ruby-lantern (procured from Watson, London), and one Thornton & Picard patent time shutter, completed my photographic paraphernalia.

I developed on the march only when there was no moon, when we chanced to camp by a clear running stream, my tent serving the purpose of a "dark room," and with such a provision found no necessity for anything more elaborate. To avoid the conveyance of heavy dishes for the "hypo" and washing, I constructed bags of rubber cloth for the purpose, tacked upon frames, and carried a box to receive exposed plates, holding two dozen, replenishing my holders always at night.

Now as to results, I leave the reader to judge how far I have been successful in obtaining truthful representations of the tribes, etc., with whom I came in contact, from those I have selected for the illustration of this book from over five hundred negatives now in my possession.

The holders provided by the Scovill & Adams Co. never failed me, and their camera, though neither brass-bound nor leather-bellowed, did not suffer even the smashing of the ground glass; while the boxes containing my photo apparatus experienced the same rough usage as my medicine-chest—carried on the head or shoulders of natives, by river in canoes, and through Bechuanaland and northward by wagon, and, like the chest, having been several times under water. Yet they are still as serviceable as when I first set out. Neither plates nor films showed the slightest sign of deterioration while they lasted. The only difficulty I experienced was with the films, which contracted three eighths of an inch, and thus could no longer be contained in the groove of the holder, but required to be kept in place by pins; this, however, could be easily obviated.

In addition to the aforenamed equipment, I had a 5×7 detective hand camera, fitted with an Eastman's roll-holder, with a good supply of rolls; but they turned out very unsatisfactory, for, although I obtained a large number of passably good snap-shot negatives, they dried after development so unevenly, puckering and crinkling, that I cannot get a decent print from them. They are the most obstreperous invention I have ever handled; nothing short of "battening down" will keep them flat. Of these thin roll films I would say, Amateurs, beware!

A parting word: Central Africa, being comparatively an unphotographed country, offers an unlimited field for the professional and amateur. The traveler will find the camera an unfailing source of pleasure, and a means of dispelling the *ennui* that will so often overtake him in that strange land, while the fascination is increased by no little danger with which his operations will be surrounded; but if successful, he carries back with him pleasing mementos of his journey that will ever remind him of the scenes and experiences through which he has passed.

www.ingramcontent.com/pod-product-compliance
Lightning Source LLC
Chambersburg PA
CBHW022134300426
44115CB00006B/184